IN EVERY SEASON

101 Devotionals for the Journey

*To Lolita.
Blessings on your
journey
Alvin*

By Alvin Frank, M.Div.

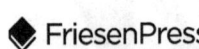 FriesenPress

One Printers Way
Altona, MB R0G 0B0
Canada

www.friesenpress.com

Copyright © 2023 by Alvin Frank
First Edition — 2023

Front cover graphics by Cathy Frank

All rights reserved.

No part of this publication may be reproduced in any form, or by any means, electronic or mechanical, including photocopying, recording, or any information browsing, storage, or retrieval system, without permission in writing from FriesenPress.

ISBN
978-1-03-919501-1 (Hardcover)
978-1-03-919500-4 (Paperback)
978-1-03-919502-8 (eBook)

1. RELIGION, BIBLICAL MEDITATIONS

Distributed to the trade by The Ingram Book Company

Unless otherwise indicated, scripture references are taken from the Holy Bible, NEW INTERNATIONAL VERSION®, NIV® Copyright © 1973, 1978, 1984, 2011 by Biblica, Inc.® Used by permission. All rights reserved worldwide.

Scripture references marked (MSG) are taken from The Message. Copyright © by Eugene H. Peterson 1993, 1994, 1995, 1996, 2000, 2001, 2002. Used by permission of NavPress Publishing Group.

Scripture references marked (NASB) are taken from the New American Standard Bible®, Copyright © 1960, 1962, 1963, 1968, 1971, 1972, 1973, 1975, 1977, 1995 by The Lockman Foundation. Used by permission.

Scripture quotations marked (ESV) are taken from The Holy Bible, English Standard Version® (ESV®), copyright © 2001 by Crossway, a publishing ministry of Good News Publishers. Used by permission. All rights reserved.

Scripture quotations marked (NLT) are taken from the Holy Bible, New Living Translation, copyright ©1996, 2004, 2007 by Tyndale House Foundation. Used by permission of Tyndale House Publishers, Inc., Carol Stream, Illinois 60188. All rights reserved.

Scripture quotations marked (NKJV) are taken from the New King James Version®. Copyright © 1982 by Thomas Nelson, Inc. Used by permission. All rights reserved.

Scripture quotations marked (CSB) are taken from the Christian Standard Bible. Copyright © 2017 by Holman Bible Publishers. Used by permission. Christian Standard Bible®, and CSB® are federally registered trademarks of Holman Bible Publishers, all rights reserved.

Scripture quotations marked (KJV) are taken from the Holy Bible, King James Version, which is in the public domain

Contents

Introduction ix
Before You Begin xii
A Bit of My Story xiv

JANUARY–MARCH 1

Chapter 1: Seasons Beyond Our Control 3
   1. God Will Make a Way 3
   2. Grief and Loss 5
   3. A Fresh Start 7
   4. The Call to Newness 9
   5. Embracing Change 11

Chapter 2: A Time to Love 14
   6. Agape 14
   7. Love Is Patient 16
   8. God's Divine Love 17
   9. Love Is Kind 19
  10. Love Forgives 21

Chapter 3: Don't Give Up 24
  11. A Steadfast Faith 24
  12. Pursue the Truth 27
  13. Keep on Trusting 28
  14. Embrace the Word 31
  15. Pray Continually 33
  16. Tell of God's Love 36
  17. Keep on Meeting Together 38
  18. Persevere in Suffering 40

Chapter 4: A Time to Un-Mask 43
  19. Uncommon Virtues 43
  20. Desiring God 46

21. The Contrite Heart 48
22. Genuine Meekness 50
23. Spiritual Hunger 52
24. Be Merciful 55
25. Having a Pure Heart. 57
26. Be a Peacemaker 59

APRIL – JUNE 63

Chapter 5: The Ancient of Days 65
27. The Bread of Life. 65
28. The Light of the World. 67
29. The Gate for the Sheep 69
30. The Good Shepherd 71
31. The Way 73
32. The True Vine 76

Chapter 6: Fruit that Lasts 79
33. The Joy of the Lord 79
34. Peace That Surpasses 81
35. Patience 83
36. Faithfulness 86
37. Goodness 88
38. Self-Control 90

Chapter 7: God's Redemption Story 94
39. The Redeemer 94
40. The Cross 96
41. The Divine Exchange 99
42. Disgrace to Grace 101
43. Death to Life 103

Chapter 8: Break Up the Fallow Ground! 106
44. Preparing Your Field. 106
45. Sow Good Seeds 108
46. Control the Weeds 110
47. Feed the Seedlings. 111
48. Reaping a Harvest. 113

    49. A Time to Uproot 115

Chapter 9: A Season for Hope **118**
    50. Renewal 118
    51. A Time to Heal 120
    52. Keeping Hope Alive 122
    53. Can You See It? 124
    54. Restoration. 126

Chapter 10: For Such a Time as This. **128**
    55. Going for Broke. 128
    56. Character Matters 130
    57. Choose for Eternity. 132
    58. Rise up and Rebuild 134

JULY– SEPTEMBER **137**

Chapter 11: Count it All Joy **139**
    59. Mirror, Mirror! 139
    60. Faith That Works. 141
    61. Sticks and Stones. 143
    62. Wisdom from Above 145
    63. Sacred Submission 147
    64. Beware of Boasting. 148

Chapter 12: Recalculating. **151**
    65. Navigating the Unknown. 151
    66. Unexpected Turns. 153
    67. Unrealistic Expectations .154
    68. Missing the Markers. 156
    69. Trusting the Navigator. 158
    70. Seasons of Restraints 160
    71. Let Justice Prevail 162

Chapter 13: New Beginnings **165**
    72. Obedience 165
    73. Change of Identity 167
    74. Patient Endurance. 169
    75. Change of Habit 171

    76. Shepherd Boy to King...173
    77. Change of Heart 175

OCTOBER – DECEMBER..................................... **177**

Chapter 14: Beauty from Ashes............................ **179**
    78. Only Ashes..179
    79. Against All Odds..181
    80. Love beyond Measure......................................183
    81. God's Kindness 185
    82. God of the Harvest 187
    83. God Covered Us 189
    84. Redemption..191
    85. Something Beautiful..193

Chapter 15: A Time for Waiting **197**
    86. Waiting on the Lord 197
    87. Soar Like the Eagle..199
    88. Run and Not Be Weary 201
    89. Walk and Not Faint..203

Chapter 16: Lost and Found................................. **207**
    90. The Lost Sheep 207
    91. The Lost Coin 210
    92. The Lost Son 212
    93. The Wanderer 214
    94. He Sets Prisoners Free 217
    95. Darkness to Light 219
    96. The Lord Our Healer 221

Chapter 17: The Season of Incarnate Love............. **224**
    97. Bethlehem, House of Bread...............................224
    98. The Awakening 226
    99. The Fulfillment 229
    100. Waiting for the Lord's Return 231
    101. Come, Lord Jesus 233
    Doxology 236

Introduction

In 1959, the late Pete Seeger wrote the lyrics to the song "Turn, Turn, Turn." He wrote:

To everything turn, turn, turn
There is a season turn, turn, turn
And a time to every purpose, under heaven.

He was reflecting on the third chapter of Ecclesiastes, written by King Solomon. The chapter begins this way: "*There is a time for everything, and a season for every activity under the heavens*" (v. 1) In this journey, we will face "the worst and best of times."

The passage contains a list of opposites, outlining the different seasons we'll face in our lives.

> A time to be born and a time to die, a time to plant and a time to uproot, A time to kill and a time to heal, a time to tear down and a time to build, A time to weep and a time to laugh, a time to mourn and a time to dance, A time to scatter stones and a time to gather them, a time to embrace and a time to refrain from embracing, A time to search and a time to give up, a time to keep and a time to throw away, A time to tear and a time to mend, a time to be silent and a time to speak, A time to love

and a time to hate, a time for war and a time for peace. (Ecclesiastes 3:2–8)

Solomon begins the book by saying: "'Meaningless! Meaningless!' says the Teacher. 'Utterly meaningless! Everything is meaningless.' What do people gain from all their labors at which they toil under the sun?" (Ecclesiastes 1:2). This is the sad cry of every person who has taken a foray into a life of meaningless indulgences, only to discover in the end the futility of it all. Solomon tried it all, did it all, lived it all. He concluded that any season you leave God out of becomes meaningless.

Seasons! They come and go—winter, spring, summer, fall, single, married, young, old. They all appear on the stage of life. How we handle them determines our conclusion in the end. If you're like me, you welcome the happy seasons but merely endure the sad and difficult ones, begging for them to quickly change.

A calendar season usually runs for about three months, but sometimes we go through dreadful seasons that seem to be without end. One of these seasons from which you may still be recovering is the pandemic of 2020–2022. We could call it the *pandemic season*. I venture to say that no one alive today had ever experienced a season like that one. To quote Charles Dickens: "*It was the best of times, it was the worst of times, it was the age of wisdom, it was the age of foolishness ...*"[1]

No matter the season we face, there's always room for grace and gratitude to God for His wisdom and insights. In every season of our lives—pandemic, sickness, marriage, divorce, financial trouble, and even bereavement—grace and gratitude can bloom brightly.

If you look closely enough into this list in Ecclesiastes 3, you'll discover that each experience reveals a loving, divine purpose and a God in whom we can put our trust.

Ecclesiastes 3:11 says: "*He* [God] *has made everything beautiful in its time. He has also set eternity in the human heart; yet no one can fathom what God has done from beginning to end.*" You see, He's in perfect control.

Knowing that God is in control, and that everything happens at the appropriate time, doesn't change the fact that we don't always understand what He's actually doing and why. But we can trust His Word and that He does everything for *His glory* and *our good*.

In every season of our lives, Jesus promises to be with us. He will never leave us or forsake us.

1. Charles Dickens, *A Tale of Two Cities* (London, UK: Chapman & Hall, 1859), 1

Before You Begin

In Every Season: 101 Devotionals for the Journey is not a daily devotional guide, although it may be used that way if you choose to read a devotional thought each day. As the title suggests, this book could be read in any time or season—not just the calendar seasons, but in every season of life. Structurally, it roughly follows the four seasons: January–March, April–June, July–September, and October–December.

During these particular groupings of months, I try to follow some of the events we observe and even celebrate. But some of the seasons we go through are beyond our control, such as suffering, misfortune, sadness, isolation, illness, death, and grief. But we discover that even during those times, the Holy Spirit of God walks with us.

This book is written primarily as an encouragement to you. I try to put a positive spin on your situation, with the hopeful expectation that God will bring you through to a brighter tomorrow. Whoever you are, wherever you've been, and whatever you're going through at the moment, please know that God loves and cares about you.

Don't get stuck where you are! Don't waste your time focusing on what you used to be or on what might have been. Remember, the hope we have in Christ means that there's a brighter tomorrow ahead. Sin has been forgiven; guilt and shame have been cancelled out. And we are no longer chained to a deep, dark pit of the past.

The very wise King Solomon wrote: "*There is a time for everything, and a season for every activity under the heavens*" (Ecclesiastes 3:1). On this journey, and in these seasons, we'll face the worst and best of times. But through it all we can take comfort in the experience of the wise king, who said "*I know that everything God does will endure forever; nothing can be added to it and nothing taken from it. God does it so that people will fear him*" (Ecclesiastes 3:14).

I invite you to come along the journey with me and experience the goodness of the Lord as He accompanies you on the way.

A Bit of My Story

One of my earliest recollections as a child is of the morning I was crawling around on the floor of our living room, when one of my uncles passed by with a tiny white coffin on his shoulder. It contained my sibling, who had died at birth. I don't know how old I was at the time, probably a toddler. I didn't know exactly what was happening then, but I remember feeling that life was full of sadness. Including that deceased baby, there were nine children in the family. I was the fifth born, so I'm the quintessential middle child.

I was born in Trinidad and Tobago, on the smaller of the two islands, but moved to Trinidad to attend school when I was seventeen years old. I remember it clearly, because it was a week following the death of my father, who passed away at the early age of fifty-nine. I had made all my plans to travel and was unable to change them. Suffice it to say, it was a very sad and lonely time of my life.

But two years later, on one of my summer vacations back in Tobago, something happened that changed my life for all eternity. One evening as I was hurrying along the street to catch up with some former school friends, a young man stopped me in my tracks and introduced me to Jesus Christ. That evening, on the side of the street, I bowed my head and invited the Lord Jesus Christ into my heart. It was the most important and happiest decision I ever made.

After graduation, I worked for a few years, after which I immigrated to Toronto, Canada. I started attending The Stone Church, where I have attended to this day. I studied Engineering Technology at Ryerson University (now TMU), and most of my working career was spent in engineering at Ontario's largest power generation company.

When I had the opportunity to retire early, I was invited to join the pastoral staff at my church. This opened the door for me to attend Tyndale Seminary, where I pursued Biblical and Pastoral Studies, graduating with a Master of Divinity degree in 2010. I held the position on staff as Discipleship & Care Pastor until my "retirement" in 2022. I am passionate about the care of people and thank the Lord always that He has given me a desire to encourage His children. I trust that this book will be an encouragement to you.

I am married to my wife Glenda, and we have two daughters, Karen and Cathy.

Rev. Alvin Frank, M Div.
Pastoral & Biblical Studies

JANUARY-MARCH

Chapter 1:
Seasons Beyond Our Control

*All streams flow into the sea, yet the sea is never full.
To the place the streams come from, there they return again.*

Ecclesiastes 1:7

1. God Will Make a Way

Difficult seasons and situations that leave us feeling alone and abandoned will happen at some point in all of our lives. You might have encountered the words, "I'm leaving. I don't love you anymore," or "You've been terminated from this company," or "We can't be friends anymore," or "The doctors have done everything they can." Heartbreaking moments like these can turn our world upside down, leaving us to pick up the pieces, with a big, gaping hole of loneliness in the middle of our souls.

Yet we have a promise from God that He will never leave us or forsake us.

God is at work in us, in our difficulties, even though the trials and challenges may not always be removed from our lives.

Hebrews 13:5 holds a promise, which is the foundation of God's love for us: "*I will never leave you nor forsake you.*"

Jesus will walk with us, even through the darkest of days—even when we may be unaware of His presence. So, let's be encouraged by

Psalm 30:5b: *"Weeping may stay for the night, but rejoicing comes in the morning."*

In reflecting on some of these contrasting seasons, Solomon reminds us of those seasons over which we have little or no control.

There is a time for everything, and a season for every activity under the heavens (Ecclesiastes 3:1).

If you're following God's will and trying to live your life according to His way, you'll eventually see that these experiences can have purpose and value in your life.

God's sovereignty over all creation covers the past, present, and future. Nothing is outside of His control. We didn't decide when we were to be born, and only God numbers the days of our lives (Psalm 90:9, 12): *"All our days pass away under your wrath; we finish our years with a moan. Teach us to number our days, that we may gain a heart of wisdom."*

As Jesus leads us through the seasons of life, we will experience times of grief and sorrow, especially in times of loss, and especially the loss of a loved one. We can't avoid or ignore sorrow, but there is a way through it in the loving arms of Jesus Christ.

Even as we grieve, we have hope … in His love, in His promises, in His care and in His strength. Jesus wants us to express how we feel, because He understands. His Word says that He is near to those who grieve, and that He was sent to heal the broken-hearted. We know He cares for us today, regardless of what we're going through. And of course, that season of mourning will come to an end, ushering in a new season that enables you to dance again.

God always has a restoration plan and is ready to watch you dance in the streets like David.

Perhaps it seems like the season you're in isn't going to end. But one of these days, a small cloud will rise from the horizon, signalling the end of your dry season. So let's keep our eyes on Jesus and stay in His presence. He will lead you through this place where you haven't been before.

Yes, there's a time and season for everything under the heavens, and God will bring it to pass in His own time in your life.

May the Lord bless you and give you hope in whatever season you're in.

2. Grief and Loss

Have you ever felt the pain and anguish of loss? Anguish is usually the result of a tragedy, or tragedies piled one on top of the other.

In 1998, my brother's wife died quite suddenly of a heart attack, just before Christmas. In fact, she was buried two days before Christmas. It was quite a difficult thing for him and the rest of the family, to say the least.

As I think about "seasons beyond our control," I remember my remarks as I tried to bring some sense of relevance to what had happened. I said at the funeral, "As I was preparing this tribute and looked at the calendar, I noticed that it was the first day of winter. But for the Frank's family, it's winter in more ways than one." Not much can prepare you for grief and loss, even when the loss is expected. But when it's sudden, the impact is ten-fold, as in the case of my dad, who died suddenly one Sunday evening when I was only seventeen years of age.

But as if the sudden passing of my brother's wife wasn't enough, he lost his thirty-year-old son to gun violence in 2007. He was shot in the abdomen and never recovered. Through the anguish and pain, my brother was able to find comfort in the knowledge that God is his refuge and strength.

Psalm 46:1–4 says"

> God is our refuge and strength, an ever-present help in trouble. Therefore we will not fear, though the earth gives way and the mountains fall into the heart of the sea, though its waters roar and foam and the mountains quake with their surging. There is a river whose streams make glad the city of God, the holy place where the Most-High dwells.

These particular verses have brought me great comfort and peace in times of grief. I trust they will do the same for you.

Anguish and pain, however, can result in bitterness that leads us away from the green pastures and still waters of Psalm 23, where the Lord promises to lead us for spiritual nourishment. Psalm 23:4 reminds us that God also leads us through the valley of the shadow of death. So how do we process all the grief, anguish, and pain we see around us without becoming bitter, even bitter at God?

If you recall, the book of Ruth starts off on a rather sour note. In Ruth 1:1–5, we learn that a family from Bethlehem, "The House of Bread," has moved to Moab due to a famine. Moab was a pagan country often in conflict with its Israelite neighbours to the west.

This migration to Moab happened during the season when the judges ruled: *"In those Days there was no King in Israel; Everyone did what was right in his own eyes"* (Judges 21:25). So it was a chaotic period in the life of the Jewish people, to say the least. During their stay in Moab, Elimelech, the patriarch of the family and husband to Naomi, died, and then both of their sons later died. However, before the sons died, they took Moabite wives.

The loss of her family caused great grief and sorrow in Naomi's heart, as well as bitterness toward God. In her bitterness, she set out to return home to Bethlehem when she heard that the famine was over. But in His sovereign mercy and grace, God provided a faithful companion, her daughter-in-law Ruth, to walk by her side as she travelled back home to Bethlehem.

God will also provide someone to walk with you through your grief and loss. He is called the Comforter, or the *Paraclete, the One called to walk alongside us.* He is the Holy Spirit of God.

Have you ever felt that the Lord has given you much more than you could bear? If so, wait on the Lord! He promises to make the end of the story more glorious than the beginning, as He did for Naomi. God promises to give you, *"Beauty for ashes, the oil of joy for mourning, the garment of praise for the spirit of heaviness; that you might be called a tree of righteousness, the planting of the* Lord, *that He might be glorified"* (Isaiah 61:3).

In the end, we see Naomi's life beautifully turned around, as God gave her a grandson through Ruth, her daughter-in-law and faithful friend. This grandson would feature prominently in the earthly genealogy of Jesus. So be patient and wait for the Lord! In due time, He will turn your sorry into joy and make you better instead of bitter. May the Lord give you great comfort and strength during your time of grief and loss!

3. A Fresh Start

I remember just how it felt as we were slowly emerging from the Pandemic in 2022. There had been almost two years of restrictions, so following the announcements that social distancing was no longer necessary, people began to take a collective deep breath.

When asked what they were looking forward to most post-pandemic, some people said, "Being able to hug again; going to group lunches with co-workers; wearing pants to meetings again; and taking off the masks." One thing that comes through abundantly clear is that we all long to be with the ones we love and care about—without the fear of being infected. What people are actually saying is, "I can't wait to get back to normal." But then I heard someone say, "Why would I want to get back to normal? Normal wasn't that great anyway!"

It is a fact that no one can go back to the beginning and recapture what had been lost. Rather, we could have a new beginning, right where we are today, if we want to ensure a great ending. We can't recapture the past, but we can begin again right where we are, allowing God to make things new in our lives. We can make a fresh start.

The apostle Paul, writing to the Ephesians, said:

> You were taught, with regard to your former way of life, to put off your old self, which is being corrupted by its deceitful desires; to be made new in the attitude of your minds; and to put on the new self, created to be like God in true righteousness and holiness. (Ephesians 4:22–24)

Are you looking to make a fresh start? The scriptures are filled with examples of people whose lives were miraculously turned around through the gracious hand of God. My prayer and hope for you is that you and the people in your life will have an amazing encounter with the grace of God. God delights in new beginnings, as we see throughout the Bible, and He's always ready to take you as you are and make you into the person He desires you to become.

As the pandemic was coming to an end, people began to experience the freedom they desired. But freedom means more than the ending of the pandemic. It's allowing God to give you a fresh start in those areas of your life that may be holding you captive. Regardless of what you've been through or may still be going through, or what you've done, no one is beyond hope. That's the great message of Jesus.

No depth of pain, sadness, loss of opportunity, or any amount of sin in your past can trump the amazing grace of God. Even though your past may be soiled, anyone can find a new beginning with God. So don't get stuck where you are or try to revert to the past! Don't waste your time focusing on what you used to be or what might have been. Remember, the hope we have in Christ means there's a brighter tomorrow ahead.

If you're a follower of Jesus, your sins are forgiven, shame is cancelled out, and you can rise to the potential the Father envisions for you. We have an inheritance in Jesus Christ laid up for us, as the apostle Peter reminds us:

> Praise be to the God and Father of our Lord Jesus Christ! In his great mercy he has given us new birth into a living hope through the resurrection of Jesus Christ from the dead, and into an inheritance that can never perish, spoil or fade. This inheritance is kept in heaven for you, who through faith are shielded by God's power until the coming of the salvation that is ready to be revealed in the last time. In all this you greatly rejoice, though now for a little while you may have had to suffer grief in all kinds of trials. These have come so that the proven genuineness of your faith—of greater worth than gold, which perishes even though refined by fire—may result in praise, glory and honor when Jesus Christ is revealed (1 Peter 1:3–7).

You may feel like you are stuck because of something from your past. Don't let it pin you to the ground with embarrassment, guilt, and fear. Don't let it cripple you. We've been given freedom by Jesus Christ. We are no longer chained to a deep, dark pit of the past. We've been made free in Jesus Christ.

Chuck Swindoll says, "We're no longer chained to a deep, dark pit of the past. Grace gives us wings to soar beyond it."[2] So break with the past and make a fresh start, with Jesus Christ leading the way.

PRAYER:
Father God, thank you that I don't need to be stuck in the past, because according to your Word, I have renounced my former way of life and put off my old self, which was being corrupted by its deceitful desires. Please help me to be made new in the attitude of my mind and to make a fresh start. In Jesus' name, Amen

2. Chuck Swindoll, *Grace to You*. Devotional - A New Beginning, November 23, 2016.

4. The Call to Newness

Do you make New Year's resolutions? If you do, you're in good company. In the United States and Canada, studies have shown that approximately forty-four per cent of adults make New Year's resolutions. However, those who have set lofty goals for the new year soon find themselves falling off the wagon just months (or weeks) later. So rest assured that you're not alone.

The beauty of goal setting is that you don't need a ball-drop or cannons of confetti to signal a fresh start—you can recommit to your resolutions at any time. In fact, June 1 is unofficially known by many as "New Year's Resolution Recommitment Day," which gives you the perfect opportunity to take stock of where you are with your resolutions so that you can hit reset if necessary and begin again.

In this devotional, "A Call to Newness," my wish is that you don't determine where your life will go by merely setting arbitrary goals, but instead, you will listen to the voice of the Lord through prayer and constantly abiding in His Word. As human beings that love the status quo, we're often resistant to change. But change can be a good thing, even if we're not quite sure where it will lead or what's in store for us—and that's where faith in God comes in.

Obedience was at the centre of the patriarch Abraham's faith. He believed, and therefore he obeyed. When God called him to something new, he went:

> Now the LORD said to Abram, "Go from your country and your kindred and your father's house to the land that I will show you. And I will make of you a great nation, and I will bless you and make your name great, so that you will be a blessing. I will bless those who bless you, and him who dishonors you I will curse, and in you all the families of the earth shall be blessed." So Abram went, as the LORD had told him. (Genesis 12:1–4)

This was quite a difficult task! But God assures Abram that if he obeys, God will both bless him and make him a blessing to others. I love how verse 4 begins: *"So Abram went."* Abram simply goes where God tells Him to. Then Abram worships God by building an altar. As you answer the call to newness and progress along the way, you too will need to build an altar. No, not a physical structure, but a daily recognition of God's faithfulness and an acknowledgement of his presence. Yet this is not Abraham's final destination—he continues to follow God as he journeys on. You see, God always has something new for us.

Can you imagine being called like Abraham was? Can you imagine God telling you that you need to leave everything you've ever known behind, pack up your family and all your possessions, and start moving? You might say, "Well, that was Abraham; he was special." In fact, he wasn't. God didn't choose Abraham because there was anything special about him; Abraham's father was an idol worshiper, which means Abraham would have been familiar with the worship of idols. This meant he had to leave behind the familiar and everything that he knew, including idols.

In North America, people wouldn't normally consider themselves idol worshippers. But anything that takes us away from wholehearted devotion to God can be considered an idol. According to scripture, the worship of idols extends beyond paying homage to images and false gods. It's a matter of the heart, associated with pride, selfishness, greed, gluttony, and love for possessions (Matthew 6:24).

Like Abraham, if you're to embrace the call to newness, you must give up certain things. The more attached you become to certain things, even those questionable things you think may not be good for us, the harder it will be to answer the call to newness. Our response to the call becomes easier when we know, either by experience or by faith, that the One who calls us to newness is faithful.

Jesus said, *"Everyone who has left houses or brothers or sisters or father or mother or children or fields for my sake will receive a hundred times as much and will inherit eternal life"* (Matthew 19:29). The call to newness can be an intimidating one for all of us. But when we step out in faith, God will bring to pass that which He has promised. So if you sense that God is calling you to leave behind the status quo for a new beginning, heed His call and move out! It may be a tough choice, and the uncertainty of the destination may cause you to hesitate, but when you step out in faith, you'll find that God never abandons you but will be with you every step of the way. Blessings on the road ahead!

5. Embracing Change

Have you ever taken a bold step after much soul searching and prayer, hoping that everything would turn out as planned? I remember when I took early retirement from my secular career in engineering and considered pursuing a Master's degree in Pastoral Studies. Even though I was convinced it was the right thing to do at the time, I was full of questions: What if I'm the oldest in all of the classes? What if I can't keep up with the work, having been out of school for such a long time?

Experiencing change or new beginnings can cause upheaval, stress, fear, and even anxiety. So it's only natural to resist it. In my case, I placed myself firmly in the hands of the Lord, being assured that He had called me and that He was going to honour His Word by being with me all the way.

When faced with new challenges and opportunities, we instinctively want to head back to *proverbial Egypt*, where the *leeks* and *onions* were at least something we could count on! But change is more than a part of life. Change is inevitable. Therefore, we need to move forward wholeheartedly, putting our hope in the unchanging One, as Paul encourages us:

> Brothers and sisters, I do not consider myself yet to have taken hold of it. But one thing I do: Forgetting what is behind and straining toward what is ahead, I press on toward the goal to win the prize for which God has called me heavenward in Christ Jesus.
> (Philippians 3:13–14)

How do you make good, healthy changes and transitions? How do you deal with change? You let go of what was and embrace the new! If you recognize God is in the change, don't resist it. Respond to it positively by embracing the opportunity.

In order to embrace something, you need to release whatever else is in your hands. I love this Corrie Ten Boom statement: "Hold everything in your hands lightly, otherwise it hurts when God pries your fingers open."[3] So Let go of what was and embrace that to which God is calling you. Our God is a God of new beginnings.

Moses experienced many new beginnings in his life. He was snatched from the River Nile as *a* baby in a basket to become a Prince of Egypt, then he later became a fugitive in the Sinai desert, where he looked after sheep. He was quite content with being a shepherd of sheep, so when God called him from the burning bush to go back to Egypt to be a shepherd of His people and deliver them from the bondage of slavery, that was the last thing he wanted to do.

Making a new start is never easy. But what God said to Moses when Moses asked, *"Who am I that I should go to Pharaoh and bring the Israelites out of Egypt?"* is the same thing He says to you today: *"I will be with you."* (Exodus 3:11-12)

Just a personal note: When I had my admission interview at Tyndale Seminary with one of the professors there, he said to me, "The courses are going to be pretty hard for you, since you've been away from school for so long. You'll need to work extra hard. You'll need at least a 2.0 GPA to graduate."

Well, I'm happy to say that I graduated with a 3.7 GPA. I told you this not to boast but to remind you of God's faithfulness. If He calls you to a new beginning, then He will see you through to completion. So embrace the call!

As the apostle Paul reminds us: *"Be confident of this, that he who began a good work in you will carry it on to completion until the day of Christ Jesus"* (Philippians 1:6).

If you believe God is calling you to something new, you should first confirm this through prayer and good counsel from someone you trust, then don't be afraid to step out in faith and begin the journey. He promises never to leave you, but He will walk with you when you're on the top of the mountain as well as through the valley.

---

3. Corie Ten Boom, *Favorite Quotes from Corie ten Boom.* (https://www.liveatthewell.org/quotes-from-corrie-ten-boom.html)

Chapter 2:
A Time to Love

*a time to love and a time to hate,
a time for war and a time for peace.*

Ecclesiastes 3:8

6. Agape

Valentine's Day is a special day on which we express our love to another. In North America alone, over 200 million Valentine's Day cards are sent each year. And if you're a spouse or a significant other, you'll probably receive flowers, chocolates, or a special dinner—something that says "I love you."

But as you know, love is not just to be shown for a day, or only to those who have shown love to you. It's to be shown at all times. You've probably heard this scripture read at weddings:

> Love is *patient*, love is *kind*. It does not envy, it *does not boast*, it is not proud. It does not dishonor others, it is not self-seeking, it is not easily angered, it *keeps no record of wrongs*. Love does not delight in evil but rejoices with the truth. It always protects, always trusts, always hopes, always perseveres. (1 Corinthians 13:4–7, emphasis added)

This is love in its purest, most *excellent* form. The Bible teaches that one of the prominent characteristics that reveals the force and nature of love is that it "is not self-seeking." Essentially, this means that those who embody true, biblical love don't insist upon their own way or their own rights. Rather, they seek the interest of others.

In a culture that is overrun with a sense of entitlement and egocentrism, true love isn't always seen exhibited in its purest form. The apostle Paul wrote this passage to the Christ followers in Corinth, who were exhibiting many undesirable traits, which they called love. He wanted to show them that there was a more excellent way—the purest form of love. He began in in 1 Corinthians 13:1–3 by saying: *"If I speak in the tongues of men or of angels, but do not have love, I am only a resounding gong or a clanging cymbal."*

What kind of love was Paul referring to? The Bible speaks of *four* unique forms of love, communicated through four Greek words: *Eros, Storge, Philio, and Agape,* or romantic, family, brotherly, and God's divine love. Each of these characteristics of love has its place in our lives. But *Agape,* God's divine, unconditional love, has the overarching effect of transforming our character.

Love describes an emotion with vastly differing degrees of intensity, which humans crave from the moment of birth. All of us have an intense desire to be loved and nurtured. This could be considered one of our most basic and fundamental needs. One of the forms this need takes is contact comfort—the desire to be held and touched.

First John 4:8 tells us, *"Anyone who does not love does not know God, for God is love."* *Agape,* God's divine love, is so unique, it could never be reciprocated to the giver. Once you've experienced it, you'll seek only to love as Jesus loves.

On what might be considered the greatest Valentine's Day in the history of the world, Jesus demonstrated His love by laying down His life on a cross for us, who were so undeserving.

Q. How is your heart toward Jesus?

Is your response to what He has done for you one of love and gratitude?

Let His love transform you. May this wonderful and life-transforming love be yours today.

7. Love Is Patient

When the apostle Paul wrote this passage to the Church, he was writing about a special type of love:

Love is *patient*, love is *kind*. It does not envy, it *does not boast*, it is not proud. It does not dishonor others, it is not self-seeking, it is not easily angered, it *keeps no record of wrongs*. (1 Corinthians 13:4–5, emphasis added)

This kind of love isn't just as an attribute but something that's put into practice. These are much-loved words, often quoted at weddings or romantic settings. But it's important to remember that Paul wasn't writing inspirational poetry here, nor was he writing a simple starry-eyed mantra. He was not a poet. No, he used to be someone who had intense hatred in his heart toward those he considered to be acting contrary to God's Word. He had no tolerance for the followers of Jesus. But one day God opened not just his eyes but his heart, and filled it with His love—*Agape*.

In this passage, Paul drives home a pointed message that this is how God expects His children to treat one another. It's less about what love *is* and more about what love *does*. When one is transformed by Jesus Christ, this kind of love should be a natural overflow of their heart, and it should be evident in everything they do.

Unfortunately, for the people in Paul's day as well as in ours, this isn't always the case. In this passage, we're urged to adopt a love that is purposeful and persistent. Patience is a fruit of the Holy Spirit.

All of us have been told at some point in our lives to "just be patient." In this age of instant gratification, nobody enjoys patiently waiting. For most people, patience can be difficult in certain circumstances. Whether it's waiting in a doctor's office past your appointment time, sitting in traffic, or trying to get the kids to do their chores, patience is sometimes hard to come by. How can we cultivate patience in relationships with our loved ones?

Patient love is waiting with grace. It enables us to live in this demanding world and still have love, joy, and peace. Patient love doesn't come simply by trying harder but by cultivating an intimate connection with the "Vine" from which this fruit of the Holy Spirit is produced.

Ask God for the patience you need to get you through all the struggles, pain, and trials you face. And may you be like Jesus more and more as He fills you with His love.

The *love* Paul speaks of in these verses is from the Greek word *agape*. These verses provide numerous descriptions of *agape*, God's divine, sacrificial love. *Patient love* actively waits for others without resentment. When we're exhausted or worried, finding patience is probably the last thing on our minds, but it should really be the first. We're told in Psalm 37:7, "*To be still before the LORD and wait patiently for him.*"

Patient love is persistent love. It should be the kind of love a wife or husband have for each other. "For better or for worse," they have chosen to be faithful and remain committed to each other, and this commitment is long-standing.

Patient love makes one more forgiving, more gracious, and more trusting. It describes God's love perfectly. Even when we're unfaithful or unloving, God remains faithful and patient. This is the kind of love God challenges His children to have for one another.

May His love shine through everything you do today.

PRAYER:
Father, in a world where I become very impatient and look for instant gratification and quick fixes, please help me to exhibit that wonderful fruit of the Holy Spirit that helps me be patient with my brothers and sisters, as you are with me. In Jesus' name. Amen

8. God's Divine Love

Do you ever beat yourself up about who you are and the situations you face? Have you ever said, "I want God to forgive me, but I don't think He can!" These phrases are usually uttered by people who don't fully understand the depth of God's love. God's love is freely given with no strings attached. It's a love that is *priceless*. True love can't be purchased. It's about heart and spirit—our very lives. Things that money can never buy.

The Bible tells us that true love isn't a passing feeling but one that endures for time and eternity.

The Apostle Paul wrote: *"But God, being rich in mercy, because of the great love with which He loved us, even when we were dead in our trespasses, made us alive together with Christ"* (Ephesians 2:4–5, emphasis added). How awesome is that?

The apostle John encourages us even further about the depth of God's love: *"Dear friends, let us love one another, for love comes from God. Everyone who loves has been born of God and knows God. Whoever does not love does not know God, because God is love"* (1 John 4:7–8). As we think of God's divine love today, we're challenged by what John says in verses 9–10:

"This is how God showed his love among us: He sent his one and only Son into the world that we might live through him. This is love: not that we loved God, but that he loved us and sent his Son as an atoning sacrifice for our sins." Isn't that an amazing thought?

So can God forgive us? The answer is a resounding YES. He can and does. You might have had a bad experience with human love. Maybe someone said, "I will always love you!" but you discovered later that they were just meaningless words. Or conversely, you might have promised to love someone till the end of time, but circumstances have changed your feeling. You see, love is not a feeling; it's a choice. God chose to love us even when we were unlovable.

God's love is a divine love that can't be reciprocated, even though we may try. It's a love of passion and selfless devotion, one that seeks only to give without any thought of receiving. It's a love that consumes us.

The apostle Paul, writing to the Ephesians, extended a challenge to them to love as Jesus loved: *"Observe how Christ loved us. His love was not cautious but extravagant. He didn't love in order to get something from us but to give everything of himself to us. Love like that"* (Ephesians 5:2, MSG).

Why should we love like that? Because it's the best way to live. When we love like Jesus, we're lifted outside ourselves. His brand of love sees beyond the normal range of human vision—over walls of resentment and barriers of betrayal. When we love like Jesus, we rise above petty demands and snobbish entitlement.

To love like Jesus, we need to think as well as feel. We need *reason* as well as *emotion*. Both head and heart, working together. It's the only way to bring perfect love into our imperfect lives.

There are many different ways to say "I love you." And because those three little words mean so much, how and when we say them can be one of the most important moments in our lives. The way God chose to say them is reflected in Romans 5:8: *"But God demonstrates His own love toward us, in that while we were still sinners, Christ died for us."*

Here's a truth for you: When you open your heart, God's love changes your mind.

Q. How has the love of God, expressed in the life and death of Jesus, affected your life? Has it made it easier to love your neighbour as yourself? Or are you still struggling to accept His love? Pray and ask the Lord to reveal Himself to you in a way that transforms you.

PRAYER:
Father God, I confess that many times I have beaten myself up, not believing that you could ever love someone like me. But I'm beginning to understand that your love for me is unconditional. Please help me to accept your love so that I'm able to demonstrate it to others. In Jesus' name, Amen

9. Love Is Kind

Have you ever been the recipient of someone's kindness and were so blown away, you were beside yourself? When the apostle Paul wrote to the church in Corinth, his main purpose was to show them a more excellent way—the Way of Love. Part of that love is expressed in God's kindness:

> At one time we too were foolish, disobedient, deceived and enslaved by all kinds of passions and pleasures. We lived in malice and envy, being hated and hating one another. But when the kindness and love of God our Savior appeared, he saved us, not because of righteous things we had done, but because of his mercy. He saved us through the washing of rebirth and renewal by the Holy Spirit. (Titus 3:3–5)

The Way of Love was prescribed by the apostle Paul for the church in Corinth and, by extension, for all of us today. Even to this day, no other description of love has surpassed these simple yet powerful words Paul put on paper nearly two thousand years ago: "*Love is patient, <u>love is kind</u>. It does not envy, it does not boast, it is not proud. ⁵ It does not dishonor others, it is not self-seeking, it is not easily angered, it keeps no record of wrongs*" (1 Corinthians 13:4–5, emphasis added).

In Galatians 5, Paul identifies kindness as a fruit of the Holy Spirit (vv. 22–23). When we exhibit the kindness of God, we are tender, benevolent, and gracious to others. Every action, every word will have the flavour of grace in it.

To maintain this attitude toward those we love is hard enough. To express kindness toward those who are against us requires the work of God. That's why kindness is a fruit of the Spirit. Love is also part of that list, revealing the close connection between it and *kindness*. Kindness is characterized by benevolence and tenderness.

The Bible repeatedly tells us to love our neighbours as ourselves and to show kindness to others. Real kindness isn't a manipulative effort to get what we want. Instead, it involves giving something without the hope of a reward. Godly love will make a person kinder. No one can be loving and unkind at the same time.

Kindness is the characteristic that led God to provide salvation for us. It's God's tender care that makes Him want to gather us under His wings to protect us and keep us close to Him. The ultimate expression of God's kindness is found in *"The incomparable riches of his grace, expressed in his kindness to us in Christ Jesus"* (Ephesians 2:7).

In Luke 6:33, Jesus fleshes out for us what it truly means to be kind: *"If you do good only to those who do good to you, what is so great about that? Even the heathens do that much!"* Kindness is patience in action without any thought of being repaid, and loving kindness motivates others toward positive change.

It's much like the famous Good Samaritan Jesus talked about in His parable. He put aside centuries of cultural hatred and religious bigotry to care for someone in need (Luke 10:25–37). That's love in action. That's kindness.

Q. Is there someone to whom you need to show God's kindness today?

As you consider how you treat loved ones, family members, and strangers, try to assimilate the truths in this passage into your own life so that God gets the glory.

PRAYER:
Father, thank you for the kindness you have shown me in Jesus Christ, who loved me even when I deserved your judgement. Please help me to show your kindness to others in such a way that they may be drawn to you. Amen.

10. Love Forgives

It's impossible to love somebody and think well of them while at the same time holding the bad things they might have done in the past against them, like a register of unpaid debts. The apostle Paul says that love keeps no record of wrongs (1 Corinthians 13:5). In this instance, he uses the word *agape*—the kind of love God extends to us.

This type of love isn't infatuation or romance, but it means to love as God loves, to wish well, or to take pleasure in. It might seem impossible to love someone that way, because we're only human. But there's good news tucked away for us in 1 John 4:16. The sentence is short, sweet, and to the point, but it provides the solution to the problem of messy humanity: *"God is love ..."* And you can guess what kind of love He is! Yes, *agape*!

The entire verse reads: *"God is love, and the one who abides in love, remains in God, and God abides in him."* How awesome is that? If that's the case, it's no longer us but the one who abides in us that enables us to *not keep a record of wrongs.*

Perhaps someone comes to mind whom you are unwilling to forgive! If so, remember Jesus' command in Matthew 5:43 to love others, including your enemy! That includes forgiving your enemy who would rater do further harm to you than apologize to you. It really is true:

> *The first to apologize is the bravest,*
> *The first to forgive is the strongest,* and
> *The first to forget is the happiest.*

In the sermon on the Mount, Jesus said:

> You have heard that it was said, "You shall love your neighbor and hate your enemy." But I say to you, love your enemies and pray for those who persecute you, so that you may be sons and daughters of your Father who is in heaven." (Matthew 5:43–46, NASB)

Don't allow the bitterness of an unforgiving spirit to rob you of your peace. Bitterness can become a barrier that prevents you from ever loving again. Someone has said, "Not to forgive a person and holding a grudge because of what they've done to you is like drinking poison and expecting the other person to die." Unforgiveness hurts you more than it hurts the other person. We have to forgive because of what Jesus has done for us. He went to the cross and took upon Himself our sins when we were still at odds with Him, and our sins separated us from the righteousness of God.

How Quickly Should We Forgive?

Pride is a major factor in keeping record of wrongs, but the exercise of humility causes us to forgive as Jesus forgives. The message of Jesus is that we are to humbly forgive others unilaterally and unconditionally. In fact, God warns us that He won't forgive us if we don't forgive others: *"For if you forgive others for their transgressions, your heavenly Father will also forgive you. But if you do not forgive others, then your Father will not forgive your transgressions"* (Matthew 6:14–15, NASB).

Even while Jesus hung on the cross, having been lashed with multiple whips that cut deep furrows on His back, and with blood streaming down His face from the crown of thorns that was pressed into His scull, He still showed forgiveness and endless grace: *"Father, forgive them*, He said, *for they do not know what they are doing"* (Luke 23:34).

Could you forgive like Jesus? Not really! But the one abiding in you will enable you to.

May the Lord fill you with His *agape*, so that you might be able to demonstrate that kind of forgiveness to others.

Chapter 3:
Don't Give Up

Consider him who endured such opposition from sinners, so that you will not grow weary and lose heart.

Hebrews 12:3

11. A Steadfast Faith

The years 2020 to 2022 will forever be engrained in people's minds. These were the years in which the pandemic was in full swing. During that time, I came across a lot of folks who said, "I'm just barely hanging on." Many were hanging on physically because they had been infected by the virus and were suffering. Some were just hanging on emotionally due to the isolation they were feeling. And still others were just hanging on spiritually, because even though they were tuning in to some online spiritual resources, they were missing the fellowship that gathering together brought.

Let me ask you: Do you feel like you're just hanging on? You might get a mental picture of someone desperately hanging on by the tips of their fingers, hoping to be rescued—rescued from isolation, from depression, from a sense of hopelessness, and from a faith that's growing weaker every day. These were very common feelings that perhaps you experienced as well from time to time. During such times, how do you strengthen your grip on the essential things of your faith so that you can find a more secure footing?

In this devotional series, "Don't Give Up!" I hope to encourage you on the essentials of your faith—those things that will enable you to stand firm during the kind of seasons that make you feel totally out of control, and in which everything you hold dearly seems to be slipping away.

The first admonition I want to give is: Don't give up—your faith." The story of faith is almost always a story of perseverance, or refusing to give up. The writer to the Hebrews reminds the followers of Jesus about what he calls "*a great cloud of witnesses.*"

> Therefore, since we are surrounded by such a great cloud of witnesses, let us throw off everything that hinders and the sin that so easily entangles. And let us run with perseverance the race marked out for us, fixing our eyes on Jesus, the pioneer and perfecter of faith. (Hebrews 12:1–2)

This great cloud of witnesses is composed of people who have gone on before us who were witnesses to the awesome power and faithfulness of God during the toughest of times.

People like Abraham and Sarah, who were childless but were promised a child by God and persevered for twenty-five years until the promise was fulfilled.

Or Moses, who witnessed the awesome power of God when, along with the freed Hebrew slaves, he came up against the Red Sea, with the pursuing army of the Egyptians after them. He witnessed the miraculous parting of the water that allowed the children of Israel to cross over on dry ground.

Or Joshua, who, timid and overwhelmed by the enormous responsibility of leading God's children into the Promised Land, witnessed the walls of Jericho crashing to the ground as an awesome display of God's power.

In the New Testament, the writer to the Hebrews speaks encouragement to the weary believers in and around Jerusalem who were facing constant discouragement and persecution, even death. But they stood their ground, held on to their faith, and saw great deliverances by God.

During these uncertain times, we too can stand strong and hold firmly to our faith as we look to what our God will do. You may be at a point where you're saying, "Enough is enough! When are these dark days going to end?" Don't give up! Instead, strengthen your grip. In 2 Chronicles 15:7, we read: *"Take courage! Do not let your hands grow weak, for your work shall be rewarded."*

Surrender your anxieties and fears to the Lord, who invites you to cast all your cares on Him, and fix your eyes on Jesus, your hope in this world.

The writer to the Hebrews goes on to say, *"For the joy set before Him, He endured the cross, scorning its shame, and sat down at the right hand of the throne of God"* (Hebrews 12:2b).

When we surrender these conflicting emotions to Him, we will see things from God's perspective. He will renew our hope—the kind of hope that comes through the resurrection of Jesus Christ.

It's a paradox that Jesus felt joy even in the midst of His suffering. But the joy set before Him was the joy He experienced in rescuing you and me and bringing us into this wonderful relationship with the Father, even through His suffering. The writer of Hebrews says, "Consider him who endured such opposition from sinners, so that you will not grow weary and lose heart." (Hebrews 12:3).

So don't give up, even though you may feel like you have more than you could bear. The apostle Peter encourages us:

> In all this, you greatly rejoice, though now for a little while you may have had to suffer grief in all kinds of trials. These have come so that the proven genuineness of your faith—of greater worth than gold, which perishes even though refined by fire—may result in praise, glory and honor when Jesus Christ is revealed. (1 Peter 1:6–7)

May the genuineness of your faith be a shield against doubts and fears and enable you to strengthen your grip on your faith.

12. Pursue the Truth

Before Jesus was handed over to be crucified, He had an interesting conversation about truth with Pontius Pilate:

> Then Pilate said to him, "So you are a king?" Jesus answered, "You say that I am a king. For this purpose, I was born and for this purpose I have come into the world— to bear witness to the truth. Everyone who is of the truth listens to my voice." Pilate said to him, "What is truth?" *John 18:37-38*

The admonition for today is: Don't give up the pursuit of truth! As I considered this passage, two things occurred to me. First, Pilate's question is one of the most important questions one can ask. In fact, how one lives and dies, what and who one values, and what one believes are dependent upon how one answers this question. I believe it's one of life's most important questions. Therefore, determining what is truth is the most essential and necessary task of our human existence.

Second, when it comes to truth, you often hear people say, "That might be truth for you, but it's not truth for me." But there can't be two types of truth. If something is true, it's true for everyone. Truth is objective. It can't be subjective. During times of suffering or when the temptation seems too much to bear, it's an easy way out to give up the truth of what you believe. This devotional is intended to encourage you to stand firm when you feel like you're just hanging on by the tips of your fingers.

For you who may be starting to let go of the truth that was once very important to you, and are now seeking to pursue your own human desires, please consider again what Jesus said in Matthew 16:26: *"What does it profit you, if you were to gain the whole world, and lose your own soul?"* In a society where absolute truth is treated as a fairy tale, an outdated idea, or even an insult to human intelligence, the motto of the day becomes, "Whatever!" Believe whatever you want. Do whatever seems best to you. Live for whatever brings you pleasure.

At a time when people are looking for quick fixes and easy solutions, it's easy to be seduced into believing a lie. How do you distinguish between falsehood and the truth? Who or what are the ultimate criteria by which truth is judged?

Jesus said, "*You shall know the truth, and the truth shall make you free*" (John 8:32). That's a wonderful promise, which when incorporated into your thinking will change your life forever. So how do you pursue the truth? Pursuing the truth isn't just searching for the truth but living the truth. It's pursuing Jesus, who said, "*I am the way the truth and the life. No one comes to the Father except through me*" (John 14:6, emphasis added). Don't exchange the truth for a lie!

In Romans 1:25, the apostle Paul addresses those who once knew the truth of God's Word but are now being influenced by falsehoods: "*They exchanged the truth about God for a lie, and worshiped and served created things rather than the Creator—who is forever praised. For this reason, God allowed their shameful passions to control them.*"

When you willfully exchange the truth for a lie, you lose your moral compass. So hold on to the truth! Don't exchange it for a lie! Keep on pursuing the truth of God's Word and allow it to take root in our heart. When you do, the truth will make you free. Yes, God has called you and has equipped you with all that you need. And He still beckons to you today to walk in truth and godliness.

In Psalm 25:5, the psalmist prays: "*Guide me in your truth and teach me, for you are God my Savior, and my hope is in you, all day long.*" If you're not pursuing the truth, make that 180-degree turn and return to reading and meditating on God's Word. Let it transform you by renewing your mind so that you no longer conform to the pattern of this world. May the Lord be with you on your journey.

13. Keep on Trusting

In this devotional, my desire is to encourage you not to give up "your trust in God," regardless of how dire the situation may be or how hopeless it might appear.

One of the greatest struggles and challenges you may encounter during difficult days is trusting God. You may have questions like:

Is He for me or against me? Does He understand what I'm going through? Does He even love me?

If you're familiar with the account of Job in the Bible, you know that there was a steadfastness about him in the midst of his suffering. Even though he didn't understand the reason or purpose for his suffering, he continued to persevere and trust God through it all. Job said, "*Though He slays me, yet will I trust in him: but I will maintain mine own ways before him*" (Job 13:15, KJV).

Trusting God is easy when you can see how everything is going to work out, or when you're in good health and have a secure job, money in the bank, and a lot of good friends. At such times, you're living on the mountain top. If you were completely honest, you'd agree that during those times, it doesn't take a lot to trust God.

The challenge comes when you go from the mountain top of joy into the valley of despair. During these periods of despair, you may become weary in body, mind, and soul—weary of waiting, weary of trying to find joy, weary of hoping for better days. Your period of despair may leave you wondering if the darkness will ever lift.

It's easy for people to become jaded as their vision gets clouded and their view of life becomes hopeless. Where do we find the strength to go on and the will to trust again? These aren't easy issues to deal with, yet in the midst of life, these two verses leap off the page from the scriptures: "*Trust in the LORD with all your heart and lean not on your own understanding, in all your ways submit to him, and he will make your paths straight*" (Proverbs 3:5–6).

There it is, laid out in front of you, the command *to trust* and not to lean on our own understanding. Yet it doesn't solve the problem of how to trust in the Lord with all your heart. More importantly, how do you do it when your world is falling apart and the walls are caving in?

Obviously, it's not easy. But it is possible to do, or else God wouldn't ask you to do it. The question remains: How do you get to this place of trust? Or even, what does it mean to trust?

Trust means to have a *firm belief* or *reliance* in the character or ability of someone or something. Certainly you'll agree that God's character and ability can be trusted. We can trust God even in the midst of adversity.

Jeremiah was called "the weeping prophet" because of his concern both for the sins and the plight of his countrymen and women. They were forcibly taken from their home, their land, and their people and forced to settle in another country with a different language and customs. More than anything, they longed to go home, to return to the land of Israel.

However, they were told that they would not go home, that they should seek to thrive where they were, because they would be in that predicament for quite a while. That's hard news. But with this hard news, God gave great assurance:

> For thus says the Lord: When seventy years are completed for Babylon, I will visit you, and I will fulfill to you my promise and bring you back to this place. For I know the plans I have for you, declares the Lord, plans for welfare and not for evil, to give you a future and a hope. (Jeremiah 29:10–11, ESV)

Personally, Jeremiah endured great perils. Picture the prophet in a dungeon, up to his armpits in mud, wrestling with the prospect that he might never see his loved ones again. He is basically in utter despair. Now listen to his answer to his own despair, and whatever despair you may be facing: "*Yet this I call to mind and therefore I have hope: Because of the* Lord's *great love we are not consumed, for his compassions never fail. They are new every morning; great is your faithfulness*" (Lamentations 3:21–23).

So how do you trust in the Lord when you are in a dungeon, up to your armpits in mud? You recall God's great love, His compassion, and His faithfulness toward you. Trust is only as good as the object of that trust. And from the Word of God, we know that God can be trusted.

Be assured today that God cares deeply about you and your present circumstances, and He will bring you through whatever satiation you're in! Don't give up your trust in God. Call to mind

His faithfulness, and allow the truth of His Word to bring hope to you today.

I began with Job, and I conclude with his remarks to God. After he came through his suffering, where his trust was strengthened in an even greater way, Job said: *"I had only heard about you before, but now I have seen you with my own eyes. I take back everything I said, and I sit in dust and ashes to show my repentance"* (Job 42:4-6 NLT).

May the Lord be with you and bring you through whatever you may be facing today, with a renewed trust in Him.

14. Embrace the Word

As you might have experienced by now, the followers of Jesus aren't immune to the hardships and struggles in this world. We experience *the same* challenges, tensions, sufferings, and struggles. In those dark and difficult moments, Jesus' presence, love, and faithfulness can become tangible and real. They enable us to persevere through suffering.

Along with the presence of Jesus, *the Word of God* has the power to encourage and strengthen us. In this devotional, I emphasize the importance of the Bible—the Word of God. "Don't give up—the Word of God!"

Why is the Word of God so essential in the life of the Christ follower? Well, it's like spiritual food. Unless you're on a fast, you don't go without your daily food. It gives physical strength to the body. In the same way, the Word of God nourishes the soul and makes us spiritually strong.

The psalmist says in Psalm 119:105, *"Your word is a lamp for my feet, a light on my path."* The Word of God is like a torch or lamp that helps us see in the dark of night. It casts light at the feet to prevent us from stumbling over obstacles, falling down precipices, or wandering off into paths that lead into danger. But it's also a light unto our path that shines on the road we take. It helps us to see the road ahead and gives us insights into our planning. It lights our path so that we may see any dangers that lay ahead and avoid them.

The scripture says that the Word of God is powerful. It's like spiritual dynamite! The writer to the Hebrews describes it in these terms: *"For the word of God is alive and active, sharper than any double-edged sword, it penetrates even to dividing soul and spirit, joints and marrow; it judges the thoughts and attitudes of the heart"* (Hebrews 4:12).

The apostle Paul, writing to the Ephesian Christians, described the Word of God as a part of our spiritual armour, calling it the *sword of the Spirit*. With the Word of God and prayer, you can demolish the strongholds of evil. So never neglect it, especially during those times when you're experiencing challenges and discouragements. Our strength lies in both the knowledge and application of God's Word.

The apostle James admonishes us:

> Therefore, get rid of all moral filth and the evil that is so prevalent and humbly accept the word planted in you, which can save you. Do not merely listen to the word, and so deceive yourselves. Do what it says. (James 1:21–22)

Don't give up on reading the Word of God. You will gain insights and wisdom by reading, meditating, and applying its truths to your life.

In writing to young Timothy, the apostle Paul reminded him not only about the power of the Word, but also the inerrancy of the Word. It is inspired by God:

> All Scripture is inspired by God and is useful to teach us what is true, and to make us realize what is wrong in our lives. It <u>corrects</u> us when we are wrong and <u>teaches</u> us to do what is right. God uses it to <u>prepare</u> and <u>equip</u> his people to do every good work. (2 Timothy 3:16–17, NLT, emphasis added)

The application of God's Word in these four distinct ways ensures that you become mature and thoroughly equipped to be and do what God requires of you. The Bible points to Jesus as the main character in the book. This is amazing! It's like one big arrow, pointing to Jesus. So when you read it, look for Jesus. Jesus says, "*You study the Scriptures diligently because you think that in them you have eternal life. These are the very Scriptures that testify about me*" (John 5:39).

There are some other benefits derived from God's Word, namely: "*They are more precious than gold, than much pure gold; they are sweeter than honey, than honey from the honeycomb. By them your servant is warned; in keeping them there is great reward*" (Psalm 19:10–11).

The Word of God is Spirit and it is life. Jesus says in John 6:63, "*The Spirit gives life; the flesh counts for nothing. The words I have spoken to you—they are full of the Spirit and life.*" My prayer is that you will hold on to the Word of God and allow it to sink deep into your heart, where it becomes a weapon against the devil's schemes. May the Lord bless you. Amen.

15. Pray Continually

As I consider the topic *Don't Give Up Praying*, I think of the biblical account of Hannah—childless and one of the two wives of Elkanah. She went up to the temple year after year to pray with Elkanah and his other wife, who had sons and daughters. Because she was barren, her rival kept provoking her in order to irritate her.

One day when Hannah could no longer bear the pain of her empty womb, she went to the temple again to present her supplication to the Lord. She cried out to the Lord and wept bitterly. She was so upset that she made a promise to the Lord in her request for a son:

> In her deep anguish Hannah prayed to the Lord, weeping bitterly. And she made a vow, saying, "Lord Almighty, if you will only look on your servant's misery and remember me, and not forget your servant but give her a son, then I will give him to the Lord for all the days of his life. (1 Samuel 1:10–11)

Not long after her visit to the temple, God answered her prayer, and she became pregnant. When she delivered her son, she called him Samuel, which means "asked of God." Hannah didn't forget her promise either; as soon as Samuel was weaned, she presented him to the Lord.

All of us at one time or another will face very difficult seasons—days when we are beset by many struggles, such as job loss, poor mental and physical health, loneliness, emotional and physical abuse, and relationship problems, to name a few. You might have prayed on several occasions, but then you've started to wonder whether God is hearing you or not. Don't give up praying! What God did for Hannah, He is able to do for you.

Jesus said to His followers: *"And so, I tell you, keep on asking, and you will receive what you ask for. Keep on seeking, and you will find. Keep on knocking, and the door will be opened to you"* (Luke 11:19). You might be asking why the answer isn't forthcoming? Jesus encourages us not to give up but to keep on persevering, even when the answer is not yet apparent.

But why pray in the first place? Since God is all-powerful and all-knowing, He must know what I want even before I ask Him. So why pray? As you know, prayer has to be more than just coming to God with a list of things we want Him to do for us. If you didn't have these needs, would you be coming to Him?

Think about it! Prayer is an opportunity to communicate with the Creator of the universe! The one who set the galaxies in place has extended an invitation for you to commune with Him. How awesome is that? Our prayers shouldn't be contingent on whether we get our needs met or not. The relationship we have with God as our heavenly Father is wonderful enough!

In Habakkuk 3, The prophet expresses his contentment with just being able to have an audience with God:

> Though the fig tree does not bud and there are no grapes on the vines, though the olive crop fails and the fields produce no food, though there are no sheep in the pen and no cattle in the stalls, yet I will rejoice in the LORD, I will be joyful in God my Savior. (Habakkuk 3:17–18)

Prayer is an opportunity for us to express our thankfulness to God and be in awe of Him—not just for what He has done but for who He is. When His disciples asked Jesus to teach them to pray, He began with this very simple phrase. *"Our Father in heaven, hallowed be your name"* (Matthew 6:9). In this simple phrase, we get a picture of the one to whom we are praying.

In it, we see the transcendence of God as well as the imminence of God. Transcendent because He is so unlike us. He is above and beyond our human wisdom. He is the Logos, the eternal Word. Imminent because He is a Father who is at hand. He can relate to His children and is touched with the feelings of our infirmities. He is never too busy to stoop and listen to the faintest cry of one of His children. What might appear as inactivity on God's part may really be Him working on your behalf.

Christian prayer is perhaps the most important activity one could engage in.

First and foremost, it develops an intimate relationship with God. Prayer involves the whole Trinity. Ephesians 2:18 reads, *"Now all of us can come to the Father through the same Holy Spirit because of what Christ has done for us"* (NLT, emphasis added).

Jesus says Matthew 6:6: *"But when you pray, go into your room, close the door and pray to your Father, who is unseen. Then your Father, who sees what is done in secret, will reward you."* So why persevere in payer? Prayer gives us perspective; it changes the way we perceive things. James 4:8 says, *"Draw near to God and He will draw near to you."* In so doing, our hearts are quieted, pride is stripped away, and we enjoy the presence of God. As my pastor says, "Prayer is a time to be cherished, not a task to be checked!"

Are you facing a *season* of struggles? Have you prayed but it seems like your prayers don't go past the ceiling of your room? Don't give up praying! The time for God's deliverance will surely come. Regardless of what the present outcome may look like, if you persevere in prayer, in the end you'll reap a bountiful harvest.

16. Tell of God's Love

Have you ever felt so discouraged that the last thing you wanted to do was to have a social conversation with someone? The pain of your discouragement might have been so intense that all you wanted was to be left alone!

Sometimes this discouragement feeds into the desire for emotional or physical isolation. This is usually brought about by grief or loss—loss of a loved one or a relationship, which has resulted in a broken heart. You may be experiencing a kind of cosmic homesickness, longing to return to the familiar. This desire can sometimes cause us to miss opportunities to connect with people. In this devotional, I encourage you not to give up sharing the good news, even during those difficult seasons of your life.

The apostle Peter, fully aware of the struggles the followers of Jesus had been facing as they were persecuted for their faith, encouraged them with these words: *"In your hearts revere Christ as Lord. Always be prepared to give an answer to everyone who asks you to give the reason for the hope that you have. But do this with gentleness and respect"* (1 Peter 3:15). Regardless of the season of life you're experiencing, you're admonished to always be prepared to share the good news of the gospel of Jesus Christ.

The exiled children of Israel were in a similar state of longing to return to the familiar, particularly their homeland, when they were being ask to tell the good news of Zion. Psalm 137:1–4 records their lament:

> By the rivers of Babylon we sat and wept when we remembered Zion. There on the poplar trees we hung our harps, for there our captors asked us for songs, our tormentors demanded songs of joy; they said, "Sing us one of the songs of Zion!" Their response: How can we sing the songs of the LORD while in a foreign land?

These aliens who had been taken from their homeland, their familiar surroundings, and the worship of God, are in great distress.

And to add insult to injury, they were being asked to sing one of the songs of Zion.

The instruments that brought them joy and with which they praised the God of Israel had been set aside. They lay silent, hanging on poplar trees. The isolation from their homeland, family, and friends was just too overwhelming for them. Understandably, their focus was turned inward, and they were having a kind of pity party. Have you ever experienced that? As followers of Jesus, wherever we are and whatever situation we find ourselves in, we must be willing to be *salt* and *light*, as Jesus says we are.

We too are aliens in this world. We are strangers and pilgrims here. Our citizenship is from another kingdom. The question "How can we sing the Lord's songs while in a foreign land" shouldn't be a rhetorical one, nor one of resignation! It is something we must do. We must share the good news at all times!

It's often during one of your most difficult seasons that someone will ask you for a song: "Sing me one of those songs of Zion! Share with me what keeps you so grounded, even during these difficult days!" Your response can't be, "If you only knew the kind of day I was having, you wouldn't ask!"

As followers of Jesus, we have the best news possible. It's news that sets prisoners free, transforms people's lives, and brings freedom from sin when people hear it and respond to the grace of God through Jesus Christ. It brings hope to the hopeless and light to those walking in darkness.

Yes, the good news of Jesus Christ is too precious to keep to oneself. Jesus came down to earth to live the life we should have lived, and die the death we should have died. Because of this, He has given us new life, abundant life, and hope for all eternity. And He has commissioned us to be bearers of this good news.

Don't ever give up sharing the good news, regardless of your circumstances. People everywhere are hungry and eager to hear good news—the good news that they can leave behind their past failures, sin, and shame for a life of victory in Jesus! What could be better news than that!

Regardless of the season you're in, don't give up sharing the good news of Jesus Christ. Because He is the hope of this world and the next. Blessings on your journey!

17. Keep on Meeting Together

Time and time again, the author of the book of Hebrews points believers back to Old Testament promises now fulfilled in Christ. And time and time again, he urges the followers of Jesus to remain in relationship with one another and to help one another through the long journey of faith.

In this devotional, I encourage you to not give up "worshiping together." Whether virtually or in person, there's something spiritually organic that happens when followers of Jesus get together. I watched with great joy and was quite encouraged by some of the "chats" on our church's "livestream services." I noticed that there was delight and hunger in people's hearts for connection. Why is that? I think it's because we're meant to be encouragers of one another. In the apostle Paul's first letter to the Thessalonians, he writes: *"Therefore encourage one another and build each other up, just as in fact you are doing"* (1 Thessalonians 5:11).

The writer of Hebrews also speaks to us about the importance of gathering together: *"Don't give up meeting together, as some are in the habit of doing, but encourage one another—and all the more as you see the Day approaching"* (Hebrews 10:25).

Fellowshipping together is one of the greatest attributes of the church. It keeps believers strong, committed, and accountable. Even though during and after the pandemic there's been a rise in the number of people who worship virtually, the need to get together isn't lost on them.

The apostle Peter also encouraged his readers to apply themselves to acquiring the true knowledge of God by saying; *"So then, dear friends, since you are looking forward to this, make every effort to be found spotless, blameless and at peace with him"* (2 Peter 3:14).

How do we apply this to our lives today? Just as the early followers of Jesus endured great trials and testing, we also will go through difficult seasons of testing and trials. These trials seem to hit us even harder when we face them alone. But when we're connected with one another both physically and spiritually, we're better able to persevere, as we are the Body of Christ. The apostle Paul wrote to the Corinthians: *"If one part suffers, every part suffers with it; if one part is honored, every part rejoices with it. Now you are the body of Christ, and each one of you is a part of it"* (1 Corinthians 12:26–27).

Believers can create dissension in multiple ways, particularly in the areas of connection and relationships. To guard against this kind of discord—both in our families and our gathering together—God's people need to remember who He is and who we are in relation to Him. Our knowledge of God through His Word is the first line of defence against the conflicts that often threaten to tear us apart. The apostle James asks, *"What causes fights and quarrels among you? Don't they come from your desires that battle within you?"* (James 4:1).

During these days of close connections, it's easy for conflicts to develop. Let's remember that as the body of Christ, the Church is called to help one another grow in grace and in the knowledge of Jesus Christ.

The followers of Jesus need to guard against a couple of things. First, putting on masks—no, not the kind that protect you from diseases, but the ones that prevent people from seeing the real you. Masks say, "Even though I'm not okay, I'll pretend that I am. Even though I don't like you, I'll pretend that I do. The other thing to guard against is presenting an exterior appearance that says "I am spiritually well" while on the inside you are hard and dry like an artificial plant with beautiful leaves and pleasant flowers to look at, but no fragrance or life.

Yes, in the Body of Christ we are called to be real, to practise love and hospitality toward one another, and in love, to correct and strengthen those who need to be encouraged. It's in these cherished relationships where faith blossoms and grows.

PRAYER:
Father God, I thank you for the wonderful relationship you have with your Church. Thank you for the sacrifice of Jesus on the cross,

where He died to purchase my salvation and set me free. Thank you for this knowledge and the reality that we are the Body of Christ. I confess that there are times when I have worn a mask because I didn't want anyone to see that I wasn't perfect. But you are the only perfect One. Please help me to lean on you as well as on the brothers and sisters you have placed in my life, so as we worship together, we will indeed encourage and strengthen one another, and so bring glory and praise to your holy name. Amen.

18. Persevere in Suffering

In the Sermon on the Mount, Jesus lists the blessings that await those who live their lives with eternity in view. In today's devotional, Jesus addresses the final beatitude: *"Blessed are those who are persecuted because of righteousness, for theirs is the kingdom of heaven"* (Matthew 5:10).

From the very beginning, Jesus prepared His followers for the inevitable—not just the possibility, but the certainty—that those who follow Him will face opposition, persecution, and even death: *"If any of you wants to be my follower, you must give up your own way, take up your cross, and follow me"* (Mark 6:34, NLT). This statement may not be very explicit to us in the twenty-first century. Many people today see the cross only as a religious icon, or a piece of jewellery to be worn around the neck. On the other hand, many people interpret the "cross" as some burden they must carry in their lives, such as a strained relationship, a thankless job, a physical illness, or disobedient children.

With self-pitying pride, they may say, "That's my cross I have to carry." But such an interpretation is not what Jesus meant when He said we are to take up our crosses and follow Him. In Jesus' day, that statement would have evoked much fear. You see, everyone knew what taking up the cross meant.

When Jesus carried His cross up Golgotha to be crucified, no one was thinking of the cross as symbolic or a burden to carry. Everyone knew that He was going to die. To someone in the first century, the cross meant one thing and one thing only—a shameful and horrible death.

The cross was the Roman instrument of torture, intended to inflict maximum pain, public humiliation, and finally death to its victims. But for Jesus, what was intended to be a cruel and shameful death resulted in peace, joy, and forgiveness for His followers. Two thousand years later, Christians everywhere view the cross as a cherished symbol of atonement, forgiveness, grace, and love. But in Jesus' day, the cross represented nothing but a torturous death.

The Roman custom was to force the convicted criminal to carry his own cross to the place of crucifixion. Therefore, "Take up your cross and follow me" means being willing to die to follow Jesus. But Jesus sees this not as a futile act of self sacrifice but one that will be greatly rewarded in heaven.

When Jesus said *"Blessed are those who are persecuted because of righteousness, for theirs is the kingdom of heaven"* (Matthew 5:10). He was assuring us that the kingdom of God belongs to those who will suffer in this life because of Him and His message. Although the call is a tough one, the reward is great. Through this beatitude, Jesus encourages His followers even today to hold fast to the righteousness of God, regardless of what happens, because the kingdoms of this world can never be compared to the kingdom of God in heaven.

When Jesus made this pronouncement, He was referring to Christians across the world where the gospel message is greeted with great hostility. Today, persecution is real. It's the daily reality for more than 360 million Christians worldwide. The words of Jesus in this beatitude must serve as a great source of assurance and encouragement to them.

Jesus ends this beatitude by elaborating on what He had just said in Matthew 5:10: *"Blessed are you when people insult you, persecute you and falsely say all kinds of evil against you because of me. Rejoice and be glad, because great is your reward in heaven"* (Matthew 5:11–12)

"Rejoice and be glad?" Is that possible? The apostle James writes, *"Consider it a great joy, my brothers and sisters, whenever you experience various trials"* (James 1:2). James tells us not to be so hasty to escape the faith-testing valleys, because those valleys contain the fertile soil needed to produce steadfastness.

We all like ease and comfort! But have you ever heard anyone say, "The deepest, rarest, and most satisfying joys of my life have come in times of extended ease and earthly comfort"? Nobody says that. Rather, what Charles Spurgeon said is true: "*Those who dive in the sea of affliction bring up rare pearls.*" [4]

As Christians, we may eagerly say, "I just want to be like Jesus." But really, we're only asking for the good stuff. Jesus said, "*Blessed are the persecuted!*" Richard Wurmbrand, who had been imprisoned in an Eastern European Communist Country and was frequently tortured for preaching the gospel, often talked about how even in the solitude of his prison cell, hungry, cold, and in rags, he danced for joy every night. What would make someone rejoice in the midst of being tortured? There is a mystery here—the mystery of joy in the midst of agony, of gladness in the midst of misery and groaning.

The very first Christian to die for the sake of the gospel was Stephen. As he was being stoned to death, listen to what he said: "'*Look,*' he said, '*I see heaven open and the Son of Man standing at the right hand of God*'" (Acts 7:56). Stephen was given a Hero's Welcome by Jesus! Jesus was faithful to His Word. Truly, the kingdom of heaven belongs to the blessed of God.

If and when persecution comes to you, please remember the words of Jesus, who said that the kingdom of God belongs to you!

4. Charles H. Spurgeon, *Charles Spurgeon* quotes *at AZquotes.com*.

Chapter 4:
A Time to Un-Mask

> Watch out for false prophets.
> They come to you in sheep's clothing,
> but inwardly they are ferocious wolves.
>
> Matthew 7:15

19. Uncommon Virtues

Can you imagine going to college, but instead of attending a formal classroom, you follow your professor from town to town, learning from His words and examples? Well, that was the way Jesus taught His disciples as well as the crowds that followed Him around.

Jesus taught a series of wonderful lessons during one of these interesting outside-the-classroom sessions. They're contained in Jesus' Sermon on the Mount, so named because Jesus gave this teaching as He sat on a mountainside, with His disciples sitting down around Him.

Jesus began His teaching by pronouncing eight blessings, commonly known as the beatitudes. "Beatitude" simply means "Blessed are you" or "Happy are you."

> Now when Jesus saw the crowds, he went up on a mountainside and sat down. His disciples came to him, and he began to teach them. He said: "Blessed are the poor in spirit, for theirs is the kingdom of heaven. Blessed are

those who mourn, for they will be comforted. Blessed are the meek, for they will inherit the earth. Blessed are those who hunger and thirst for righteousness, for they will be filled. Blessed are the merciful, for they will be shown mercy. Blessed are the pure in heart, for they will see God. Blessed are the peacemakers, for they will be called children of God. Blessed are those who are persecuted because of righteousness, for theirs is the kingdom of heaven." (Matthew 5:1–10)

In this devotional series, I'll be looking at each of these blessings individually. But first, I want you to get a good idea of the kinds of people Jesus considers to be blessed. They are people with uncommon virtues, which is the topic of this devotional today. Culturally speaking, the people on whom Jesus is conferring these blessings are not the ones society cherishes. They aren't the kind of people typically featured on magazine covers or invited to awards shows. Yet they are exactly the ones Jesus is speaking about—the ones He considers blessed.

His words are especially designed for and targeted at those we might call *losers*. But Jesus was not aloof from such persons. They typify His own life here on earth. He was born in a smelly stable, grew up in a dirty seaside village, of which the question was asked, "Can anything good could come from there?" He wasn't afraid to touch the oozing wounds of lepers, and He knew what it was like to be poor and destitute. He went to dinner with outcasts and the marginalized, both religious and irreligious. His closest friends were a collection of crude fishermen and cultural misfits.

The Sermon on the Mount was a harbinger of the things that the righteous Son of God would later suffer. It began with the disciples gathered at His feet with the crowds listening in. The crowd might have come out of curiosity, skepticism, or even genuine need. But regardless of their reasons for being there, Jesus addressed everyone present, with the hope that they would find in Him the answer to their needs.

In a world where riches seem to mean the most, what could Jesus mean by these words? In our day, people commonly seek every opportunity to advance themselves. They seek the highest seats in government, seek to be honoured by all, while accumulating the wealth of this world. Yet Jesus' words flow contrary to such thinking and seeking. As followers of Jesus, we're called to live a life that is totally counter-cultural. But if you were honest, you'd confess that it's not easy to do. It's hard to take the solitary road.

Yes, the Beatitudes are important because they inform us that the things that need pursuing, the treasures that are priceless, are not the ones to be found in this world but are laid up for us in heaven. They teach us that life includes setbacks and challenges, but our rewards will be worth the struggles. They teach us that we shouldn't repay evil with evil, that we should seek to bring peace into the world, and that even our best intentions at times may be met with persecution.

Through these beatitudes, we learn that the rewards spoken of are mostly to be had in the future, although there may be glimpses of them in this present life. Jesus brought the kingdom of heaven to earth in His own kingly power, so at times we may enjoy a foretaste of it here and now.

But Jesus doesn't want us to focus on achieving these rewards here on earth; He wants us to have our priorities in order: *"But seek first his kingdom and his righteousness, and all these things will be given to you as well"* (Matthew 6:33). The full experience of the life of the kingdom will be realized in the age to come.

Through these Beatitudes, Jesus speaks to believers of our day as well, emphasizing that riches are not blessings. Being famous, or popular, is not to be our goal. Rather, we must seek the things of Jesus, which are never popular, but they are the ones that will earn eternal dividends.

If you find that Jesus' Sermon on the Mount is challenging, strive to acquire the virtues that are enumerated there. Because they are uncommon virtues. Keep living as Jesus calls you to do, even when it becomes difficult. Because great will be your rewards in heaven. Amen.

20. Desiring God

It's been said that the most uplifting sermon Jesus ever preached was the Sermon on the Mount. It describes what our life should be like while we live in faith—in our thoughts, words, and actions.

In this devotional series, I'm looking at how Jesus, in His Sermon on the Mount, paints a picture of an upside-down kingdom—a picture quite different from what His audience, especially the religious leaders, envisioned.

Jesus describes a kingdom where the poor in spirit—those who desire God and are dependent on Him—are considered blessed, where only the ones with repentant hearts will see Him, and where the ostracised and the marginalized are brought from the fringes into the centre of God's redeeming love.

Today, our focus is on the first Beatitude: *"Blessed are the poor in spirit, for theirs is the kingdom of heaven"* (Matthew 5:3).

Some people, especially those who do social work, find it very difficult to fathom Jesus' statement that poor people are blessed. Because they see how poor people are suffering around the world.

In Mark 14:7, Jesus says, *"You have the poor with you always."* What does it mean to be poor in spirit? Is it low self-esteem, or low interest in spiritual things? Many religious people in Jesus' day called themselves "the poor," for they often *were* poor materially. Poor people know that they have needs, and they look to God to supply their daily needs. But Jesus wasn't referring to that.

To be poor in spirit suggests something more. The truth is, regardless of our cleverness, our achievements, and our technological gadgets, we are spiritual paupers without God. Those who are poor in spirit know that they need God; they feel a lack in their lives. They feel unworthy even to think that God would care about them.

But Jesus says that the kingdom is for people such as these. It's the humble, the God-dependent, the unworthy who are given the kingdom of heaven. The poor in spirit have a desire for God and trust in His mercy. There are famous and wealthy people who are "pitifully poor" in spirit. Jesus' message wasn't only for the financially poor, the socially poor, or the intellectually poor. It was meant for those who recognized their own spiritual poverty and their need for God. They are the ones who are blessed. "*Blessed are the poor in spirit, for theirs is the kingdom of heaven*" (Matthew 5:3).

This is the first Beatitude. It's the dominant note on which the remainder of the message was composed. Jesus was speaking to all people of all beliefs, ages, and financial status, revealing to them the secret of happiness.

Jesus stated clearly that those qualities lead not just to a different lifestyle that pleases Him but to one that will reap eternal dividends in the kingdom of heaven. Therefore, a close examination of each is essential in order to identify and demonstrate these traits in our own lives.

Attached to each character trait is a corresponding promise. Jesus holds out a particular benefit for each particular quality. And what great promises they are! A promise of the kingdom of God, to be comforted, to be filled, and so forth. But that's not all. The Beatitudes also contain an implicit invitation to all to become this kind of person.

The disciples sitting at Jesus's feet would have heard these words as congratulations. "Oh, how blessed you are, my dear brothers!" It's no wonder that when He finished the sermon, we read, "*the crowds were amazed at His teaching; for He was teaching them as one having authority*" (Matthew 7:28–29). Never before had His audience heard such marvelous truths presented in such a graceful and meaningful manner. They longed to have those promises incarnate in their own lives, as all of us should this wonderful day. Please examine your heart to see if you are God-dependent or self-dependent!

In the fallen world, poverty of spirit may seem to be a hindrance to success and advancement. But that's only an illusion. Jesus is saying that no matter your status in life, you must recognize your spiritual poverty before you can come to God in faith to receive the salvation He offers.

The phrase the "kingdom of heaven" can be broad in meaning. It's the domain of God and our future home, but it's also the eternal quality of life with God we can enjoy even now. Jesus says in John

10:10: "*The thief comes only to steal and kill and destroy. I came that they may have life and have it abundantly.*"

Whether you have it all together socially, financially, or intellectually, and consider yourself to be rich, if you don't have a desire for God in your life, you are spiritually poor. God in His mercy and grace wants you to confess that you're spiritually poor so that you can lay hold of the wonderful riches and blessings of the kingdom of heaven He has in store for you. Be blessed.

21. The Contrite Heart

In Ecclesiastes 3, Solomon says, "*There is a time for everything, and a season for every activity under the heavens … a time to weep and a time to laugh, a time to mourn and a time to dance.*" Through the various seasons of our lives, we have to expect the unexpected.

When my father passed away quite suddenly at the age of fifty-nine, it was quite a sad time for me. I was only seventeen years old, and even though I didn't have a personal relationship with the Lord at the time, looking back, I believe I received comfort from Him. There was a traditional wake called "nine nights," when family and friends showed up to sing hymns and have a time of fellowship. To my family, this was a time of mourning. But mourning can take on many forms based on tradition or customs, and people mourn for various reasons.

Today as we look at the second Beatitude, it takes us to Jesus' pronouncement about the blessedness of those who mourn" "*Blessed* (happy) *are those who mourn, for they will be comforted*" (Matthew 5:4).

What did Jesus mean? Is it not our goal in life to be happy? Why then would mourning be a blessing?

As Jesus spoke on the mountainside that day, it was clear to everyone that He was about to disturb the status quo. He was turning everything upside-down. It's after a loss or catastrophe that we're more attuned to spiritual things. As a matter of fact, the Sunday after 9/11 occurred, church buildings across North America reported record attendances.

According to Solomon, the house of mourning causes us to think about the end of life, which has a profound affect on how we live. However, the words of Jesus in Matthew 5:4 point to another aspect of mourning.

The Bible tells us that the Lord is close to the broken-hearted and to those who are remorseful about their sins. When Jesus spoke these words, He wasn't necessarily thinking of those who had just lost something of value or suffered a catastrophe. Rather, He was referring to those who are of a contrite heart and remorseful about their sins.

Mourning in this context refers to a deep sadness over sin. Jesus is saying that those who are remorseful about their sins shall receive comfort from God. Those who mourn are the ones who acknowledge their lost and sinful state and, in repentance, receive comfort from the Lord.

Along with the disciples and the crowd on the mountainside that day were the ultra-religious leaders, known as the Pharisees. They were unrepentant in their attitudes and their insistence on following their own man-made laws and religious customs. In spite of Jesus' teaching to the contrary, they expressed no sorrow or remorse for their persistent sin and self-righteousness. Jesus' words were intended to help them see their own sinfulness. His words included an implicit invitation for them to come to Him in contrition and have their sins forgiven.

How easy it is for us to pridefully live each day as though there's no end to the comforts and pleasures we enjoy! But as Jesus reminds us, there is no comfort for those who are not remorseful about their sin. Jesus extends this wonderful invitation:

> Come to me, all you who are weary and burdened, and I will give you rest. Take my yoke upon you and learn from me, for I am gentle and humble in heart, and you will find rest for your souls, for my yoke is easy and my burden is light. (Matthew 11:28–30)

For the believer, mourning reminds us that this world is not really our home. Our true home is in heaven with the Lord Jesus, and all of life is a travail that will end with the perfect peace of eternity with our Lord's comfort.

If you're looking for comfort from this world, you'll find that it's fleeting. But if with a contrite heart you lay hold of God's grace and, with genuine contrition, confess your sins to Him, you will receive comfort from the Lord that will last throughout eternity. So when godly sorrow overcomes you in this life, experience the comfort of the Lord as He wraps His loving arms about you.

In this life, the Lord comforts us with a comfort that no one else could give. But the ultimate comfort comes when you see Him face to face and know that it is well with your soul. So why are those who mourn blessed? Because they shall receive the ultimate comfort from the Lord.

22. Genuine Meekness

What's the one word you typically won't see in your average Facebook or Twitter post? It's the word "meek." Meekness is usually absent both in word and attitude. In a world where we seek to put our best face forward and boast about our possessions and achievements, there's no room for meekness in our vocabulary.

When people do use this word, they generally mean *weak, easily lead,* or *impressionable*. But Jesus sees meekness in a different light. In His Sermon on the Mount, Jesus made this statement as the third beatitude: "*Blessed are the meek, for they shall inherit the earth*" (Matthew 5:5, emphasis added). What did Jesus mean by this pronouncement? He was speaking an incredibly counter-cultural truth to those people sitting on the mountainside that day, as this was a world that didn't understand gentleness or meekness.

The disciples, the crowd, and especially the religious leaders (the Pharisees) understood what it meant to be powerful. This was a world where armies made people in rebellion submit to their incredible might. Those were the ones, it would appear, who had already inherited the earth.

Meekness is probably the least admired character trait in the world today, yet the greatest person who ever lived was a meek and humble man. Jesus said, *"Take my yoke upon you, and learn from me; for I am <u>meek and lowly in heart</u>: and you shall find rest unto your souls"* (Matthew 11:29, emphasis added).

Meekness, as used by Jesus, is different from what the world considers it to be. Meekness is not weakness. It is power under control. The literal interpretation is "gentleness," but it goes even deeper in meaning. It means to have great power to do harm but choosing to suffer insults upon yourself rather than using your power to cause injury.

The person who exemplifies this virtue best is Jesus. Remember His words when He suffered beatings and mocking and was nailed to the cross by cruel soldiers: *"Are you not aware that I can call on My Father, and He will at once put at My disposal more than twelve legions of angels?"* (Matthew 26:53). But of course, we know that He endured these insults and cruelty by praying for His offenders instead.

According to Jesus, those who inherit the earth will be those whose stories may never be known on this earth—the oppressed, the persecuted, the marginalized, and those who live their lives with eternity in view. One day when we're standing in heaven, we might discover that the poor misunderstood, maligned person is the one God used to change the course of history. You can never know the end of the story until you get to it.

Jesus said, *"Blessed are the meek, for they shall inherit the earth"* (Matthew 5:5). So who are the meek? Would you consider yourself to be a meek person? If you have humbled yourself before God and have embraced the truth of the gospel, that is the beginning of being meek. A meek person considers others more important than themself. And if you strive to lead others, you must first be willing to become a servant in obedience to the gospel of Jesus Christ.

The apostle Paul, writing to the Philippians, said: *"Do nothing out of selfish ambition or vain conceit. Rather, in humility value others above yourselves, not looking to your own interests but each of you to the interests of the others"* (Philippians 2:3–4).

The apostle Paul continues to encourage the Philippians by explaining that their attitudes and mindset should be the same as the Lord Jesus Christ's:

> In your relationships with one another, have the same mindset as Christ Jesus: Who, being in very nature God, did not consider equality with God something to be used to his own advantage; rather, he made himself nothing by taking the very nature of a servant, being made in human likeness. And being found in appearance as a man, he humbled himself by becoming obedient to death—even death on a cross! (2 Philippians 2:5–8)

Everything in our culture and experience says the meek and the humble will get run over. But Jesus says that these are the very ones who shall receive the earth as an inheritance. They will become co-heirs with Jesus.

Ask the Lord daily to give you a spirit of humility, gentleness, and meekness in your dealings with others. By exhibiting these virtues, you will bring glory to your Father in heaven. May the Lord bless!

23. Spiritual Hunger

Having five Great Lakes on the North American continent can desensitize us to the needs of people who live in arid lands and for whom water is a precious commodity. Water for us is something we take for granted.

But as Jesus sat on a hillside in Northern Israel on the Korazim Plateau, where He delivered His famous sermon, His audience would have been quite hungry and no doubt very thirsty. Fresh water for them was a precious commodity. This might have inspired Jesus' fourth Beatitude. Looking at the crowd around Him, Jesus said, *"Blessed are those who hunger and thirst for righteousness, for they will be filled"* (Matthew 5:6).

In this Beatitude, Jesus speaks about our longings and desires. Hunger and thirst are frequent human urges. It's wonderfully satisfying to eat a meal when starving or to have a drink of water when parched. Hunger is often used metaphorically to convey a consuming desire, like a young and inexperienced sports team hungry for a win (or even an experienced one like the Toronto Maple Leafs, hungry for another shot to play for the Stanley Cup). This same hunger can be experienced by an individual who, after a string of failures, is hungry for success.

The Bible often uses hunger and thirst to exemplify powerful desires. In Isaiah 55:1–2, we read:

> Come, all you who are thirsty, come to the waters; and you who have no money, come, buy and eat! … Why spend money on what is not bread, and your labor on what does not satisfy? Listen to me, and eat what is good, and your soul will delight in the richest of fare.

Jesus used these references to communicate a blessed appetite for a particular pursuit: righteousness. *"Blessed are those who hunger and thirst for righteousness, for they shall be satisfied"* (Matthew 5:6).

Perhaps you find yourself today with the realization that, according to the prophets Isaiah and Jeremiah, you have been drinking from broken cisterns and eating bread that does not satisfy. C.S. Lewis said, *"If I find in myself a desire which no experience in this world can satisfy, the most probable explanation is that I was made for another world."* [5] And indeed we were!

In the previous three Beatitudes, Jesus pronounced a blessing on those who recognized their emptiness and didn't try to justify or defend themselves. They were the poor in spirit, they that mourn, and the meek. Jesus now makes a transition from emptiness to fullness by saying that those who hunger and thirst for righteousness will be filled.

What is the essence of this righteousness for which we must hunger and thirst? I assure you that it can be found only in an intimate relationship with God, through Jesus Christ. This relationship will enable you to exhibit the fruit of the Holy Spirit in your life.

That is the essence of what Jesus is asking us to seek. It means to have a strong desire—a passionate force inside the soul—that makes us unrelenting to have this hunger satisfied. This hunger shouldn't be something that just comes and goes—it's a hunger that keeps on going until it's satisfied. It's not like Israel's love for God, as described in the book of Hosea, which was just transient: "*What shall I do with you, O Ephraim? What shall I do with you, O Judah? Your love is like a morning cloud, like the dew that goes early away*" (Hosea 6:4). What do morning clouds do? They go away. What happens to dew? It goes away. It doesn't remain. Jesus expects our hungering and thirsting for righteousness to remain. It's the way to be truly blessed.

In reality, the righteousness we're seeking is the righteousness of God. When we hunger and thirst for the righteousness of God, we aren't looking to the broken cisterns of our own making. No, we're looking to God. And Jesus says that when we do, we will be filled.

Restlessness and longing are universal traits of the human heart, placed there by God. How is it with your soul today? Is your soul hungry and your spirit thirsty for something that really satisfies? Perhaps everywhere you turn, the grass seems much greener than where you stand. The great tragedy is that we don't always recognize this longing, this dissatisfaction with the status quo, for what it truly is—the Spirit of God drawing us to something more lasting and eternal. He's drawing us to the righteousness of God.

Don't turn away to some short-term, temporary, backfiring pleasures of this world. They only turn to ashes in your hand. When the thrill disappears, it leaves you only with the sediment of guilt and loneliness. Jesus beckons you to something much better: "*Seek ye first the kingdom of God and his righteousness, and all these things will be yours as well*" (Matthew 6:33).

When it comes to righteousness, people who follow Christ must desire it so much that they hunger and thirst for it. Righteousness means wanting the same things God wants. Do you hunger and thirst for that? If you do, Jesus says you will be filled! Filled by God! How awesome is that?

5. C. S. Lewis, *Mere Christianity* (London, U.K: Harper Collins, c1952).

24. Be Merciful

Have you ever been the recipient of mercy from someone who was well within their right or had the authority to punish you for something you had done? Perhaps it was the police officer who let you off with a warning for going fifteen kilometres over the posted speed limit. Having mercy is to have compassion or forgiveness toward someone over whom you have the power to punish or harm.

As Jesus delivered His Sermon on the Mount, He must have looked around at the crowd and seen many types of people straining to catch every word. There were the disciples, Pharisees, slave masters, as well as slaves. As Jesus looked at some of the inhumane ways in which the marginalized were treated, it must have inspired the fifth Beatitude: *"Blessed are the merciful, for they will be shown mercy"* (Matthew 5:7). Just who are the merciful?

One day when the disciple Peter was feeling rather benevolent, He asked Jesus, *"Lord, how many times shall I forgive my brother or sister who sins against me? Up to seven times?"* (Matthew 18:21). In order to answer Peter's question and drive home the point about forgiveness, Jesus tells the parable of the unmerciful servant. This servant owed a massive debt that was beyond his ability to repay, so his master forgave him. But in response, the servant refused to forgive a smaller debt owed to him, going as far as torturing his debtor for what he owed.

Mercy consists of treating people better than they deserve. Forgiveness is a type of mercy, and so is helping someone to whom we have no obligation to help. Jesus is saying that if you extend acts of kindness to someone who definitely doesn't deserve your kindness, you will be shown mercy by the Lord.

In James 2:13, the apostle says, *"Judgment without mercy will be shown to anyone who has not been merciful. Mercy triumphs over judgment."* In the Beatitude, Jesus says, *"Blessed are the merciful, for they will be shown mercy"* (Matthew 5:7). James provides the converse of that statement in saying, in essence, "Cursed are the unmerciful, for they will be shown no mercy."

The parable of the unmerciful servant teaches us first that it is beyond our capacity to repay *our* own massive *sin* debt. And second, it teaches us that this sin debt is greater than any offense we have suffered—or could suffer—at the hands of others.

Without seeing ourselves as impoverished sinners, we can't appreciate God's grace or truly forgive others as we should. In the parable, when the master got wind of what this servant had done, He said:

> "You wicked servant, shouldn't you have had mercy on your fellow servant just as I had on you?" In anger his master handed him over to the jailers to be tortured, until he should pay back all he owed. Then Jesus said to the crowd: This is how my heavenly Father will treat each of you, unless you forgive your brother or sister from your heart. (Matthew 18:32–35)

From the heart: In other words, we're not to just pay lip service when we say "I forgive you." We must do it willingly and graciously because of what Jesus has done for us.

One of the qualities of the Christian is that he/she shows mercy and compassion toward others. The apostle James says that mercy triumphs over judgement! Where mercy and judgement seem to be in conflict, mercy should always win out. James 2:13 tells us that since God will judge us with mercy, we should judge others with mercy as well.

Being merciful is an act that shows our thankfulness for all God has done, and it's made possible through the Holy Spirit's indwelling presence. As recipients of this wonderful mercy, we are to be dispensers of His amazing grace.

We can't make a rule for forgiveness. By putting a limit on the maximum number of times we forgive someone, we miss the point of mercy. When we understand the magnitude of what we've been forgiven, we won't be tempted to keep a spreadsheet, documenting the number of times we've shown mercy to someone else. As Jesus says, *"Freely you have received; freely give"* (Matthew 10:8b).

Mercy is the driving force behind Christ's coming to earth. Through Him, our sins are forgiven and we receive the gift of God's mercy. As gospel song writer Gordon Jensen put it: *"I should have been crucified, I should have suffered and died. I should have hung on the cross in disgrace; But Jesus my Lord took my place."* [6]

That's mercy! Are you merciful? If so, you will be shown mercy by God. May the Lord bless you today!

6. Gordon Jensen, *I Should Have Been Crucified* (John T. Benson Publishing Co. INC. 1969)

25. Having a Pure Heart

One day, the Pharisees and some of the teachers of the law gathered around Jesus and saw some of His disciples eating food with unwashed hands. So they asked Jesus, *"Why don't your disciples live according to the tradition of the elders instead of eating their food with defiled hands?"* (Mark 7:5).

Jesus replied:

> What comes out of a person is what defiles them. For it is from within, out of a person's heart, that evil thoughts come—sexual immorality, theft, murder, adultery, greed, malice, deceit, lewdness, envy, slander, arrogance and folly. All these evils come from inside and defile a person. (Mark 7:20–23)

In all of His messages, Jesus always focuses on the heart. In this devotional today, we are looking at having a pure heart, as we've come to the sixth Beatitude. During His Sermon on the Mount, Jesus said, *"Blessed are the pure in heart, for they will see God"* (Matthew 5:8).

What did He mean by the "pure in heart"? Jesus is presenting us with the concept of purity. The word "pure" in the Greek refers specifically to that which is made clean by going through the fire or being pruned, as in the case of a vine or a tree. The prophet Malachi speaks of Jesus the Messiah as being like a *"refiner's fire."* He says, *"But who can endure the day of his coming? Who can stand when he appears? For he will be like a refiner's fire or a launderer's soap"* (Malachi 3:2). Jesus also refers to Himself as the true vine, and believers as being the branches (John 15:1–17). For a vine to produce fruit, it must be pruned. Those who are truly "pure" are those who are being sanctified by His refining fire and pruning process.

To be pure in heart means having no hypocrisy, no guile, no hidden motives. It's marked by transparency and a desire to please God in all things. It's more than an *external* purity of behaviour.

When Jesus speaks of the "pure in heart," He is referring to internal purity. On the mountainside that day, He wanted His audience to know that their hearts needed to be transformed by the power of God.

The "heart" Jesus is referring to here is not that muscle between the lungs that circulates blood throughout the body. No, it's our inner self, where thoughts, desires, character, and sense of purpose originate and reside.

I don't have to tell you that it's hard to be pure in heart in your own strength! As human beings, it's much easier to give in to greed, jealousy, anger, lust, selfishness, and pride than it is to keep one's thoughts and actions pure. So much in our world today vies for our attention and tries to lure us away from the things of God. But you know what? That's why Jesus came. God forgave us our sins! And He keeps on purifying us until we're like silver that has gone through the refiner's fire.

Someone once asked a silversmith, "How do you know when all the impurities have been burnt up from the silver?" He replied, "When I'm able to see my face in it." That's what God wants to do to our hearts; like silver, He wants to take us through the crucible until our hearts reflect the face of the Master.

If you're a child of God, your heart has been made pure by God. Your responsibility then is to have such a close and intimate relationship with Jesus that your heart is constantly being purified by

His presence. The psalmist David asks: "*Who shall ascend the hill of the Lord? And who shall stand in his holy place? He who has clean hands and a pure heart, who does not lift up his soul to what is false, and does not swear deceitfully*" (Psalm 24:3–4 ESV).

In replying to the Pharisees and the teachers of the Law, Jesus said, "*Isaiah was right when he prophesied about you hypocrites; as it is written: 'These people honor me with their lips, but their hearts are far from me'*" (Isaiah 29:13). Jesus called them hypocrites because they paid lip service to God, while their hearts were full of impurities.

What is the condition of your heart? Can you say, with the help of the Holy Spirit, that your heart is pure? If not, ask the Lord to come and purify your heart so that it becomes like pure silver or gold.

The virtue God looks for in you is a pure heart, but the reward is the wonderful pleasure of seeing Him. We will see God as we are able to understand more clearly His will for our lives and walk in a way that pleases Him. But ultimately, if you abide in Him, you will be eternally admitted into His presence and be awestruck by His glory. May the Lord continue to keep your heart pure!

26. Be a Peacemaker

As Jesus gave His Sermon on the Mount that day, there was the ever-present threat of war, as the religious zealots and insurrectionists were all preparing to do battle with the occupying Roman army. In His seventh Beatitude, Jesus addresses the reward for making peace: "*Blessed are the Peacemakers, for they will be called children of God*" (Matthew 5:9). The reward for being a peacemaker, as Jesus proclaimed, is the high honour of being called a child of God.

In modern history, the first prize given out to honour someone who had sought to bring warring factions together was awarded in 1901. It was called the Nobel Peace Prize, named after Alfred Nobel, a Swedish industrialist who, ironically, was the inventor of dynamite. According to Nobel's will, the prize was to be awarded to the person who in the preceding year had done the most or the best work in bringing nations together or for holding and promoting peace congresses.

Peacemaking requires taking the initiative to get involve wherever there are conflicts, with the intention of building bridges between the parties at odds. As such, Jesus Himself is to be recognized as the greatest peacemaker of all time.

In Colossians 1:19-20, Paul writes, "*For God was pleased to have all his fullness dwell in him* (Jesus), *and through him to reconcile to himself all things, whether things on earth or things in heaven, by making peace through his blood, shed on the cross.*"

Those who have been reconciled to God by Jesus' death on the cross have been given the task of reconciling others to God. It should come as no surprise, then, that a peacemaker is someone who emulates Jesus. You see, Jesus is called the "Prince of Peace." While the human race was at odds with God because of our sinful nature, Jesus came to make peace and to restore our relationship with God through His sacrifice on the cross.

The ministry of reconciliation, or peacemaking, is addressed by Jesus in this Beatitude. A peacemaker is someone who reconciles people with God and with one another. It entails spreading the good news that all people, everywhere can have a restored relationship with God through Jesus Christ. Peacemakers are those who build bridges to end conflicts.

According to the apostle Paul, we are Christ's ambassadors when we live out this call to be peacemakers. When you act as a peacemaker in this way, Jesus says that you exhibit a *family resemblance.* Peacemakers are blessed because they will be called sons and daughters of God. In other words, we will have the honour of being identified as children of the God of peace: "*That's when you discover who you really are, and your place in God's family*" (Matthew 5:9b, MSG).

To live as a child of God is to have the greatest relationship in the world. It's a relationship made possible by the Prince of Peace Himself. The apostle Paul says, "*For in Christ Jesus, you are all sons and daughters of God, through faith*" (Galatians 3:26).

There's a great need for peacemakers who can put an end to all the conflicts we see in the world today. But as far as Jesus is concerned, today's greatest peacemaker may never win a Nobel Peace Prize. You see, the kind of peace that Jesus came to bring is not the absence of conflicts or war. Jesus came to bring inner peace.

Have you experienced that kind of peace from Jesus? If not, ask the Lord to take away that which is robbing you of the wonderful experience of His peace, and to come by His Spirit and fill you with His peace today. Perhaps you've already experienced His peace. If so, are you actively engaged in being a peacemaker? Seek to be one who reconciles others to Jesus by introducing them to the Prince of Peace.

Having been reconciled to God by the Prince of Peace, we have been given the ministry of reconciliation—reconciliation with others and with our enemies. That day in His Sermon on the Mount, Jesus made this revolutionary statement that would have caused many to recoil: *"You have heard that it was said, 'Love your neighbor and hate your enemy.' But I tell you, love your enemies and pray for those who persecute you, that you may be children of your Father in heaven"* (Matthew 5:43–45). As joint heirs with the Prince of Peace, let us recognize the ministry of reconciliation given to us by God so that we may be used of Him to bring lost people into a relationship with Him. May the Lord bless you!

APRIL - JUNE

Chapter 5:
The Ancient of Days

"Very truly I tell you," Jesus answered,
"before Abraham was born, I am!"

John 8:56

27. The Bread of Life

When Moses first encountered God through the burning bush and was told to go and lead the Israelites out of slavery, he asked God what he should say if the people asked who had sent him. God replied, *"This is what you are to say to the Israelites: 'I AM has sent me to you'"* (Exodus 3:14, emphasis added). "I AM" refers to the name by which the Lord Almighty is known. He is the Alpha and Omega, the beginning and the end. He ever was and always will be. He is known as the Ancient of Days.

Jesus was nearly stoned to death by the Pharisees one day for blasphemy when He identified Himself with this God who had made Himself known to Moses He spoke to them about being set free:

> They answered him, "We are Abraham's descendants and have never been slaves of anyone. How can you say that we shall be set free?" Jesus replied, "Very truly I tell you, everyone who sins is a slave to sin … So if the Son sets you free, you will be free indeed. I know that you are Abraham's descendants. Yet you are looking for a way to

kill me, because you have no room for my word ... Very truly I tell you," Jesus answered, "before Abraham was born, I am!" At this, they picked up stones to stone Him ..." (John 8:33–34, 36–37, 58–59a)

In the gospel of John, Jesus made seven profound "I Am" statements: the *bread of life*, the *light of the world*, the *gate for the sheep*, the *good shepherd*, the *resurrection and the life*, the w*ay, the truth and the life*, and the *true Vine*. In these statements, Jesus identifies himself as the Great "I AM"—the Lord of "What Is." This devotional deals with the first of these "I AM" statements. I AM *"the bread of life"*

Many of us struggle with powerful negative emotions like guilt, shame, fear, or anxiety that threaten to overwhelm us. But sometimes we don't realize that the emotions that cause our anxiety involve us living either in the past or the future. The gospel, on the other hand, is a powerful call to stay in the now—the present—because the great "I AM" is the Lord of the NOW.

Remember how you felt the first time you saw a picture of a starving child? Perhaps guilty or ashamed for not having done enough? Often we don't realize that we might be that starving child. Oh, we may not be starving for physical food. But we need something even more sustaining and eternal—spiritual food. In John 6:35, Jesus says, *"I am the bread of life; whoever comes to me shall not hunger, and whoever believes in me shall never thirst."* This is a phenomenal statement!

By equating Himself with bread, Jesus is saying that He is *essential* for life. This is an invitation for us to commit ourselves wholly to His Lordship, in order that He might provide for our total being—body, soul, and spirit.

Committing to Jesus involves making a choice to forsake the world and follow Him wholeheartedly. If the history of human religion teaches us anything, it's that people seek to earn their way to heaven. Our dilemma is that we have a desire we can't fulfill, no matter what we do. That's where Jesus comes in. He alone can fulfill that desire in the human heart for righteousness. He does this by taking our sin and imputing to us His righteousness.

At times we may be seeking for the wrong kind of bread, and in all the wrong places, but when we seek the Lord with all of our hearts, He will be found by us. Let's express our total dependency on Him as we seek Him daily in prayer so that He will provide not just the daily bread that nourishes our bodies but that which nourishes the soul as well.

He satisfies our deepest needs and gives us the assurance that He will always be our daily bread! No matter what you're experiencing, it's never beyond the ability of Jesus to supply, because He is the bread of life.

28. The Light of the World

This devotional address another of Jesus' "I AM" statements: "*I AM the Light of the World*" (John 8:12). One day when Jesus was speaking with some of the religious authorities, He was almost stoned to death for blasphemy. His crime? He identified Himself with the almighty God who had made Himself known to Moses: Jesus said to them: "*Very truly I tell you, before Abraham was born, I am!*" At this, they picked up stones to stone Him …" (John 8:58–59a, emphasis added).

This "I AM" statement points to Jesus' unique and divine identity and purpose. In declaring Himself to be the *light of the world*, Jesus was claiming that He is the exclusive source of spiritual light. No other source of spiritual truth is available to humanity.

Jesus was at the Feast of Tabernacles—a week-long festival when the temple court was lit with some powerful torches as people celebrated the time when their ancestors journeyed through the wilderness. It was said that the light from these torches was so bright, it penetrated every courtyard in Jerusalem. It was at this same feast that Jesus gave this powerful invitation:

On the last and greatest day of the festival, Jesus stood and said in a loud voice, "Let anyone who is thirsty come to me and drink. Whoever believes in me, as Scripture has said, rivers of living water will flow from within them." By this he meant the Spirit, whom those who believed in him were later to receive" (John 7:37–39). Jesus must still have been at the temple on the eighth day, when after the celebration, the lights were extinguished, rendering the courtyard quite dark. John records, *"When Jesus spoke again to the people, He said, 'I am the Light of the World. Whoever follows me will never walk in darkness but have the light of life'"* (John 8:12).

The joy associated with the lights and water rituals of the Feast of Tabernacles was in anticipation of the Messiah coming to the temple. They had been waiting for centuries, yet there He was, and no one recognized that He was in their midst. Let us be careful never to miss the opportunity to recognize His presence among us.

The metaphor used by Jesus in this verse speaks of the light of His *truth*, the light of His *Word*, and the light of His eternal *life*. With Jesus as the light of the world, the world has no other light but Him. He is the true light, and in Him there is no darkness.

In Hebrews 1:3 we read, *"The Son (Jesus) is the radiance of God's glory and the exact representation of his being, sustaining all things by his powerful word."* In Colossians 1:19-20, we read, *"For God was pleased to have all his fullness dwell in him (Jesus), ²⁰ and through him to reconcile to himself all things, whether things on earth or things in heaven, by making peace through his blood, shed on the cross."*

Yes, Jesus is the light of the world, which means that one day this world will be filled with this light, as the waters cover the sea. All darkness, and all the works of darkness, will be cast out. If we follow the light, we will never walk in darkness. Rather, it will lead us into the presence of the Holy One.

If we follow the light, we will reflect the light of Life. Just as Jesus came as the light of the world, He commands His followers to be "lights" as well. This light will be evident to others by the good deeds we do in faith and through the power of the Holy Spirit.

If you were to take a small candle into the darkest room, it would overcome the darkness. Likewise, the light of Jesus Christ has to be taken into the darkness of this world so that it can engulf the hearts and lives of those who are not yet following Him. As Jesus commands, *"Let your light so shine before others, that they may see your good deeds and glorify your Father in heaven"* (Matthew 5:16).

Just as the moon has no light of its own but reflects the light from the sun, so the Father wants you to shine by reflecting the light from His Son. May the Lord bless you!

29. The Gate for the Sheep

One day, Jesus was in a serious discussion with some of the Pharisees, who had just investigated the claims that He had healed a man who'd been blind from birth. Some of them had come to the conclusion that Jesus had done this miracle through a demon. But others believed that no one who was unrighteous could have done this miracle. They were divided and asked how a sinner could perform such signs. They were right. You see, Jesus had already told them in a previous conversation that *"Before Abraham was born, I AM."*

Now Jesus was making another "I AM" pronouncement. Jesus said, *"Very truly I tell you, I am the gate for the sheep"* (John 10:17). This is a profound statement, because Jesus is using the gate and sheep metaphor not just to show the relationship between Himself and His followers, but also the exclusivity of the door to heaven.

In this devotional series I want to encourage you to keep trusting Jesus, regardless of what you may be going through, because He is the gate for the sheep. In this pluralistic world, many will try to make you believe that there are many gates that lead to the one destination. But Jesus clearly identifies Himself as *the* gate.

To get a clear picture of Jesus' meaning in this statement, it's helpful to understand a little of that ancient culture, especially regarding sheep and shepherding. There were two kinds of sheepfolds or pens. One was a public sheepfold found in the cities and villages, and another in the countryside. The one found in the cities and villages would be large enough to hold several flocks of sheep. This sheep pen would be in the care of a keeper, whose duty it was to guard the door to the sheep pen during the night and to admit the shepherds in the morning.

As the shepherds arrived in the morning, they'd call their sheep, each of which knew its own shepherd's voice. When the shepherd had brought out his own sheep, he'd go on ahead of them, and his sheep would follow because they knew his voice. He would lead them out to pasture.

But Jesus said to them that they would never follow a stranger; in fact, they would run away from him because they don't recognize a stranger's voice. *"Jesus used this figure of speech, but the Pharisees did not understand what he was telling them. Therefore Jesus said again, 'Very truly I tell you, I am the gate for the sheep'"* (John 10:6–7).

The second kind of sheep pen was in the countryside, where the shepherds would keep their flocks in good weather. This type of pen was nothing more than a rough circle of rocks piled into a wall, with a small open space to enter. Through this open space, the shepherd would drive the sheep at nightfall.

Since there was no gate to close—just an opening—the shepherd would keep the sheep in and wild animals out by lying across the opening. He would sleep there at night, literally becoming the door to the sheep. In this context, Jesus is saying to the Pharisees, and by extension us, that He is not just the shepherd of the sheep. He is also the door of the sheep.

Jesus explicitly contrasts Himself with the Pharisees with whom He's conversing. He describes them as thieves and robbers: *"All who have come before me are thieves and robbers, but the sheep have not listened to them"* (John 10:8).

When Jesus says, "I am the gate," He's reiterating the fact that only through Him is salvation possible. Jesus makes it clear that any religious leader who offers salvation other than through the teachings of Christ is a "thief" and a "robber." As the scriptures repeat on so many occasions, the one who believes the gospel of Jesus Christ and repents of sin is assured of being in "the fold" and of having entered by "the door." He is both our *Shepherd* and the *door* to the *sheepfold*. He provides for all our needs.

Knowing that the world is full of predators whose sole intent is to destroy us, we are always under the Shepherd's protection. More importantly, we are fully confident that when the Chief Shepherd appears, we will receive the crown of glory that doesn't fade away.

Jesus goes on to say:

> I am the gate; whoever enters through me will be saved.
> They will come in and go out, and find pasture. The
> thief comes only to steal and kill and destroy; I have
> come that they may have life, and have it to the full.
> (John 10:9-10)

In these two passages, Jesus gives us the assurance that in Him we have salvation, and that He provides all that we need. He also cautions us to look out for the predators of our soul that come to kill and destroy. Conversely, as the Shepherd, He has come to bring us life. Yes, life in the hereafter, but also life now, abundant life, as we follow Him today. As the gate to the sheep, Jesus is our one defence, but also our righteousness.

May this knowledge give you confidence and a feeling of security as you rely on your Master for His care and provision today.

30. The Good Shepherd

To the Pharisees and teachers of the law, Jesus was someone to be cautious of. On the other hand, tax collectors and those considered sinners loved Him and were always seen hanging around Him. This infuriated these religious leaders, and they were heard to be muttering, *"This man welcomes sinners and eats with them"* (Luke 15:2).

Jesus tells three parables about things that had been lost but were later found—the lost *sheep*, the lost *coin*, and the lost *son*. In these parables the religious leaders, who were steeped in their own self-righteousness, would hopefully understand the purpose of Jesus coming to earth. Jesus had previously said to them, "*I have not come to call the righteous, but sinners to repentance*" (Luke 5:32).

At the end of the parable of the lost sheep, after the sheep had been found, Jesus says, "*And when he* [the shepherd] *finds it, he joyfully puts it on his shoulders and goes home. Then he calls his friends and neighbors together and says, 'Rejoice with me; I have found my lost sheep'*" (Luke 15:5-6). Clearly, in this parable Jesus is portraying Himself to be the Good Shepherd who goes after the lost sheep.

In this devotional series, I'm reflecting on Jesus' I AM pronouncement "I am the Good Shepherd." This is the fourth of seven "I AM" declarations of Jesus recorded only in John's Gospel. These proclamations point to Jesus' unique, divine identity and purpose.

Immediately after declaring that He is "the door" in John 10:7, Jesus declares "I am the good shepherd." He describes Himself as not just "the shepherd" but the "good shepherd." What does this mean?

> I am the good shepherd. The good shepherd lays down his life for the sheep. The hired hand is not the shepherd and does not own the sheep. So, when he sees the wolf coming, he abandons the sheep and runs away. Then the wolf attacks the flock and scatters it. (John 10:11–12)

"I am the good shepherd!" This is such a short statement from Jesus, yet it's filled with so much truth and encouragement. Why is Jesus the Good Shepherd? He's the only one who can truly protect and save His people—His flock. But instead of honouring Jesus, the Pharisees figured He was disrespecting God as opposed to being God Himself, made flesh.

In this passage, Jesus contrasts a Good Shepherd with a hired hand (John 10:13). The hired hands run away when the flock is in trouble because they don't love the flock as Jesus, the Good Shepherd does.

Of all domesticated animals, sheep are the most helpless. They'll spend their entire day grazing, wandering from place to place, never looking up. As a result, they often become lost. Additionally, sheep are easily susceptible to injuries and are utterly helpless against predators. This is why David in Psalm 23 tells us of the shepherd who "*makes* [us] *to lie down in green pastures; he leads* [us] *beside the still waters. He restores* [our] *soul*" (Psalm 23:2–3a, NKJV). David tells how he killed a lion and a bear while defending his father's flock as a shepherd boy (1 Samuel 17:36). In the same way, Jesus the Good Shepherd is our defender.

After a sheep has gone missing, the shepherd will search for days, if necessary until he finds it. Shepherds, after doing exhaustive searching, have been known to find their sheep quite week and sometimes very close to the edge of a precipice. They usually don't attempt a rescue at that point, lest the sheep struggles to get to its feet, and no doubt fall to its death. The shepherd usually waits for several hours, until the sheep is incapable of struggling, before he tries to rescue it.

That's what the Good Shepherd does. Perhaps like that lost sheep you're wondering why the Lord hasn't come to your rescue after all this time. Well, perhaps He's waiting for the right time, until all the fight, bitterness, anxiety, and self-reliance have diminished, before He comes to your rescue. Otherwise, you'll try to help in the rescue process and make matters worse. You see, as humans, we like to boast that we've done it our way. So be patient! Be of good cheer! The Good Shepherd hasn't forgotten you.

Through His willing sacrifice, the Lord made salvation possible for all who come to Him in faith. In proclaiming that He is the Good Shepherd, Jesus speaks of "laying down" His life for His sheep, which He did when He laid it down on the cross for you and me.

Let's be thankful for this wonderful gesture of grace and sacrificial love bestowed on all of us through Jesus Christ our Lord, the Good Shepherd.

31. The Way

It's almost vacation time, and there are many ways to travel: highway, back roads, bus, train, plane, etc. In the same way, the world tells us that there are many ways, or roads, to reach God: go to church, be a good person, lists of dos and don'ts, different religions, etc. Do whatever feels best to you and what is right in your own eyes. However, the Word of God tells us a different story: *"There is a way that seems right to a man, but its end is the way of death"* (Proverbs 14:12).

The world says the road is wide open. You get to choose which path is right to get to God. But the Bible says something very different: *"Enter by the narrow gate; for wide is the gate and broad is the way that leads to destruction, and there are many who go in by it"* (Matthew 7:13). This devotional focuses on Jesus' claim that He and the Father are One. And today, we're looking at Jesus' statement: "I am the way."

On the last night before His betrayal and death, Jesus was preparing His disciples for the dark days ahead. For over three years, these men had been following Him and learning from His teaching and example. They had placed their hopes in Him as the Messiah, the promised deliverer. Yet they still didn't understand how He was going to accomplish that deliverance.

On that last night together, the atmosphere in the room was emotionally charged, as the disciples could sense that things weren't going to be the same anymore. Jesus had mentioned to them on several occasions that He would be put to death, but somehow the reality hadn't quite set in yet.

> Now Jesus was going up to Jerusalem. On the way, he took the Twelve aside and said to them, "We are going up to Jerusalem, and the Son of Man will be delivered over to the chief priests and the teachers of the law. They will condemn him to death and will hand him over to the Gentiles to be mocked and flogged and crucified. On the third day he will be raised to life!" (Matthew 20:17–19)

Jesus assured them that although He was going away, they should be of good comfort. As the time drew near for Him to say goodbye, His last words to them were filled with hope. But when in grief, hope does not come easily. If you've ever had to say goodbye either to a friend or family member who was departing this life, or to someone leaving for an indefinite time, you'll appreciate the sadness the disciples felt.

> Do not let your hearts be troubled. You believe in God; believe also in me. My Father's house has many rooms; if that were not so, would I have told you that I am going there to prepare a place for you? And if I go and prepare a place for you, I will come back and take you to be with

me that you also may be where I am. You know the way to the place where I am going. (John 14:1–4)

This led to even more questions from His disciples. Thomas (yes, doubting Thomas) said, "*Lord, we don't know where you are going, so how can we know the way?*" (v. 5). Jesus answered with some of the most compelling words in scripture: "*I am the way and the truth and the life. No one comes to the Father except through me*" (v. 6). In these words, Jesus declares Himself the great "I AM," the only path to heaven, the only true measure of righteousness, and the source of both physical and spiritual life. He stakes His claim as the very God of creation, the Lord who blessed Abraham, and the Holy One who inhabits eternity.

He gave these encouraging words so that His disciples would be able to face the dark days ahead and carry on the mission of declaring the gospel to the world. The Christian life is often compared to a journey. Whether you're starting out for the first time or taking up from where you left off, you can only take up a journey from where you actually are.

Your present circumstances may not be all that you had hoped for, whether you're struggling in a bad relationship, coming to grips with the loss of a loved one, or battling a dreaded disease or an addiction. The fact remains, that's where you are on your journey. But Jesus offers to be your navigator. He has promised not just to show you the way—He is the WAY. So follow Him the same way the disciples did long ago. They followed Him, resting on His promises.

> In all this you greatly rejoice, though now for a little while, you may have had to suffer grief in all kinds of trials. These have come so that the proven genuineness of your faith—of greater worth than gold, which perishes even though refined by fire—may result in praise, glory and honor when Jesus Christ is revealed. (1 Peter 1:6–7)

When we follow Him in "this way," we can be assured of following Him all the way to heaven.

So wherever you may be on your journey, Jesus, the Great "I AM" and Lord of the Way extends this wonderful invitation: "*Come to me, all you who are weary and burdened, and I will give you rest*" (Matthew 11:28). Let Him show you the way today.

32. The True Vine

Have you ever felt really parched and dry? Wilted and lifeless? That's the description of a branch that has been severed from a tree or vine. Conversely, there are those who may look like they're full of life and bursting with colour, but they're not real. They're artificial branches with artificial flowers. In both cases, both are dead and only good for the fire.

Jesus was almost stoned to death for blasphemy by the religious leaders one day when He identified Himself as "I AM." "I AM" is the ultimate statement of self-sufficiency, self-existence, and immediate presence. "I AM" is God Himself. In this statement, Jesus is saying, "I am the ever present One." Jesus said to them, "*I am the true vine, and my Father is the gardener. He cuts off every branch in me that bears no fruit, while every branch that does bear fruit, he prunes so that it will be even more fruitful*" (John 15:1–2).

We're not first-century farmers and may not be workers of the land, so we may not be accustomed to metaphors like this. Indeed, many of us have only ever seen vines in pictures or on television. We may understand the concept of what it means but not the actuality. What does it mean that Jesus is the true vine? And how does this truth apply to us today? In this devotional series, I'm looking at Jesus' pronouncement "I am the true vine" and what it means to us today.

A vine, as defined by Merriam-Webster Dictionary, is a plant whose stem requires support and which climbs by tendrils or twining or creeps along the ground. A grapevine, for example, has a main vine that sends nutrients from the root of the plant to the branches, which then thrive and bear fruit. Vines were used throughout the Old Testament as a symbol of Israel, an old and holy image.

But along the way, the vine grew wild, off-path; it stopped bearing good fruit, withered, and was consumed by fire (Jeremiah 2:21). Most times, the vine was used as an illustration of how Israel had strayed from the Lord. But when Jesus said He was the "true vine" and that the disciples were to remain in Him, this was an illustration of how His followers could get back on track by nourishing themselves only through Jesus.

Jesus elaborated on this in John 15:4-6: *"I am the vine; you are the branches. If you remain in me and I in you, you will bear much fruit; apart from me you can do nothing."* No branch can bear fruit by itself; it must remain in the vine. Neither can you bear fruit unless you remain in Jesus. A true circle of life-sustaining support exists for us, but we have to stay connected.

Jesus wanted His friends throughout all time to know that He wasn't going to desert them, even though they would no longer enjoy His physical presence. His living energy—His spiritual reality—would continue to nourish and sustain them, just as the roots and trunk of a grape vine produce the energy that nourishes and sustains its branches while they develop their fruit. He wanted us to know that even though we can't see Him, we're as closely connected to Him as the branches of a vine are connected to its stem.

As we stay connected to the vine, our desire to know and love Him and the energy to serve Him will keep flowing into and through us. But if we don't abide in Him, we can do nothing.

All true branches bear fruit. Just as we can know a healthy, living tree by the good fruit it produces, we can recognize fruitless branches as having no connection to the true vine. This is why Jesus tells us, *"By their fruit you will recognize them"* (Matthew 7:16). Those who don't produce good fruit are cut away and burned. Jesus said, *⁶ If you do not remain in me, you are like a branch that is thrown away and withers; such branches are picked up, thrown into the fire and burned"* (John 15:6).

Here He's speaking to those who profess to know Him but whose relationship is insincere. Just like an artificial branch that looks healthy but is lifeless, so are those branches that profess to be alive but bear no fruit. Jesus says that they'll be picked up, thrown into the fire, and burned.

So stay connected to Jesus! Abide in Him because we depend on Him for everything, starting with our very life: *"For in Him we live and move and have our being"* (Acts 17:28). He has reconciled us with God through His death on the cross and remains our only connection with the Father, who produces in us a fruitful life of righteousness and peace.

Chapter 6:

Fruit that Lasts

> Jesus said of us, "You did not choose me,
> but I chose you and appointed you
> so that you might go and bear fruit
> —fruit that will last."
>
> John 15:16

33. The Joy of the Lord

During the various seasons of our lives, there will be times of physical and sometimes social isolation, such as when ill-health prevents you from having the kind of fellowship to which you've become accustomed. Or perhaps it's the kind of isolation we experienced during the pandemic. Regardless of the reason for your feeling of isolation, please remember that the Lord loves you and wants you to continue growing in your walk with Him.

During those times of solitude, please continue to seek the Lord and endeavour to cultivate an intimate relationship with Him as you delve into His Word, meditate on what it reveals to you, and remain in constant prayer.

In this devotion today, I begin a series on the "Fruit that Lasts."

Jesus said of us, *"You did not choose me, but I chose you and appointed you so that you might go and bear fruit—fruit that will last"* (John 15:16).

A list of the "fruit of the Spirit" can be found in Galatians 5: *"But the fruit of the Spirit is love, joy, peace, patience, kindness, goodness, faithfulness, gentleness and self-control. Against such things there is no law"* (5:22–23). Today, I'm sharing on the second characteristic of the fruit of the Spirit, which is joy.

Fruit is the natural result of growth, and "of the Spirit" explains exactly who causes that growth to take place—it's the power of the Holy Spirit in you. Sometimes we mistake happiness for joy, and vice versa. Is there a difference between *joy* and *happiness*? Certainly there is!

Happiness is based on circumstances. If you're in good health, have a good job, and things are going well, chances are you'll be happy. Joy, on the other hand, as a fruit of the Spirit, is created when the Holy Spirit indwells a believer. The presence of the Holy Spirit produces joy.

Joy isn't based on circumstances but comes with a deep, settled peace from God. It's the work of the Holy Spirit cultivating a godly character in the heart of the one who trusts in Jesus Christ. The Greek word for "joy" is *chara*. It's related to *charis*, which is the Greek word for grace. So you could say that joy comes through the grace of God.

Joy, like *agape* love, is not a feeling but something one possesses from the Holy Spirit. The apostle Peter tells us how this works: *"Though you have not seen him, you love him. Though you do not now see him, you believe in him and rejoice with joy that is inexpressible and filled with glory"* (1 Peter 1:8). Expressing joy is a choice. When you yield to the Holy Spirit, He opens your eyes to God's grace around you and fills your heart with joy.

Perhaps at this moment you're experiencing sadness brought about by loss, brokenness, or grief. You might see the possibility of joy only as an impossible dream. But that dream can become a reality.

A farmer can't make anything grow. He can only provide the conditions necessary for growth, namely preparing the soil, planting good seeds, and provide the nutrients. The rest is up to God. In like manner, we have to prepare our hearts and nourish our souls and spirit by the Word of God and seek His face in prayer. As we do, the

Holy Spirit cultivates in our hearts the fruit of joy. Because only God can make things grow.

We can experience joy even in the midst of suffering—even in the midst of physical isolation. This is totally counter-intuitive! Joy in the midst of suffering or trials? But this is only possible if the author of joy, Christ Himself, is living within you.

Do you have that kind of joy today? Let me encourage you with the words the apostle James wrote to comfort those who were experiencing tremendous suffering, trials, and persecution: "*Consider it pure joy, my brothers and sisters whenever you face trials of many kinds, because you know that the testing of your faith produces perseverance*" (James 1:2–3, emphasis added).

To the natural human mind, this is totally inconceivable. Joy in suffering? Yet during such times, God in His mercy and grace can fill you with inexplicable joy. You might have already discovered that the things of this world don't bring you joy. We get joy and feel joyful only when we're spiritually connected to God through Jesus Christ our Lord.

The joy of the world is hollow, but the joy of the Lord is rich and abundant. The world's happiness will fade with time, but the joy of the Lord will last forever. May the Lord bless you this day and fill your heart with His joy.

34. Peace That Surpasses

One day I observed a duckling gliding along a pond in such a serene manner. I thought, *How peaceful!* But it captured my attention when I observed a little closer; its feet were going a mile-a-minute beneath the surface of the water.

In this devotional series, I'm reflecting on what it means to exhibit the fruit of the Spirit as identified in Paul's epistle to the Galatians. After outlining the acts of the sinful nature, he goes on to give a warning: that those who live like that will not inherit the kingdom of God.

Today, I'm reflecting on peace—"Peace that surpasses."

We've seen that the fruit of the Spirit is not as a result of our striving or straining, but the power of the Holy Spirit in us. Peace cannot be manufactured. So what is peace? How do we describe this kind of peace mentioned as a fruit of the Spirit? It's certainly not just the absence of conflict or war. That's the way the world defines it. The Bible gives us a more excellent notion of the word peace. The Hebrew word for "peace" is *salom*, translated in the Greek as *eirēnē*. It has a wide semantic range, including the notions of totality or completeness and harmony.

The apostle Paul, writing to the Philippians, said:

> Do not be anxious about anything, but in every situation, by prayer and petition, with thanksgiving, present your requests to God. And the peace of God, which transcends all understanding, will guard your hearts and your minds in Christ Jesus. (Philippians 4:6–7)

The opposite of peace is not war. It's more likely anxiety. Only as we present our situation before the Lord can the Holy Spirit produce in us that peace that defies understanding. Sometimes you hear people say, "I don't know how you could be so calm under the circumstance." The answer is simply this: the peace that comes from the Holy Spirit transcends understanding.

In Romans 12:18, Paul exhorts, "*If possible, so far as it depends on you, be at peace with all men.*" We cannot manufacture the fruit of the Spirit. No gritty determination or self-will can produce it. Only God can create peace through the work of the Holy Spirit—a harmonious relationship with God. You see, we were born at war. At birth, our sinful nature had already declared war on God and His truth. Our heart's desire was to be separated from God, and if left to our own devices, we will just keep drifting. But Jesus bought our peace with His life.

God's methods of warfare are not what we'd expect. Instead of a battle, He sent us the Prince of Peace (Isaiah 9:6). Jesus' goal in coming to earth was more than simply to cease hostilities; He came to bring about a full and abiding relationship of restoration and love. The cost of this peace was His life.

The prophet Isaiah says, *"But he was pierced for our transgressions, he was crushed for our iniquities; the punishment that brought us peace was on him, and by his wounds we are healed"* (Isaiah 53:5).

The apostle Paul says:

> So I say, walk by the Spirit, and you will not gratify the desires of the flesh. For the flesh desires what is contrary to the Spirit, and the Spirit what is contrary to the flesh. They are in conflict with each other, so that you are not to do whatever you want. But if you are led by the Spirit, you are not under the law. (Galatians 5:16–18)

When we find ourselves striving to live by the letter of the law, there is no peace, just the fearful question of "What if I do mess up?" The law brings death, but the Spirit brings life and peace.

Once the Spirit draws us, and we believe in Jesus, the Bible says that we are justified, which makes us at peace with God. Paul gives us this assurance: *"Since we have been justified through faith, we have peace with God through our Lord Jesus Christ"* (Romans 5:1).

That is the kind of peace referred to in Galatians 5:22 as a characteristic of the Holy Spirit. Yes! It includes a peace that surpasses our understanding. It is a sweet relationship with God through Jesus Christ.

Are you experiencing this kind of peace? If you are, then you know the joy of sins forgiven. But if you're not experiencing this kind of peace, please ask the Lord, the Prince of Peace, to come in to your heart and give you this kind of peace.

35. Patience

Sometimes you'll hear people say, "You have the patience of Job." What do they really mean? Well, Job was a man of great wealth. He had ten children, many servants, and his livestock numbered in the thousands. *"He was the greatest man among all the people of the East"* (Job 1:3). He was great by man's standards and by God's.

Incredible. We can surmise that every need Job had was met, and every desire was fulfilled. But he suffered many tragedies. Following the first four, Job mourns ("*tore his robe and shaved his head*") and then worships God (Job 1:20–21). Job utters these famous words: "*Naked I came from my mother's womb, and naked I will depart. The Lord gave and the Lord has taken away; may the name of the Lord be praised*" (Job 1:21).

Having the patience of Job speaks to the ability to remain patient even when you are beset by many tragedies or setbacks in life, and to do what you think you should do, despite having many problems. In this devotional series, I'm focusing on cultivating the fruit of the Spirit, and today I'm reflecting on patience. These characteristics or virtues help us to develop a greater intimacy with God.

Our society describes patience as the capacity to accept or tolerate delays, trouble, or suffering without getting angry or upset. But that's not the patience spoken of as a fruit of the Spirit. As you can see, the world's kind of patience rests entirely on your ability to wait or tolerate.

The virtue of patience, on the other hand, comes entirely from the Holy Spirit. So what part do we play in this? Just as a farmer can't make a plant grow but simply provides the environment and nutrients conducive to growth, so we too don't have the ability to make this virtue grow in us.

How do we become more patient? How do we develop a greater measure of this virtue in our lives?

- By abiding in Christ,
- By going deep in His Word,
- By prayer,
- By having fellowship with others, and
- By putting what we learned about patience into practice!

Patience, like any other virtue, has to be put into practice before we can see the fruit.

The Greek word translated as "patience" in Galatians 6:22 is *makrothumia*,[7] which literally means "longanimity", i.e. (objectively) forbearance. It's "the capacity to hold one's temper for a long time." The King James Bible translates it as "longsuffering."

A patient person can endure much pain and suffering without complaining—not because they're without feeling but because the Holy Spirit provides the ability to do that. Patience is closely related to meekness, which Jesus exhibited so well, even when He was being abused and insulted. With the Holy Spirit's enablement, we too can exhibit such patience.

The thought I want you to take away from this devotional today is this: Patience comes from a position of power—power through the Holy Spirit! What exactly does that mean? When a person exercises self-restraint, or responds with a loving deed even though they might be in a position to get even or take revenge, that is exhibiting patience.

Patience is power under control. Losing patience is a sign of weakness. Exercising patience is a sign of strength. As the Holy Spirit produces patience in you, He is making you more Christlike.

The apostle Paul says: *"May the Lord lead your hearts into a full understanding and expression of the love of God and the patient endurance that comes from Christ"* (2 Thessalonians 3:5).

We should be patient even as He is patient. When we're patient, we leave room for God to work in our hearts and relationships. Let's lay aside the tyranny of our own schedules and the desire to lash out when we believe we're being taken advantage of and trust in God's own timing.

During these days when everyone seems to be in a hurry, when waiting in line causes us much frustration, let's make room in our hearts for the Holy Spirit to produce this wonderful virtue in our lives. As the saying goes, "patience is a virtue." May the Lord enable you to exhibit this fruit in your life today.

7 Strong's Concordance #3115: *makrothumia* (pronounced mak-roth-oo-mee'-ah)

36. Faithfulness

In today's devotional, I'm looking at the characteristic of faithfulness, a fruit of the Holy Spirit. It's something that remains when others fail because it's produced in us by God. You might say, "Well, if God is the one who produces it in me, that lets me off the hook." But is that really the case? What part do we play in exhibiting faithfulness?

In Luke 16, Jesus tells a parable about a manager who had been careless with the resources entrusted to him by his master to invest. So when the time came for settling his accounts, he found that he had not been very wise in the way he managed what had been given to him. Realizing the seriousness of this offence, he quickly and shrewdly made amends.

Whatever faithfulness we exhibit as children of the Lord must come from a close relationship with Him and a realization that all we possess comes from God. We have to submit ourselves, first of all to Him, and then our possessions, realizing that He possesses us. In the parable in Luke 16, Jesus says:

> If you are faithful in little things, you will be faithful in large ones. But if you are dishonest in little things, you won't be honest with greater responsibilities. And if you are untrustworthy about worldly wealth, who will trust you with the true riches of heaven? (Luke 16:10–11, NLT)

You see, if you're a child of God, your possessions are the property of God. You are only a steward of them. God has only permitted you the use of it. This steward in Jesus' parable wasted his master's goods before he realized the consequences. We're all liable to the same charge if we haven't been faithful in investing our time and talents—that which God has entrusted to us—for His glory and honour.

Fruit grows out of our relationship with Jesus Christ as we allow the Holy Spirit to manifest Himself in us and through us. So what is *faithfulness*? How would you define it? *Marriam-Webster's Dictionary* defines it this way: "Faithfulness—The virtue of being steadfast in affection or allegiance, loyal, a faithful friend, firm in keeping promises or in observance of duty." [8]

Biblically, we see faithfulness as the virtue by which we demonstrate obedience to God and to His children. The Bible speaks of this type of faithfulness as an attribute of God, an essential characteristic of a Christ follower, and when you lack it, it results in disobedience. As you can see, faithfulness demands quite a bit. So how are we able to measure up to these expectations? Biblical faithfulness requires belief in what the Bible says about God—His existence, His works, and His character. The Bible also warns us of the consequences of unfaithfulness. These warnings are necessary because, as the old hymn says, we are prone to wander. "*Prone to wander, Lord I feel it; Prone to leave the God I love. Here's my heart Lord, take and seal it. Seal it for Thy courts above.*" [9]

After all that God has done for us, why would we want to wander away from Him? *Because we are like sheep*. Our hearts are often very fickle, despite our best intentions. The Bible says that we were born in sin and shaped in iniquity, so our natural tendency is to go our own way, do our own thing, disobey. If we're exhibiting this characteristic in our lives, we have nothing to boast about, because left on our own, we'd be the most unfaithful and disobedient person there is.

The apostle Paul, in explaining the war that goes on within us—the sinful nature against the righteousness of God—exclaims: "*What a wretched man I am! Who will rescue me from this body that is subject to death?*" (Romans 7:24). There you have the words of a person who has come to the end of himself. In the previous verses, he's described how he had struggled and wrestled in his own power to obey the holy law of God but failed. In answer to his own question, he now finds the truth and cries out, "*Thanks be to God, who delivers me through Jesus Christ our Lord!*" (Romans 7:25).

Perhaps you've found this to be true: you've failed in your effort to be faithful—faithful in relationships, faithful at your vocation, faithful as a friend, faithful in promise keeping, and most of all, faithful to God and His Word. Like the apostle Paul, you're discovering that faithfulness doesn't just come by trying harder or making resolutions. You need to make space for God in your life and allow the virtues from the *true vine*, Jesus Christ, to flow through you.

Do you long to have the power and liberty of the Holy Spirit? Then why not bow before God in one final cry of despair and pray: "Oh God, must I go on in my own strength forever? Please deliver me from the clutches of unfaithfulness and give me the power to overcome."

When you seek the power of Jesus to dwell and work in you, God will create in you the capacity to be faithful. He will fill you with the Holy Spirit and enable you to be victorious. That is what God wants, and nothing else will enable you to live a life of power, peace, and faithfulness.

8. The Merriam-Webster Dictionary, New Edition, 2022 Copyright
9. Robert Robinson (1758); *Come, Thou Fount of Every Blessing*.

37. Goodness

In today's devotional, I'm focusing on the characteristic of goodness, a fruit of the Holy Spirit.

What is goodness? Goodness isn't about doing elaborate things to gain recognition. Oftentimes, it's the small acts of kindness we do throughout our day that mean the most to those around us. Jesus equates this to being a visible town built on a hill. Goodness is like a landmark.

Whenever I travel out of town and am on my way home, I always look to see when the CN Tower in Toronto becomes visible. When it does, I feel good on the inside. I know that I'm close to home. In His Sermon on the Mount, Jesus said:

> You are the light of the world. A town built on a hill cannot be hidden. Neither do people light a lamp and put it under a bowl. Instead they put it on its stand, and it gives light to everyone in the house. In the same way, let your light shine before others, that they may see your

good deeds and glorify your Father in heaven. (Matthew 5:14–16, emphasis added)

Humanly speaking, goodness is moral excellence and human virtue. But goodness, as found in Galatians 5:22, is not just a virtue. It's also holiness in action, characterized by deeds that are motivated by righteousness and a desire to be a blessing to others—*deeds that glorify our Father in heaven.*

The Greek word for "goodness" in Galatians 5:22 is *agathosune*, meaning "uprightness of heart and life." It's goodness for the benefit of others, not simply for the sake of being virtuous. This goes much deeper than our natural desire to be good. It's not just being good; it's also doing good.

In Galatians 5:22, "fruit" means "beneficial results." It's the good things that come from the Holy Spirit's presence in the life of the Christ follower. As the Holy Spirit works in your life, He changes your character. No one exudes goodness naturally! Our natural inclination is to defy God and do that which is evil. But once God's Spirit is at work within us, He produces the wonderful fruit of the Spirit: love, joy, peace, patience, kindness, *goodness,* faithfulness, gentleness, self-control" (Galatians 5:22).

Goodness reflects the overall character of God. GOD is GOOD! Goodness is not a quality we can manufacture. The apostle James says, "*Every good thing given and every perfect gift is from above, coming down from the Father of heavenly lights who does not change like shifting shadows*" (James 1:17). As you hand over the reins of your life to the Holy Spirit, He blesses you with the fruit of *goodness.*

When I speak of the Holy Spirit's control, I'm not saying that we become robots that move as the Holy Spirit pushes a button. NO! Control comes out of a relationship with God through Jesus Christ. It's as if the Holy Spirit is laying down tracks that are in accordance with God's Word and His will for you to follow. The prophet Ezekiel of old, speaking God's Word, told us how this was going to happen:

> I will give you a new heart, and I will put a new Spirit in you. I will take out your stony, stubborn heart and give

you a tender, responsive heart. And I will put my Spirit in you so that you will follow my decrees and be careful to obey my regulations. (Ezekiel 36:26–27, NLT)

Yes, the Holy Spirit has and will lay down tracks for you to follow. He has done so by giving us His Word. The psalmist says, "<u>Your word is a lamp for my feet, a light on my path</u>" (Psalm 119:105). And He will do so for anyone who has made a heartfelt and genuine commitment to follow the Lord in true obedience.

Perhaps you've been struggling to be good. I've met someone who has struggled most of their life to be good, without any success. That person was told from a very early age that they would amount to no good. How cruel! Although humanly speaking that's a cruel and debilitating thing to hear, spiritually speaking, without God, it's a self-fulfilling prophecy.

In his Epistle to the Romans, the apostle Paul writes:

> As it is written: "There is none righteous, no, not one; There is none who understands; There is none who seeks after God. They have all turned aside; They have together become unprofitable; There is none who does good, no, not one." (Romans 3:10–12, NKJV)

The bottom line is this: Your goodness cannot come through your own striving. It comes only as you develop a wonderful relationship with God by allowing the Holy Spirit to shape and mold you from the inside out. As you exhibit goodness in your daily lives, Jesus says this brings glory to God our Father. May the Lord bless you today and fill your heart with the goodness of the Lord.

38. Self-Control

You can't watch or listen to the evening news without seeing or hearing the result of people who fail to exercise self-control in dealing with others. The dreadful thing about this is that this phenomenon isn't just limited to the ordinary "man on the street." So what is self-control, and how do we get it? In today's devotional, I'm focusing on self-control, a fruit of the Holy Spirit.

In Galatians 5:22–23, we read: "*But the fruit of the Spirit is love, joy, peace, patience, kindness, goodness, faithfulness, gentleness and self-control. Against such things there is no law.*" Merriam-Webster dictionary defines self-control as: "Restraint exercised over one's own impulses, emotions, or desires." [10]

The apostle Paul describes self-control in these terms: "*I discipline my body and keep it under control, lest after preaching to others I myself should be disqualified*" (1 Corinthians 9:27). Even Paul knew the power of the flesh could wreck his ministry. Like Paul, we're to refuse our flesh those carnal things it craves, in order that we might develop strength of character.

Today's news headlines often remind us of Christian people who weren't able to exercise self-control and the damage it caused to them and their families. When a Christian leader falls, it's usually due to a lack of self-control and personal discipline. But it's not just Christian leaders; Christians as a whole have to be alert and exercise self-control.

Self-control, by its very name, almost sounds like something we could do on our own. Like, if I try very hard, I'll be able to master it. You hear people ask, "Don't you have any self-control? Why do you keep doing the same thing over and over?" This quotation, attributed to Albert Einstein, is so true: "Insanity is doing the same thing over and over and expecting different results!" Self-control as a fruit of the Spirit doesn't come from trying harder. Biblical self-control doesn't mean "counting to ten" or trying your hardest not to lust at something that could be called evil.

Self-Control, like the other eight fruits of the Spirit, comes from a close walk with Jesus Christ and allowing the Holy Spirit to manifest Himself in your life. So again, the fruit of the Spirit is the change in our character that comes about because of the Holy Spirit's work within us.

We don't become a Christian on our own, and we certainly can't grow on our own. Think of it in terms of a plant. We do the planting and watering, but only God can make it grow. The apostle Paul wrote, "*It is God who is at work in you, both to will and to work for His good pleasure*" (Philippians 2:13).

Self-control is the ability to control oneself. Pay attention to the word *ability*. Where does that ability come from? It comes from God the Holy Spirit. It involves the ability to say "no" to our baser desires and fleshly lusts. You might say, "I don't have a lot of base desires or fleshly lusts." Well, just listen for a moment to Paul as he shows us what it's like for the Christian who isn't allowing the Holy Spirit to control his or her thoughts and actions:

> So I find this law at work: Although I want to do good, evil is right there with me. For in my inner being I delight in God's law; but I see another law at work in me, waging war against the law of my mind and making me a prisoner of the law of sin at work within me. (Romans 7:21–23)

Don't for a moment misunderstand the word "control." God doesn't want us to become puppets by pulling the strings for us to behave or act in a certain way. No, it's more like a train. The track is already laid down. Laying down tracks is painstaking work to ensure the train doesn't derail. But once the track is down, the train moves within those parameters. Spiritual disciplines such as reading and practicing the Word of God, prayer, fasting, church attendance, and spiritual accountability are equivalent to laying down tracks.

How do we ensure we keep the track clear? Derailments can happen. The apostle Paul urges us this way:

Therefore, I urge you, brothers and sisters, in view of God's mercy, to offer your bodies as a living sacrifice, holy and pleasing to God—this is your true and proper worship. [2] *Do not conform to the pattern of this world, but be transformed by the renewing of your mind. Then you will be able to test and approve what God's will is—his good, pleasing and perfect will.* (Romans 12:1-2)

Like a vulnerable city, we must have defenses. A wall around an ancient city was designed to keep out the enemy, and judges were placed at the gates to determined who should be allowed in and who should remain outside. Soldiers and gates enforced those decisions. In similar ways we should have defenses in our lives. They help us along with the Holy Spirit's presence to maintain and exhibit self-control. May the Lord be with you.

10. The Merriam-Webster Dictionary, New Edition, 2022 Copyright

Chapter 7:
God's Redemption Story

> For you know that it was not with perishable things
> such as silver or gold that you were redeemed
> from the empty way of life handed down to you
> from your ancestors,
> but with the precious blood of Christ.
>
> 1 Peter 1:18–19

39. The Redeemer

As we approach the Easter season, our thoughts naturally turn to the events of Jesus' death, burial, and resurrection. Today I'll be looking at Jesus entering Jerusalem on Palm Sunday to the cheers and adulation of a large crowd that had gathered.

It was a springtime Sunday when Jesus rode into the Holy City on a donkey. The city was crowded with pilgrims who had come for the annual Passover celebrations. Jesu had spent the last three-and-a-half years travelling through the towns and villages of Palestine, where He'd healed the sick, opened blind eyes, and even raised the dead. He was now ready to present Himself as God's Redeemer of the world.

> A very large crowd spread their cloaks on the road,
> while others cut branches from the trees and spread
> them on the road. The crowds that went ahead of him

and those that followed shouted, "Hosanna to the Son of David!" "Blessed is he who comes in the name of the Lord!" "Hosanna in the highest heaven!" When Jesus entered Jerusalem, the whole city was stirred and asked: "Who is this?" (Matthew 21:8–10)

That's the question for us today. "Who is this?" Have you discovered in your own heart the answer to this very important question? Well, He is the central figure in God's redemption story. He is the Redeemer. God's redemption story can be summed up with one verse of scripture—that well-known verse from the Gospel of John: *"For God so loved the world that he gave his one and only Son, that whoever believes in him shall not perish but have eternal life"* (John 3:16).

But why did we need to be redeemed in the first place? The Bible says we have all sinned and fallen short of God's glory. Like an archer, we didn't just miss the target. In our disobedience, we turned around and shot the arrow in the opposite direction.

The penalty, or wages, of sin is death. And since we all have sinned, then we all have been appointed to die. But the good news is that God sent us a redeemer, a substitute to take our place.

Ironically, the same crowd who had welcomed Jesus into the City of Jerusalem with shouts of praises on Palm Sunday were the same ones to shout "Crucify Him" in response to Pontus Pilate's question on Good Friday: "Who shall I release? Jesus or Barabbas?" Barabbas was a well-known criminal who had been imprisoned *"for an insurrection in the city, and for murder"* (Luke 23:19).

In response to Pilate's question, the crowd cried out for him to release Barabbas. But Pilate insisted that he found no fault in Jesus. Earlier, Pilate had said to them, *"You have brought this Man to me, as one who misleads the people. And indeed, having examined Him in your presence, I have found no fault in this Man concerning those things of which you accuse Him!"* (Luke 23:14).

This pronouncement from Pilate was directed by God. In order to be a redeemer in this context, the Redeemer had to be one of us (human) but without sin. This claim could only be made about the righteous Son of God, and not by His own mouth, but by Pilate, a Roman governor. Yes, *only* the sinless Son of God had the qualifications to be our Redeemer:

> For this reason this sinless Redeemer had to be made like us, fully human in every way, in order that he might become a merciful and faithful high priest in service to God, and that he might make atonement for the sins of the people. (Hebrews 2:17)

What seemed like bad news that day for Jesus' followers was good news for us. What seemed like the worst day in history, has become the best day. And what seemed like a bad Friday has become a Good Friday. All because He who knew no sin paid our sin debt.

Today, He ever lives to make to make intersession for us as our faithful and merciful High Priest. That's why we're able to enter God's throne room at anytime, because Jesus has made a way for us.

"Who is this?" the crowd asked. Thanks be to the Lord that we have come to know Him as our Redeemer and Lord. The Bible tells us that we are redeemed, not with perishable things such as silver or gold, but with the precious blood of Jesus Christ. So during this Easter season, may your mouths be always filled with praises.

40. The Cross

This is a season of reflection—reflection on the cross. The cross has inspired many hymns and poems, but no matter how beautiful we make the cross appear, it's shame and ugliness can't be covered up. Today's devotional is about the cross and your response to it

In modern times, the cross has been adorned with gold and silver and beautified with precious stones, but it still remains that cruel instrument of shame and disgrace. George Bennard, an American hymn composer, is best known for composing the famous hymn, "The Old Rugged Cross." He sees beauty in the cross, but only because of the One who was nailed to it:

> *In the old rugged cross,*
> *stained with blood so divine,*
> *a wondrous beauty I see.*
> *For the dear Lamb of God,*
> *left His Glory above,*
> *To pardon and sanctify me* [11]

When seen from that vantage point, the cross has a wondrous beauty. The One on the cross had the power to save and sanctify all those who would come to Him.

The prolific hymn writer Isaac Watts also wrote about the cross. He saw the cross in another light. Like a beautiful diamond, there are so many different facets to the cross! He wrote:

> *When I survey the wondrous cross*
> *On which the Prince of Glory died*
> *My richest gain I count but loss*
> *And pour contempt on all my pride.* [12]

It's easy to see why Isaac Watts called it the "wondrous cross." We are awestruck when we gaze upon the cross. It's an emblem of torture, of disgrace, and of shame and suffering for the one who is hung from it. It depicts shame, public humiliation, and eventually death. Yet today, it's worn as a piece of jewellery around the neck. It symbolizes hope and commitment for the ones who wear it.

Why would God choose such a horrific instrument of death for His Son? The cross was reserved for the most dreadful offenders—murderers, thieves, and insurrectionists. Jesus didn't fit into any of these categories. In fact, when Jesus was tried, Pilate, the Roman Governor, declared that he could find no fault in Him.

No, I believe God's choice for Jesus' death speaks to the horrible nature of sin, and that the penalty had to be paid in the severest form. But seen another way, God must have used this form of punishment on His Son so that when we go through any kind of suffering, we might know that there is One who has gone through even more and is able to empathize with us. That was significant, because Jesus was taking our place, dying the death we should have died.

The apostle Paul wrote about Jesus: "*God made him who had no sin to be sin for us, so that in him we might become the righteousness of God*" (2 Corinthians 5:21). On the cross, a *divine exchange* took place. God laid our sins on Jesus and gave us His righteousness. God laid on Him the darkest, grossest, most inconceivable human atrocities and nailed them to the cross. That's why the prophet Isaiah, about seven hundred years earlier, made this prophetic utterance: "*Surely, he took up our pain and bore our suffering, yet we considered him punished by God, stricken by him, and afflicted*" (Isaiah 53:4).

Why was this necessary? Isaiah tells us: *We all, like sheep, have gone astray, each of us has turned to his own way; and the LORD has laid on Him the iniquity* (sin) *of us all*" (Isaiah 53:6).

Isaac Watts ends his hymn about the wondrous cross with these words:

> *Were the whole realm of nature mine*
> *That were an offering far too small*
> *Love so amazing so divine*
> *Demands my soul my life my all.* [13]

And that's the bottom line: this amazing love of God demands a response.

The Psalmist asks, and answers, this question: "*What can I offer the LORD for all He has done for me? I will lift up the cup of salvation and praise the LORD's name for saving me*" (Psalm 116:12–13).

During the season in which you're reading this devotional, whether it's the Easter season or some other, I trust that you will respond as the psalmist did: that you will lift up the cup of salvation that the death of Jesus on the cross made possible for you, and that you will praise the Lord's name for saving you. Amen

11 George Bennard (1912); *The Old Rugged Cross*
12 Isaac Watts (1707); *When I Surveyed the Wondrous Cross*
13 Isaac Watts (1707); *When I surveyed the Wondrous Cross*

41. The Divine Exchange

When I was in my teens (a very long time ago), I saw a movie called *Barabbas*. Barabbas was a notorious murderer and insurrectionist on death row in Jerusalem awaiting his crucifixion for crimes he had committed against Rome. The movie opens with the screen in total darkness, and then a voice over says: "You are witnessing an actual eclipse of the sun. On just such a day, almost two thousand years ago, an obscure carpenter from Galilee, gave up His life in exchange of this man." [14]

Then we see Barabbas, stumbling unshackled as his prison door swings open and he walks away a free man. As the movie continued, I discovered that the One who was called an obscure carpenter from Galilee was actually Jesus of Nazareth, the sinless Son of God, who didn't just exchange His life for Barabbas but for me and for anyone who would put their trust in Him.

Yes, two thousand years ago, a divine exchange took place—Jesus took your sins and mine and gave us His righteousness: "*Surely, he took up our pain and bore our suffering, yet we considered him punished by God, stricken by him, and afflicted*" (Isaiah 53:4). Jesus chose the way of the cross to redeem us from the curse of sin. In Galatians 3:13, Paul writes, "*Christ redeemed us from the curse of the law by becoming a curse for us, for it is written: "Cursed is everyone who is hung on a pole."*"

As you go through seasons of struggle, journey with Jesus and allow the Holy Spirit to help you to absorb His passion, as He willingly laid down His life on that cross to rescue you from the curse of sin.

Today, our devotional is about the divine exchange that took place on the cross. What was the problem? What needed to be exchanged? The prophet Isaiah had prophesized, several hundreds of years earlier, that "*We all like sheep had gone astray; we had turned—every one—to his own way; and the* LORD *has laid on him* (the Messiah) *the iniquity of us all*" (Isaiah 53:6).

If the problem was sin, the solution was the righteousness of God. About one thousand years earlier, Isaac, son of Abraham, walked up that mountainside with his father, carrying wood on his shoulders. The wood was meant to be made into an altar on which Isaac would be sacrificed to God.

> Abraham took the wood for the burnt offering and placed it on his son Isaac, and he himself carried the fire and the knife. As the two of them went on together, Isaac spoke up and said to his father Abraham, "Father?" "Yes, my son?" Abraham replied. "The fire and wood are here," Isaac said, "but where is the lamb for the burnt offering?" Abraham answered, "God himself will provide the lamb for the burnt offering, my son." And the two of them went on together. (Genesis 22:6–8)

Abraham's answer could be paraphrased, "*Jehovah Jireh,*" meaning, "the Lord will provide" or "the Lord will see to it." Just in the nick of time, God intervened and saved the life of Isaac. Well, a thousand years later, God saw to it. He provided Jesus, the spotless Lamb of God.

As Jesus walked up that Calvary hillside that day, carrying the wood on which He would be nailed, He fell beneath the weight of our sins. His followers were hoping and praying that just as Isaac escaped the knife, Jesus would escape the cross. But that wouldn't be the case. Jesus had come to die. He willingly laid down His life for you and for me.

At mid-day, as He hung there on that cruel cross, the sun refused to shine. The One who'd created the universe and turned darkness into light was now Himself engulfed in utter darkness. At that point He cried out to His Father, *"Eli, Eli, lema sabachthani?"* (which means "My God, my God, why have you forsaken me?") (Matthew 27:46). Our sins, as it were, had separated Him from the Father.

What Jesus did that day brought freedom for us and reconciled us to God our Father! So our only response today is to thank God for the grace He has bestowed on all of us, undeserving servants, whose penalty should have been death. With gratitude, let's live our lives abiding in Jesus, because as we do, we are being transformed daily into His image. He has made provision for us to be set free because of His victory on the cross. Most of all, His death brought eternal life to you and me.

What wondrous grace! What a divine exchange! May the Lord bless you.

14. Barabbas (1961); *Religious Epic Movie.*

42. Disgrace to Grace

Have you ever been through a situation so hopeless that despite assurances from your friends that better days were ahead, you couldn't be consoled? The disciples of Jesus and His friends and family would have been quite inconsolable with every strike of the hammer that pushed the nails through His hands and feet. All hope had been lost, as no one, probably with the exception of His mother, who had kept in her heart all the prophetic renderings about her Son, would have expected a glorious outcome from the death of Jesus.

Today, we're looking at how the disgrace of the cross has turned into grace that is greater than all our sins. It's hard for the human mind to fathom the depth of torture, pain, and suffering the sinless Son of God underwent. He was perfect in every way, yet He came to earth in human form to be a sacrifice and to pay the penalty for our sins. But what was intended to bring shame, disgrace, and humiliation to the Son of God resulted in His grace being bestowed on all of us.

Sometimes we try to describe GRACE by spelling out what the letters represent: God's Riches At Christ's Expense. Grace is unmerited favour, kindness from God that we don't deserve. We can never earn this favour. It's a gift from God: *"For the grace of God that brings salvation has appeared to all people, teaching us that, denying ungodliness and worldly lusts, we should live soberly, righteously, and godly in the present age"* (Titus 2:11–12).

Our response to the grace of God, should be a life that honours Him in all that we do. When we look at what Jesus went through on the cross on our behalf, it should fill our hearts with gratitude for His amazing grace toward us. What did He accomplish? In Colossians 1:13–14, we read, "For he has rescued us from the dominion of darkness and brought us into the kingdom of the Son he loves, in whom we have redemption, the forgiveness of sins."

To rescue someone means to forcibly deliver them from their captivity or from our calamity. And that is just what Jesus' death and resurrection accomplished for us. He opened the door of our prison cell and brought us out and into the kingdom of God: *"For it says: When he ascended on high, he took the captives captive; and He gave gifts to people"* (Ephesians 4:8).

He rose victorious from the grave after paying the price for the sins of the world through His sacrificial death. Through His resurrection, He broke the power of sin, Satan, death, and hell forever in the lives of *all* who would trust in Him.

Jesus led captivity captive! What does that mean for us today? This paints a vivid picture of Christ's wonderful and victorious entrance into heaven after having triumphed over everything that sought to overcome Him. Because of Christ's victory, God saw it fit to bestow gifts and graces on *all* those who trust in Him. We have all been endowed with a variety of spiritual gifts by the Holy Spirit, so let's strive to use these gifts and graces for the glory of God and in service for the benefit of the Body of Christ, His Church.

As Jesus' body was taken down from the cross that Good Friday, His followers were filled with sadness and grief. But what seemed hopeless and futile on Friday turned into joy and celebration on Sunday. The resurrection of Jesus wasn't the reversal of a defeat but the manifestation of a victory.

He rose victoriously to bring hope to all of us. When you're at the graveside of a loved one and the casket is slowly lowered into the grave, the grief is intense, and the situation seems hopeless. But Jesus rose from the dead. His resurrection instils hope and says to us "Because He lives, we shall live also."

The Bible says that just as in Adam all die, so in Christ all will be made alive. The apostle Paul says it best in in Galatians 2:20: "*I have been crucified with Christ, nevertheless I live, yet not I, but Christ lives in me."*

May the resurrection power of Jesus Christ bring renewed life to you today!

43. Death to Life

On several occasions, Jesus spoke of His death with His disciples, but they were in such denial, they couldn't come to grips with the fact that He was going to depart this world—and not in a peaceful or pleasant way but by being crucified.

> From that time on, Jesus began to explain to his disciples that He must go to Jerusalem and suffer many things at the hands of the elders, the chief priests and the teachers of the law, and that he must be killed, and on the third day be raised to life. Peter took him aside and began to rebuke him. "Never, Lord!" he said. "This shall never happen to you!" (Matthew 16:21–22)

Jesus had told them that unless a grain of wheat falls to the ground and dies, it stands alone. But if it dies, it produces a great harvest. Jesus was alluding to His own death and resurrection, and how being raised from the dead would bring a glorious harvest to His followers.

His crucifixion was predicted by the prophets centuries before, but the time had come for the fulfilment. The disciples became so afraid and distraught that many of them went into hiding as the crowd that had visited Jerusalem for the Passover festival began to disperse, returning to their own homes.

On the Sunday evening following the burial if Jesus, two of His disciples set out from Jerusalem on their journey home. They had a long walk ahead of them, as they were travelling to a village called Emmaus, about seven miles away. They were quite despondent as they reflected on what had transpired over the weekend. As they travelled along in their despondency, someone drew alongside them, but they didn't recognize that it was Jesus Himself.

> He asked them, "What are you discussing so intently as you walk along?" They stopped short; sadness written across their faces, then one of them, Cleopas, replied, "You must be the only person in Jerusalem who hasn't heard about all the things that have happened there the last few days." [19] "What things?" He asked. (Luke 24:17–19)

They went on to tell their companion the reason for their despondency. They poured out their grief about what had happened to Jesus, the man from Nazareth whom they'd hoped would be their Messiah. How He was handed over to the authorities, sentenced to death, crucified, and buried.

How many times have you and I, in our grief and suffering, been unaware of the resurrected Lord walking by our sides? Be assured today of our living hope. Jesus went from death to life, and today through His Holy Spirit, He walks with us. Hebrews 7:25 tells us: *"Therefore, He is able to save completely those who come to God through him, because He always lives to intercede for them."*

The life-changing power of the cross and the resurrection clearly present Jesus as the only way and our only hope: *"Jesus answered, 'I am the way and the truth and the life. No one comes to the Father except through me'"* (John 14:6).

Today, the cross is empty, and so is the tomb. Neither the cross nor the grave were able to hold Jesus! You can try to bury power, but it won't stay down. You can try to bury truth, but it can't be silenced. You can try to bury love, but it can't be contained. Jesus is alive! He rose victoriously from the grave, giving us hope not only in this life but also for the life to come.

When the two despondent disciples reached their destination, they begged this mysterious traveller to abide with them for the evening: *"As they sat down to eat, He took the bread and blessed it. Then he broke it and gave it to them. Suddenly, their eyes were opened, and they recognized him"* (Luke 24:30–31).

It had been Jesus with them all along! What made the difference? Did He call them by name? Was it the familiar way in which

He broke the bread that opened their eyes? Perhaps like doubting Thomas, it was when they saw the nail prints in His hands.

Whatever season you may be in, let this be a wonderful reminder that Jesus rose victoriously to bring hope to all of us. He has sent His Holy Spirit to walk with you and be your comforter in all your sorrows.

Perhaps your journey has become lonesome and weary. Don't give up or give in! Allow the resurrected Lord to open your eyes and fill you with hope for today and in the days to come

Chapter 8:
Break Up the Fallow Ground!

Sow for yourselves righteousness;
Reap in mercy; Break up your fallow ground,
For it is time to seek the LORD,
Till He comes and rains righteousness on you.

Hosea 10:12

44. Preparing Your Field

The May 24 weekend is traditionally planting season for amateur gardeners like myself. The ground that had been left barren during the winter months is now hard and dry, so a lot of work goes into breaking up the hard soil and working in some fresh top soil and manure in order to make the ground ready to receive seeds or tender plants.

In ancient times, land was allowed to lie fallow—that is, remain unplowed for a season—so that it might become more fertile. But when left in this condition, it soon became overgrown with thorns and weeds. The cultivator of the soil was careful to break up his fallow ground and clear the field of weeds before sowing seed in it.

In this devotional, I'm reflecting on preparing your field for planting. Here is the prophet Hosea's admonition to his people; he says that it's time to attend to those unplowed fields: "*Sow for yourselves righteousness; Reap in mercy; Break up your fallow ground, For it is time to seek the* Lord, *Till He comes and rains righteousness on you*" (Hosea 10:12).

In Jesus' Parable of the Sower (Matthew 13), He describes what happens to seed when the soil is not prepared. The ones that fell *by the wayside*, the ones that fell *on stony places*, and the ones that fell *among thorns* didn't produce. Only the ones that *fell on good soil* produced a bountiful crop. Therefore, soil preparation is vitally important if we're to reap a great harvest.

Yes, we need to prepare the soil of our hearts in readiness to receive the seed that the Holy Spirit is waiting to plant. A life that bears much fruit is one that glorifies the Lord (John 15:8). So prepare the soil of your heart!

This involves digging up, or plowing, to break up the hardness. It just sounds painful, doesn't it? When our hearts are hardened to God's Word, perhaps hardened by our own life experiences, we need to plough it up. We need to make ourselves more receptive by being honest about what's under the surface of our hearts and the state of our spiritual garden.

Looking into our hearts can be quite painful, and being honest with ourselves isn't easy. But the level at which we're prepared to go through the pain and examine what's in our hearts is the level to which our hearts will be receptive to the seeds that will bring us a great harvest. We must honestly examine our hearts and take a good look at ourselves so that the Holy Spirit can show us the path to healing, restoration, and growth.

As you might have surmised by now, that which is important in the physical is of even greater importance in the spiritual. The prophet admonished his audience to *"Break up your fallow ground, for it is time to seek the* Lord*!"*

Spiritually speaking, we're to break off all those things that so easily entangle so that our hearts might be prepared for the seed of righteousness So start cultivating the soil of your heart and allow the good seed of the Word to grow.

Sin is insidious; it may seem harmless in the beginning, but it brings destruction and separation from God in the end. Don't allow it to germinate in your heart. Ask God to reveal to you those areas that need to be attended to by the Master Gardener. With God's help, you'll prepare the right conditions in your heart so that as you sow the seed of His Word, watered by the Holy Spirit, it will produce a bountiful harvest

As you prepare, look to the heavens, heavy with blessing. Lift your eyes and offer your heart as Jesus Christ, Lord of the Harvest, opens the floodgates to pour out His rain.

PRAYER:
Father God, I want to make myself more open to you by being honest about what's under the surface of my heart and the state of my spiritual garden. As painful as it may be to look into my heart, I just want to be honest with myself and seek your help. Please examine my heart so that the Holy Spirit can show me the path to healing, restoration, and growth, In Jesus' name. Amen.

45. Sow Good Seeds

The apostle Paul writes in Galatians 6:7, *"Do not be deceived. God will not be made a fool. For a person will reap what they sow."* While the text was written to awaken those who were engaged in careless living, we must not forget that it's equally fitted to cheer and encourage the faithful. This seems to have been its original purpose. Paul was writing to the members of the household of faith and was calling them to Christian service.

To encourage these Galatian Christians to labour earnestly, he tells them that their labour cannot be in vain. Their spiritual work is in sowing, and by the eternal law of the universe, it must be followed by a reaping. Therefore, if we sow good seeds, we should expect a bountiful and beautiful harvest.

In the prophet Hosea's day as well as in ours, people with hardened hearts sow seeds of discontent and strife. Hosea's admonition to us is to sow seeds of righteousness in order that we may reap mercy.

Did you know that our words and actions are like "seeds" that we sow into the hearts and lives of those around us? Those seeds produce fruit in our lives, and in the lives of others. But what kind of fruit do they produce? If we sow bad seeds (such as anger, strife, resentment, bitterness, fear, etc.), we will experience the repercussions of having sown these bad seeds. The results will be a bitter harvest. But when you sow seeds of righteousness, such as love, joy, peace, and harmony, you will experience a harvest of righteousness. James 3:18 says, *"Peacemakers who sow in peace reap a harvest of righteousness."*

In scripture, God introduces the word-picture of *sowing* and *reaping* to describe His relationship with us. Every day we sow seeds that will one day sprout and produce a harvest. So there is going to be a season of reaping. For some that harvest will be incredibly joyful, but for others, the fruit of that harvest will be bitter.

In Galatians 6, the apostle Paul uses a well-known law of botany, namely that a given seed can re-produce only after its own kind. God's parallel law of sowing and reaping in the moral and spiritual realms is equally set and can't be violated.

The kind of seed we sow determines the kind of harvest we will realize. Hosea says, "They sow the wind and reap the whirlwind" (Hosea 8:7). In other words, there is a multiplication factor that comes into play when you sow. For example, the farmer sows one grain of corn, but that one grain produces many ears of corn. In the same way, if you sow seeds of righteousness today, the harvest will be multiplied tomorrow.

The process of sowing isn't always a pleasant or easy one. It takes work to change rocky soil into fruit-producing soil. In the same way, God wants us to work on those fallow places of the heart so that they become a great harvest field. That's why the psalmist says in Psalm 126:5, *"Those who sow with tears will reap with songs of joy."* The joy of the harvest will far outweigh the toil of sowing when we produce the peaceable fruit of righteousness.

Q. Have you been noticing the kind of fruit that is produced by your labour? Even though it may be abundant, are they the right kind of fruit? Are they the peaceable fruit of righteousness?

Q. Just what kind of fruit have you been producing? If per chance they're not the right kind, ask the Lord to change the condition of your heart!

PRAYER:
Father, it appears that what I've been reaping is a result of what I've been sowing. I confess that I have sown bad seeds (such as anger, strife, resentment, bitterness, and fear), which resulted in a harvest of turmoil. Please forgive me and help me to sow seeds of righteousness so that I may reap a harvest of peace. Amen.

46. Control the Weeds

As followers of Jesus, we must never be under the impression that since God gives us His Spirit to mold and shape us into the image of Jesus, we can quit trying to grow the garden of our hearts. The Holy Spirit has a work to do, but we must do our part if we're to exhibit the fruit of the Spirit.

I think Proverbs 24:30–31 applies as much to our hearts as it does to our gardens: "*I passed by the field of a lazy and careless person, by the vineyard of a man lacking sense, thorns had come up everywhere; the ground was covered with weeds, and its stone wall was broken down.*"

It's not only the weeds that come up naturally that we're to be concerned about. We have to the careful that the *boundaries* we set up around our hearts are kept intact and in good repair. Otherwise, we will unwittingly or by choice allow weeds to enter and grow.

Don't ever let the conditions described in Proverbs 24:20–31 be the state of your heart. We need to work on the field of our hearts and put up a guard around our heart: "*Above all else, guard your heart, for everything you do flows from it. Keep your mouth free of perversity; keep corrupt talk far from your lips. Let your eyes look straight ahead; fix your gaze directly before you*" (Proverbs 4:23–25).

The Weeds

In explaining the parable of the sower and the seed that fell among thorns, Jesus gave a threefold description of "heart weeds" and what they do: "*Still others, like seed sown among thorns, hear the word; but the cares or worries of this life, the deceitfulness of wealth and the desires for other things come in and choke the word, making it unfruitful*" (Mark 4:18–19).

The word, "cares" literally means something that has become a *distraction* for you. That's what worries or cares are—things that distract our minds and absorb our energy, time, and resources. Legitimate worries can become weeds, or cares, when we make them our main focus.

Jesus said, "*But seek first the kingdom of God and his righteousness, and all these things will be given to you as well*" (Matthew 6:33). Weeds are anything that competes with our earnest desire to be what God wants us to be.

Q. How do you fight the weeds in your heart?

One of the greatest herbicides is our desire to seek first the kingdom of God and His righteousness. As we submit to the Lord and His Word, denying the desires of the old nature and applying godly principles, we will see the weeds eradicated.

If you take care of the weeds, the Holy Spirit will take care of the seeds. He is the one who gives the increase.

PRAYER:
Father, thank you for Your blessed Holy Spirit, whom you have given to mold and shape me into the image of Jesus. I'm beginning to realize that I can't quit trying hard to grow the garden of my heart free of weeds. Please help me recognize those things that secretly creep in to choke out your Word. My desire is to be a productive follower of Jesus Christ, so please help me! Amen.

47. Feed the Seedlings

Just as tender plants require the right nutrients to make them grow healthy and strong, our heart, soul, and mind require the right nourishments to make them fruitful. When the garden of our heart receives the right nourishment, it will grow and produce the fruit of the Holy Spirit (Galatians 5:22–23).

Opposed to the fruit of the Spirit, are the acts of the sinful nature (Galatians 5:19–21). When we allow these acts to enter our hearts, they bring a harvest of bitterness. The apostle Paul clearly says in this passage, *"I warn you, as I did before, that those who live like this will not inherit the kingdom of God."* He goes on to say, *"But the Fruit of the Spirit is love, joy, peace, patience, kindness, goodness, faithfulness, gentleness and self-control"* (Galatians 5:22–23).

It's common knowledge that what we consume directly affects the health and workings of our bodies. Unfortunately, we aren't always as careful with what we feed our souls and minds. God is the ultimate gardener, and He is the one who causes things to grow: *"So, neither the one who plants nor the one who waters is anything, but only God, who makes things grow"* (1 Corinthians 3:7).

Only the Holy Spirit can transform us and produce this fruit in our lives. But we can co-operate with His work by feeding our minds with truth. Let's ask God to show us where our thinking may be out of line with His truth, and so renew our minds and transform our spiritual health.

In Romans 12:2, Paul tells us how to do that: *"Do not conform to the pattern of this world, but be transformed by the renewing of your mind. Then you will be able to test and approve what God's will is—his good, pleasing and perfect will."*

God's Word tells us to think on things that are true, noble, right, pure, lovely, admirable, excellent, and praiseworthy (Philippians 4:8), so what we think about does matter. What our culture considers "good, moral, and acceptable" may be a far cry from the truth of God's Word, but the Bible shows us time and time again that there's a direct correlation between the way we think and our spiritual wellbeing.

So how can we start applying these spiritual nutrients to our heart, soul, and mind so that they will be renewed and produce the fruit of righteousness? We can:

- Read the Bible regularly
- Meditate on scripture
- Participate in the ministry of the church

- Join a Bible study small group
- Listen to music that edifies our soul

Jesus says in John 15:1–2: *"I am the true vine, and my Father is the gardener. He cuts off every branch in me that bears no fruit, while every branch that does bear fruit, he prunes so that it will be even more fruitful."*

Do your part in providing the environment necessary for growth and so allow the Holy Spirit to produce in you the fruit of righteousness.

PRAYER:
Father, I'm not always as careful with what I feed my soul and mind as I am with the things I feed my body. Please help me *not* to conform to the pattern of this world but to be transformed by the renewing of my mind, in order that I may glorify you in all that I do. Amen.

48. Reaping a Harvest

The harvest has always been a beautiful and important part of life on earth. The time when, after a season of sowing and nurturing, the seed produces a crop. Proverbs 20:4 says, *"A farmer too lazy to plant in the spring has nothing to harvest in the fall."*

Reaping a great harvest is not only contingent on sowing the right seed but also on the soil in which it's sown. In this passage, The Living Bible translates Proverbs 20:4 as, *"If you won't plow in the cold, you won't eat at the harvest."* Like all of Proverbs, this is a piece of plain, practical common sense. It teaches that people should diligently seize the opportunity while it's theirs.

Israel celebrated their times of the harvest with a feast, appropriately named the "Feast of Harvest" (Exodus 23:16). Just as it takes work to produce a harvest by first preparing the soil, it takes much more careful preparation of the soil of the heart if we hope to see a bountiful harvest. By now you've experienced that preparing the heart is not just a seasonal thing but a lifelong pursuit.

The prophet Jeremiah describes it in these terms:

> The human heart is the most deceitful of all things, and desperately wicked. Who really knows how bad it is? Only the Lord knows! He searches all hearts and examines deepest motives so He can give to each person his right reward, according to his deeds—how he has lived. (Jeremiah 17:9, NLT)

We have to constantly examine our hearts and also ask the Lord to do the examination, as the psalmist implores: "*Search me, O God, and know my heart; test me and know my anxious thoughts. Point out anything in me that offends you, and lead me along the path of everlasting life*" (Psalm 139:23–24).

To reap a harvest of righteousness, certain spiritual disciplines must be incorporate into one's life: "*No discipline seems pleasant at the time, but painful. Later on, however, it produces a harvest of righteousness and peace for those who have been trained by it*" (Hebrews 12:11). Taking care of the heart by careful discipline and constant nurturing will result in a great spiritual harvest. But an even greater harvest can result—a harvest of souls resulting from sowing the seed of the good news of the Word.

Jesus used the same metaphor of the field and harvesting after sowing the seed of the Word to the woman at the well in Samaria. Jesus asked His followers: "*Don't you have a saying, 'It's still four months until harvest?' I tell you, open your eyes and look at the fields! They are ripe for harvest*" (John 4:35). In the days following this statement, many Samaritans became followers of Jesus. In nourishing our own hearts with the seed of God's Word, a spiritual overflow takes place into the lives of others. Therefore, sow the seed, being assured of this one thing: Every seed, buried with sweat and tears, God will call forth in His time, because He is Lord of the harvest, and He will give us the increase.

Q. Have you been reaping a harvest of righteousness?

Q. Have you been providing the necessary spiritual nutrients to the soil of your heart in order to receive a spiritual harvest? Ask the Lord to search your heart to see if it needs to be purified by the Holy Spirit!

PRAYER:
Father, I confess that I haven't been diligently seizing the opportunity to edify my soul and purify my heart as your Word commands. I'm discovering that the harvest produced by my labour is not that of righteousness but of bitterness, folly, and strife. Please search my heart to see if there are any contrary ways in me, and lead me in the path of righteousness. Amen.

49. A Time to Uproot

Last spring after preparing the soil that had laid fallow for a year, I planted some green beans. They sprang up quite quickly, as the growing conditions of warmth and moisture were in great abundance. The plants grew healthy and strong, and they produced quite a crop, which came in handy at dinner time.

But even after the last bean pods were harvested, the plants remained healthy and strong. They looked hardy enough to survive another year. I had to keep reminding myself that they are annuals, and even though they may look healthy and strong, the stalks had to be uprooted, reluctantly.

Is there something in your personal life or ministry that has served you well but has now become something that is comfortable but needs to go? In Ecclesiastes 3:2, we read, *"There is a time to plant and a time to uproot, a time to tear down and a time to build."*

The concept of planting and reaping is a universal one. However, we have to be careful what we sow, because fruit will follow. Sometimes after the fruits have been harvested, the plant that is left behind seems to remain healthy and strong. But if it's a seasonal plant, regardless of how healthy it looks, it has to be uprooted.

As difficult as this may be, Solomon invites us to embrace this experience as an important part of life. *There is a time to plant and a time to uproot.* Like plants that have outlived their usefulness, we sometimes tend to hold on to things in our lives that were once useful but now have no redeeming value.

As you might have experienced, God uses change to bring us to better, newer-and-improved places in our lives. It's important to recognize that changes do happen, and we shouldn't try to hold on to things that need to be uprooted or torn down.

In life, we always have to keep moving. God gives us dreams and ambitions to inspire us to move ahead. Still, we tend to find a comfort zone and settle there. *But there is a time to plant and a time to uproot.*

Some things are necessary to uproot in order to embrace the next season of our lives, for example, tradition. The spirit of religiosity thrives on tradition. It makes us inflexible and legalistic, causing us to stagnate. Even as a pastor, some of your ministry initiatives that were once flourishing have run their course. Even though it would be nice to keep them going, there comes a time when they need to be uprooted, because God has something better for you.

God usually provides a season of pause in the action for us to reflect and plan for the next growing season. Most of all, we should be grateful for the reminder that even when our efforts to create come to an unceremonious end, we are sustained by Creator God, who provides for us in every season. That seems to be the lesson that reverberates throughout the contrasting seasons of Ecclesiastes 3.

At some point, we all must face the reality of giving up our self-sufficiencies and the illusion of independence. In uprooting some of these things, we find the *seeds of faith and life* in a God who loves and sustains us. So take a good look again at some of those areas of your life—things that have stopped growing and producing, things you just can't bring yourself to uproot.

In Ecclesiastes, we're challenged to consider the strange irony of death—not just in the garden, but also in some of the things in our lives that need to be uprooted. In John 12:24, Jesus says, *"Truly, truly, I say to you, unless a grain of wheat falls into the earth and dies, it remains alone; but if it dies, it bears much fruit."*

Take a good look at your life and the comfort zone you've created for yourself, and ask the Lord if something needs to die in order that He might grow something new in you.

PRAYER:
Father God, please help me to recognize and accept those things in my life that need to die in order that you might birth something new in my heart and life. Help me to let go and to trust you more for better and greater fruits. Amen.

Chapter 9:
A Season for Hope

*Praise be to the God and Father of our Lord Jesus Christ!
In his great mercy he has given us new birth
into a living hope through the resurrection
of Jesus Christ from the dead.*

1 Peter 1:3

50. Renewal

What do you think of when you hear the word "renewal"? Does it give you a sense of hope? Renewal is like a seed that has been buried in the ground, covered over with snow. But at the first sign of spring, it pushes new sprouts through the stubborn soil and begins to grow.

Jesus says in John 12:24, *"Yes, indeed! I tell you that unless a grain of wheat that falls to the ground dies, it stays just a grain; but if it dies, it produces a big harvest."*

People often say "Hope springs eternal." But it may not always feel that way. Feelings of hopelessness can affect you if you're struggling with heavy emotions like anger, anxiety, depression, or loss. These are all emotions that can drain people of their hope. I know that during the pandemic, many people were finding it hard to hold on to hope. Perhaps for you there was a significant loss—your job, or rough patches in a relationship.

Springtime is usually a season for renewal, a season for hope. I have titled this series of devotionals "A Season for Hope." Today, we're looking at "Renewal."

During periods of extreme uncertainty, we often feel overwhelmed. But through the wonderful provision God has made for us though Jesus Christ, we can have hope—not just for today, but for the future. The apostle Peter writes:

> Praise be to the God and Father of our Lord Jesus Christ! In his great mercy he has given us new birth into a living hope through the resurrection of Jesus Christ from the dead, and into an inheritance that can never perish, spoil or fade … In all this you greatly rejoice, though now for a little while you may have had to suffer grief in all kinds of trials. (1 Peter 1:3–6)

For all the struggles life may throw your way, moments of unexplainable joy can be found. Hope may present itself in unexpected ways, whether you find it in quiet moments of peace with your loved ones, a funny conversation, a meditative walk, or in a conversation with God.

The Bible reminds us that there is hope to be found even in the darkest of days: *"And the God of all grace, who called you to his eternal glory in Christ, after you have suffered a little while, will himself restore you and make you strong, firm and steadfast"* (1 Peter 5:10).

The biblical account of Job tells the story of a man whose life became unbearably difficult through suffering and unbelievable loss of family and all his possessions. It wasn't an easy time for him. His friends were no longer supportive, nor was his wife, who encouraged him to just curse God and die. But Job was buoyed by his hope and steadfast faith in God, who was looking out for him.

Perhaps your struggles have drained your hope and caused your faith to weaken, such that you're finding it hard to trust God for better days ahead. You may be at a point where you're beginning to question everything, even the goodness of the Lord.

Job said, "*If someone dies, will they live again? All the days of my hard service I will wait for my renewal to come*" (Job 14:14). From the scriptures we know the answer to this question is a resounding yes. And it is the same answer to the question, "If hope dies, will it live again?" Yes, indeed! Job says he will wait for his renewal to come.

Like Job, God is looking out for you, and there is light to be found, even in the darkest moments of life. Job connects this idea of hope to the possibilities that exist for a tree:

> For a tree there is always hope.
> Chop it down and it still has a chance—
> its roots can put out fresh sprouts.
> Even if its roots are old and gnarled,
> its stump long dormant; At the first whiff of water it
> comes to life. (Job 14:7–8)

In the same way, hope springs eternal for those who put their trust in God. So whatever you may be going through today, or have been through in the recent past, don't give up! Wait on the Lord to be renewed in spirit.

51. A Time to Heal

When you think of hope, what comes to mind? Is it wishful thinking, hoping something good will happen? Hope is more than wishful thinking. It's a desire accompanied by an expectation that something like a promise will be fulfilled. And when it comes to the hope that a belief in God inspires, it's the evidence of things not as yet seen. The hope that this devotional focuses on today is the confident expectation of what God has promised!

Spring is a season for hope, a season of excitement and change, a season for growth and new beginnings. We plant seeds and water them while we wait for signs of new life. But we also watch as flowers bloom in the garden—flowers produced by seeds that have gone through the harsh winter, buried in the depths of the earth.

This is a metaphor for what the world has gone through over the past few years (2020 to 2022). We're now into the fourth year of the pandemic, and though there are some hopeful signs that it's coming to an end, we can't be certain. Our medical officers are hopeful. But hope, they say, is not a substitute for planning. You plan for the worst but hope for the best.

In today's devotional, hope says it's "A Time to Heal" In Ecclesiastes 3:1, Solomon says: *"There is a time for everything, and a season for every activity under heaven."* This is a "time to heal" after a long period of physical and emotional pain.

In Lamentations 3, the prophet Jeremiah gives us a gruesome description of the atrocities that devastated the City of Jerusalem during the time of the Babylonian occupation. Then we suddenly come to one of the most unexpected and jarring literary pivots in all of scripture. Nothing about the horrific circumstances of the city, the nation, or the prophet gives any reason for hope. By all appearances, all had been lost. But suddenly, unexpectedly, the lamenting prophet breaks into this beautiful, and now beloved, declaration:

> But this I call to mind, and therefore I have hope: The steadfast love of the Lord never ceases; His mercies never come to an end; they are new every morning; great is your faithfulness. The Lord is my portion," says my soul, therefore, I will HOPE in him. (Lamentations 3:21–24)

The steadfast love of the Lord is also called His *Hesed*. It's a Hebrew word that means "God's unconditional love." It's a love that the recipient, trying as hard as they could, could never reciprocate.

Perhaps over the past three years, you've suffered the anguish and pain of the dreaded pandemic or some other debilitating disease. Your pain, which is still ongoing, has robbed you of your joy and taken your peace and hope away. But with the help of the Lord, it is a time to heal!

During this season, allow the steadfast love of the Lord and His mercies that are new every morning to restore your health in every area of your life.

PRAYER:
Father God, I pray right now for this one who is reading this devotional and, have identified with what has been said, is suffering immensely from an ailment that has taken their hope and health away. Please restore their hope and their health, I pray, through the precious name of Jesus Christ our Saviour. Amen.

52. Keeping Hope Alive

In tough and uncertain times, it can be quite difficult to look beyond what's currently happening in your life to see the light at the end of the tunnel, so to speak. Whether you're going through a big life change, a hard time with your family, or personal health concerns, an optimistic frame of mind can help you see a difficult challenge as an opportunity for gratitude.

As the flowers start to bloom and the sun stays out a little longer, we're reminded that spring is the ultimate time of renewal. It's a time to reset ourselves and spiritually prepare for the harvest ahead, hoping for an overflow of blessings from the Lord. In Romans 15:13, the apostle Paul says, *"May the God of Hope fill you with all joy and peace as you trust in him, so that you may overflow with hope by the power of the Holy Spirit."*

When you're feeling low or going through some hardships, try to find the silver linings in your circumstances that will bring you hope. In 2 Corinthians 4:17–18, Paul encourages us:

> For our light and momentary troubles are achieving for
> us an eternal glory that far outweighs them all. So we
> fix our eyes not on what is seen, but on what is unseen,
> since what is seen is temporary, but what is unseen
> is eternal.

In the recent past, I've had the privilege as Care Pastor to hear from people in the midst of turmoil in their lives. Some have gone through bereavements and relationship breakups; some have lost their jobs, while others are struggling with illnesses. One thing they all have in common is that they're grasping for something to give them hope.

When the children of Israel were going into exile due to their disobedience, God didn't abandon them. Instead, He gave them this wonderful hope-filled promise:

> "For I know the plans I have for you," declares the Lord, "plans to prosper you and not to harm you, plans to give you <u>hope</u> and a future." Then you will call on me and come and pray to me, and I will listen to you. You will seek me and find me when you seek me with all your heart." (Jeremiah 29:11-13, emphasis added)

The children of Israel were to keep their hope alive by focusing on that time in the future when God was going to bring them back from their captivity. Do you feel like you've become a captive? Perhaps it's not a physical captivity, but emotional or spiritual captivity can be just as debilitating.

The good news is that when you focus on what will happen once the storm has passed, you'll receive the strength you need to overcome your present moments of doubt and fear. Be patient, therefore, and seek the Lord. When you seek Him with all your heart, He will be found and will change your doubts and fear into a hope-filled future.

How do you keep hope alive? You may ask lots of questions, chief among them being, "Why?" "Why me?" "Why, Lord?" "Why this?" "Why" is the question that first comes to mind as you struggle to keep hope alive, and it's the one that lingers the longest. But don't give up the things you know for the things you don't know.

The things you know are: *God loves me. He sent His Son to die on a cross for me. He promises to be with me and to never leave me or forsake me.* So don't turn away in the darkness from the things God has shown you in the light. Let His many promises give you strength and keep your hope alive. Because in due time, you will receive a bountiful harvest, if you don't give up.

PRAYER
Father God, in these tumultuous times in which we live, it's getting increasingly difficult to be hopeful about the future. People are

struggling with homelessness, and there are illnesses and diseases all around us. Regional conflicts are escalating into global threats of war, and our hope is turning into fear. But your Word encourages us to look up, because when we see these things coming to pass, our redemption is drawing near. So please give me courage and fill me with hope for brighter and better days ahead. Please help me to keep my hope in you alive. In Jesus' name. Amen.

53. Can You See It?

You probably remember as a little child being at a parade with your parents or caregivers. Your vision was obscured by the crowd, only allowing for small glimpses of the procession between slivers of light as people shifted about.

Oh, but how things changed when your dad lifted you up above the crowd and placed you on his shoulders. Everything suddenly became clear and you could see—not just the immediate surroundings, but what seemed to be miles away. That's what perspective does for you.

To be able to get a better view, you need to see things from a better vantage point. You need to lift your sights from the darkness and discouragement around you at ground level so that you can get a better perspective of what God is doing.

You may have been going through a very tough time. You might even call it a drought—a spiritual drought. But at the invitation of the Lord, you can look to the heavens, because that is where your help comes from: "*I lift my eyes toward the mountains. Where will my help come from?* ² *My help comes from the* LORD, *the Maker of heaven and earth*" (Psalm 121:1–2, CSB). Let's look up, because the upward look gives us a greater perspective.

After three-and-a-half years of drought, the prophet Elijah sent his servant to look toward the sea for any sign of rain. So the servant went up and looked and said:

> "There is nothing." And seven times Elijah said, "Go again." Then it came to pass on the seventh time, that the servant said, "There is a cloud, as small as a man's

hand, rising out of the sea!" So, Elijah said, "Go up, say to Ahab the king, 'Prepare your chariot, and go down before the rain stops you'" (1 Kings 18:43–44).

When we see what's happening in the world around us—the chaotic nature of politics, wars, the atrocities, and man's inhumanity to man—I wonder if there's any room for hope in your heart? In this series of devotionals, I encourage you to find hope even amid the gloomiest of circumstances. Today, "Can You See It?"

Even before the small cloud appeared, Elijah's hope was rising. He saw in his spirit, and felt in his bones, that rain was about to come. His hope was becoming sight. He said to King Ahab: "*Go, eat and drink, for there is the sound of a heavy rain*" (1 Kings 18:41).

Based only on the sighting of a cloud as small as a man's hand, Elijah knew a torrent was on its way. When we see God moving, even in small ways, among us, it should increase our faith and hope for an even greater demonstration of His power. Many people may be cautiously optimistic because there are some small signs signalling a better day ahead, while we who have hope see those little signs as the sound of a torrent to come.

Zechariah the prophet said, "*Do not despise these small beginnings, for the LORD rejoices to see the work begin*" (NLT). The evidence of imminent rain came slowly and in a small way, but out of this small beginning, God brought a mighty torrent. So too in our day, God is poised to shower us with an abundance of blessings if we do not faint. You might feel like you've been in a drought for a number of years, but there is a cloud. Can you see it?

Lift your eyes to the heavens. That's where our help and hope come from. So with great anticipation, we await the promise to come. Everything that God has ordained, He will bring to pass; just as He quickens in the spring, the seed that had been buried deep beneath the winter snow.

So reach out to Jesus the Son. He is the hope of the world.

PRAYER

Father God, please lift me up and let me stand by faith on your promises. Help me to see things from your perspective and so transform my despair into life-giving hope. In the name of Jesus Christ, my Saviour. Amen.

54. Restoration

Have you ever been so filled with joy due to an unexpected gesture of grace that it all seemed like a dream? I remember as a youth when one day my best friend, Mac, and I couldn't get tickets to the World Series of Cricket between the West Indies and England. It was being played at the Queen's Park Oval in Port-of Spain, Trinidad. So we decided to scale the wall surrounding the ballpark, only to land in the arms of a police officer.

We were expecting to be placed in confinement for the day, or at best escorted to the exit gate. But instead, the officer took us to the ticket booth, where we were able to purchase tickets to see the game. We were expecting the worst, but we were over the moon with joy due to this unexpected gesture of grace.

I think that must have been how the children of Israel felt after they were released from their Babylonian captivity. The Psalmist writes in Psalm 126:1–2:

> When the LORD restored the fortunes of Zion, we were like those who dreamed. Our mouths were filled with laughter, our tongues with songs of joy. Then it was said among the nations, "The LORD has done great things for them."

Today I'm looking at "Restoration." When God restored the fortunes of Israel, it was so unbelievable that the people felt like they'd been walking in a dream. Imagine their joy: The year was 538 B.C, and the Jews, after being in exile in Babylon for seventy years, had been set free.

Seventy years is a long time. The people had settled down. But even though they had established homes and families in their new land, there was always a longing for restoration. Psalm 137:1 gives a sense of what the exiles felt while in captivity *"By the rivers of Babylon we sat and wept when we remembered Zion."*

There was a kind of cosmic homesickness for the familiar. But then suddenly, Cyrus, the new king, made a proclamation allowing all the Jews to go home (Ezra 1:1–4). It was as if they were dreaming.

We aren't in captivity today, although at times over the past few years, it might have felt that way. We faced many restrictions during those days of the dreaded pandemic. The isolation and the social and physical distancing caused us to feel like we were being held captive.

When all the restrictions come to an end and our lives return to normal, I'm sure it will take some getting used to. No more wearing masks, and being able to walk side by side, sit close to one another in church, and hug again.

In a spiritual sense, we're also aliens and captives on this earth. Our home is in heaven, and there is a kind of cosmic homesickness for our redemption to come. Speaking of Abraham, the writer to the Hebrews says: *"For he was looking forward to the city with foundations, whose architect and builder is God"* (Hebrews 11:10). And again, *"For here we do not have an enduring city, but we are looking for the city that is to come"* (Hebrews 13:14).

Yes, there is a time of restoration coming, when that which has been taken will be restored. But we're looking forward to an even greater restoration, when the Lord Himself will bring peace to a world that is so steeped in conflicts and ravaged by war. After a time of suffering in this life, like Job, we will wait for our restoration to come.

Let Psalm 126:5 be a source of comfort to you today. It reminds us of this great truth: *"Those who sow in tears will reap with songs of joy."* So be encouraged by this thought, and allow the Lord to fill you with hope—the kind that only He alone can give.

Chapter 10:
For Such a Time as This

> But Moses said to God, "Who am I that I should go to Pharaoh and bring the Israelites out of Egypt?"
> And God said, "I will be with you."
>
> Exodus 3:11-12

55. Going for Broke

Have you ever had an encounter that left you with a feeling of guilt? You re-live the situation over and over in your mind, thinking you could have done more, you could have spoken up, or you could have come to the aid of your friend or colleague. But the cost would have been too high. So you remained silent while some innocent one suffered.

Whether they were slaves in Egypt, exiles in Babylon, or scattered across the provinces of Persia, God always chose someone to bring deliverance to His people whenever their wellbeing is in jeopardy. Queen Ester is the inspiration for this devotional series, which I have titled "For Such a Time as This."

Today, we're "Going for Broke." It was around 475 BC, and due to her disobedience to King Xerxes, Queen Vashti was banished. A contest was held to find a successor. This resulted in a young and beautiful Jewish girl being chosen to be queen. Her name was Hadassah, but she was given the Persian name Esther, meaning Star.

She was an orphan who'd been brought up by her cousin Mordecai. But Esther 2:10 tells us, *"Esther did not reveal her ethnicity or her family background, because Mordecai had ordered her not to make it known."*

After Esther became queen, Mordecai became embroiled in a power struggle with Haman, the second in command in the king's palace. Mordechai had refused to bow before Haman, which infuriated him, so he resolves not only to put Mordecai to death, but also to slaughter all the Jewish people. Haman secured the king's permission to carry out this edict, which was set to take place during Purim, a popular Jewish festival.

When Mordecai learned of Haman's plans, he sent this message to Esther:

> He said, "Don't think that you will escape the fate of all the Jews because you are in the king's palace. If you keep silent at this time, relief and deliverance will come to the Jewish people from another place, but you and your father's family will be destroyed." (Esther 4:13–14a)

God always finds someone to do His bidding. Mordecai ended his message to Esther by saying, "*Who knows, perhaps you have come to your royal position for such a time as this*" (v. 14b).

Esther felt helpless. To approach the king without being summoned by him could mean death. However, due to Mordecai's incessant prodding, she said, "*I will go to the king, even though it is not permitted, and if I perish, I perish*" (Esther 4:16b).

We're living at a time when the authority of God's Word is being challenged by seductive humanistic views and doctrines contrary to God's will. Can you afford to remain silent? Who knows, perhaps God has positioned you where you are for *such a time as this*.

There comes a time in all of our lives when we need to make the hard choices. Do we choose self-preservation and status? Or do we make a choice for God, trusting Him for the outcome? On the third day, after Esther's people had prayed and fasted, Esther went in to see the king.

The prayers of God's people were answered, praise the Lord! The king received Esther, and not only was Esther's life spared, but the Jewish people were saved as well. Haman's evil plot was overthrown, Mordecai was honoured, and Haman was hanged from the gallows he had fashioned for Mordecai.

Yes, God does respond to the prayers of His people—not just when their lives are in peril, but also when they have disobeyed Him and are pursuing the evil ways of the world. We can count on this, because God has promised in His Word that He will come to our rescue:

> If my people, who are called by my name, will humble themselves and pray and seek my face and turn from their wicked ways, then I will hear from heaven, and I will forgive their sin and will heal their land. (2 Chronicles 7:14)

For all those times when you felt guilty due to apathy caused by fear of reprisal, or just not wanting to rock the boat, be aware that the God we serve is a God of the second chance and more. Think about it! Perhaps God has positioned you where you are for a particular purpose, to be "salt" and "light," as He said in Matthew 5. He has called you for such a time as this!

56. Character Matters

He was the favoured son of his father but hated by his brothers. Their hatred was so intense that one day they sold him as a slave, reporting to their father that he had been devoured by wild beasts. Joseph ended up in Egypt, where he worked as a servant in his master's house. Hindsight is always 20/20. But in retrospect, Joseph would say that he was chosen by God "for such a time as this."

This devotional focuses on those times when, through God's providence, someone who is elevated to a position of influence is looked upon to deliver God's people. Today, as we consider Joseph, we see that "Your Character Matters."

Working as a servant in his master's house, Joseph was of such impeccable character that his master, Potiphar, put him in charge of his household and entrusted to his care everything he owned.

Genesis 39:4 tells us, *"Joseph found favor in his eyes and became his attendant."* Genesis 39:6–7 goes on to say, *"Now Joseph was well-built and handsome, and after a while his master's wife took notice of Joseph and said, 'Come to bed with me!'"* But Joseph's commitment to God and respect for his master's wife wouldn't permit him to entertain such a sinful request. His refusal to engage in a sinful act against God and his master so infuriated his master' wife that she brought some false acquisitions against Joseph. This, of course, landed Joseph in prison. Joseph had purposed in his heart that regardless of the cost, he was not going to allow a few fleeting moments of the sinful pleasures of this world to rob him of the destiny God had in store for him.

We are living at a time when the world's standards are accepted as the norm, when anything is permissible if it feels good. How do you go against the pressures to conform and instead stand up for what you believe to be right? Perhaps you're called to God's kingdom for such a time as this to exhibit a godly character that is exemplary to your peers.

After spending several years in prison, Joseph was taken from his dungeon to appear before the Pharaoh. Pharaoh had had a disturbing dream, which none of his wise men could interpret. But he'd heard of Joseph's ability to interpret dreams, so he sent for him.

> Pharaoh said to Joseph, "I had a dream, and no one can interpret it. But I have heard that when you hear a dream you can interpret it."
>
> "I cannot do it," Joseph replied to Pharaoh, "but God will give Pharaoh the answer he desires."
> (Genesis 41:15–16)

Joseph's interpretation of the Pharaoh's dream later enabled Egypt to survive seven years of famine: *"Then Pharaoh dressed Joseph in robes of fine linen and made him second in charge over all of Egypt"*

(Genesis 41:42). When the years of famine began, Egypt was well positioned to survive. People from all over came to Egypt to buy their grain. This included Joseph's brothers, who had sold him into slavery. In His providence, God had positioned Joseph in Egypt, "for such a time as this."

When Joseph's brothers arrived, they bowed down to him, with no thought that this was their brother. Joseph could have avenged himself for what his brothers had done to him, but instead he treated them with kindness. Joseph said to them, "*You intended to harm me, but God intended it for good to accomplish what is now being done, the saving of many lives*" (Genesis 50:20).

God has made it possible for you to have a character like Joseph as you continually abide in Him and allow His righteous virtues to flow through you. Because character matters! Who knows, perhaps God has positioned you where you are "for such a time as this."

57. Choose for Eternity

With God, timing is everything. We may try to run ahead of Him with our own plans and ideas of how He'll accomplish His will, but in the end, God has the final say. As humans, He has given us free choice—two paths from which to choose. The choices we make will determine our destiny.

This baby was snatched from the River Nile by the daughter of the King of Egypt and was raised in the palace as her own son. His name was *Moses*, meaning, *I drew him out of the water*. But he was really the son of Hebrew slaves.

Today in this devotional, we're focussing on the choices we make, especially when we're in a position of influence, which God by His sovereign power has orchestrated. Today, I'm encouraging you to "Choose Heavenly Treasures."

During and after the famine in Canaan, the Hebrews moved to dwell in Egypt, where their numbers increased so greatly that they became a threat to the Egyptians. So in an effort to slow the growth of the Hebrew population, the king had all the male babies killed by having them tossed into the river at birth.

But God preserved the life of Moses. He saved him from the river and enabled him to grow up in a life of privilege in the palace of the king. But the turning point came for him one day as he went out to where the Hebrews were and watched them at their hard labour. As he observed the brutality to which the slaves were subjected, he took matters into his own hands to avenge one of the Hebrews being abused by an Egyptian. As a result, he had to flee for his life.

There comes a time in all of our lives when we have to make the hard choices! Do we choose riches, self preservation, and status? Or do we choose the path of righteousness, even though it may lead to all kinds of hardship, pain, and suffering?

In his quiet lifestyle as a shepherd in the land of Midian, to which Moses had fled, God got his attention one day through a burning bush to remind him why he'd been saved from the river. God had heard the cries of the Israelites and had seen their oppression at the hands of the Egyptians and was ready to rescue them. God said to Moses, *"'Go. I am sending you to Pharaoh to bring my people the Israelites out of Egypt.' But Moses said to God, 'Who am I that I should go to Pharaoh and bring the Israelites out of Egypt?'"* (Exodus 3:10–11)

"Who am I that I should go?" Moses' question might be one that you have asked, feeling secure in your own position, and not wanting to make waves. Or perhaps you felt inadequate for the task. Either way, God may have called you to the kingdom for such a time as this.

After many questions to God concerning His mission, Moses finally returned to Egypt. There in Egypt, Moses' appeal to the king to set God's people free was rejected time and time again. But Pharaoh finally relented, realizing it was God and not Moses he was fighting against. So with great reluctance, he set the Israelites free (Exodus 12:31). That night, God used Moses to lead the Israelites out of bondage and into freedom.

The writer to the Hebrews summarizes Moses' choice this way: *"By faith, Moses, when grown, refused the privileges of the Egyptian royal house. He chose a hard life with God's people. Because he valued suffering in Messiah's camp far greater than the wealth of Egypt"* (Hebrews 11:24–25).

Moses, to his own peril, could have turned a blind eye to the plight of the Hebrew people and continued to live the life of a prince in the palace of Pharaoh. He could have considered the wealth of Egypt something to be grasped. But instead, he chose something of far greater worth, something with eternal value. He chose to suffer in the wilderness with the people of God rather than enjoy the pleasures of sin for a season.

Perhaps like Moses, God has positioned you where you are "for such a time as this." Look around and see the injustices in the world today, in your country, in your city, in your neighbourhood, perhaps even in your home. Or maybe you're faced with an ethical dilemma that could result in you being very well off for the rest of your life. Choose wisely! Make your choice for the eternal. Choose heavenly treasures.

58. Rise up and Rebuild

In this devotional series, I'm focusing on those times when, through God's providence, someone rises to the occasion to fulfill God's divine purpose. Have you ever considered that your particular vocation, the people in your sphere of influence, or the place where you find yourself may have been orchestrated by God? Today's devotional is called, "Rise up and Rebuild."

He was living a life of ease in the palace of the Persian King Artaxerxes, so nothing really should have shaken him from his opulent lifestyle. This man's name was Nehemiah, and he was born to Jewish parents in Persia during their exile from Jerusalem.

He had never been to Jerusalem, but he had a keen interest in what was transpiring there after most of the exiles had returned. He held an honoured and influential position—that of cupbearer to Artaxerxes, King of Persia (Nehemiah 2:1).

This may sound like a glamorous position, but being a cupbearer to the king was a way to protect the king in case someone wanted to poison him. Nehemiah had to taste everything that was brought to the king before the king partook of it. So the job was a little dangerous, but it had its perks.

The turning point came for Nehemiah one day when he received some sad news about what was happening in his ancestral homeland. These are Nehemiah's words:

> In the month of Kislev in the twentieth year, while I was in the citadel of Susa, Hanani, one of my brothers, came from Judah with some other men, and I questioned them about the Jewish remnant that had survived the exile, and also about Jerusalem. They said to me, "Those who survived the exile and are back in the province are in great trouble and disgrace. The wall of Jerusalem is broken down, and its gates have been burned with fire." When I heard these things, I sat down and wept. For some days I mourned and fasted and prayed before the God of heaven. (Nehemiah 1:1–4)

As a follower of the Lord, you no doubt can bear testimony to the fact that prayer changes everything! Whatever the situation, no matter how dire it might appear, when we bring it to God in prayer, He works on our behalf. So in great sadness, and with fear and trepidation, Nehemiah approached the king to ask a favour.

> In the month of Nisan in the twentieth year of King Artaxerxes, when wine was brought for him, I took the wine and gave it to the king. I had not been sad in his presence before, so the king asked me, "Why does your face look so sad when you are not ill? This can be nothing but sadness of heart." I was very much afraid, but I said to the king, "May the king live forever! Why should my face not look sad when the city where my ancestors are buried lies in ruins, and its gates have been destroyed by fire?" The king said to me, "What is it you want? How can I help you?" (Nehemiah 2:1–4)

As a result of prayer, Nehemiah was given an audience with the king, with the queen sitting beside him. Nehemiah related to the king the plight of the city and petitioned him to give him leave, to provide the material necessary for rebuilding, and to ensure safety on his journey. Quite a tall order! Amazingly, due to God's divine provision, Nehemiah, who seemingly was at the right place at the right time, was given all that he needed to travel to Jerusalem. The king granted all his requests. So Nehemiah journeyed to Jerusalem and started the rebuilding of the walls.

No one can forget the dreaded pandemic that plagued the whole world at its peak from 2020 to 2022. It wreaked havoc among the families of the world—death, severe illness, separation, anxiety, physical and social isolation, loss of employment, broken relationships, loss of faith, disruption in religious gatherings, etc. As we emerge from over two years of this world-wide virus, many things have been devastated by it and lie in ruins. Like Nehemiah, this may be causing you sadness of heart. But it calls for a determined effort to rise up and rebuild, with God's enablement, that which has been broken. Nehemiah encountered great hostility from the enemy as he tried to rebuild the wall.

There will always be hostility and opposition as the child of God is made aware of things that have been ruined by the enemy and seeks to rebuild. But with the help of the Lord, it is possible to not just rebuild but to exceed our own expectation. In the space of fifty-two days, under the direction of Nehemiah, the wall was rebuilt.

Whatever you may be facing today, even if it's all in pieces, with God's enablement, you can put it back together again. My Father's hands can fix anything in this world. If it all lies in pieces, seemingly without a hope or a prayer, it is never beyond the loving repair of my Father's hands.

Pray and ask God for His enablement, which will help you to fulfill His divine purpose. Who knows, perhaps God has called you and placed you exactly where you are for such a time as this!

JULY- SEPTEMBER

Chapter 11:
Count it All Joy

> Anyone who listens to the word but does not do what it says
> is like someone who looks at his face in a mirror
> and, after looking at himself, goes away
> and immediately forgets what he looks like
>
> James 1:23–24

59. Mirror, Mirror!

The apostle James, a biological brother of Jesus, knew what it was like to disbelieve, even in the face of all the wondrous and miraculous deeds Jesus did. He didn't come to believe in Jesus until after Jesus was resurrected from the dead. James' transformation, like all the followers of Jesus Christ, was brought about miraculously.

He writes in James 1:22, "*Do not merely listen to the word, and so deceive yourselves. Do what it says.*" In these devotional thoughts from the apostle James, "A Season to Get Real," I want to look at the practical side of our faith in Jesus Christ.

James likens the Word of God to a mirror. You've heard the saying, "The mirror doesn't lie."

> Do not merely listen to the word, and so deceive yourselves. Do what it says. Anyone who listens to the word but does not do what it says is like someone who looks at his face in a mirror and, after looking at himself, goes

> away and immediately forgets what he looks like. But whoever looks intently into the perfect law that gives freedom, and continues in it—not forgetting what they have heard, but doing it—they will be blessed in what they do. (James 1:22–26)

To read the Word without acting on it leads to self-deception. James underscores his command to obey the Word with an illustration about a mirror. What does a mirror do? A mirror gives you information about yourself. It doesn't change your condition. It only alerts you to the condition. We can apply James' illustration to our lives in a practical way.

You got out of bed this morning, but you're late for work. You take a quick look in the mirror and notice that your hair isn't really presentable, but you figure no sweat, no time to fix it. So you quickly rush out the door, even though you look like you've just gotten out of bed.

The mirror showed you the problem, but you didn't do anything to fix it. If it tells you your hair is messy and you walk away without taking any action, when you return the information will be the same: "Your hair is messy!"

The Word of God is like a mirror that reveals to us the very thoughts and intentions of our hearts (Hebrews 4:12). It shows us our ugly, self-centred attitudes. It exposes our pride. It confronts our contempt for others. It even uncovers our deception, greed, and lust. But if we only take a quick glance at the Word once in a while and rush out the door, without doing anything to address the problem, it won't do us any good.

The main point of James' illustration about the man in the mirror is that he quickly forgets what he has seen in the mirror. The mirror isn't at fault. It tells it like it is. It shows us what we really look like. But the man who takes this quick look soon forgets what he has seen (1:24)

In the same way, a brief look at the Word of God may enter the person's ear, or even his eyes. But the power of the Word doesn't penetrate to the heart. The Word has to be acted upon.

One of Yogi Berra's quirky comments was, "You can see a lot just by looking." That's true when you spend time looking into God's Word. You can see a lot about yourself: *"But if you look carefully into the perfect law that sets you free, and if you do what it says and don't forget what you heard, then God will bless you for doing it"* (James 1:25).

Let's purpose in our hearts to not just hear the Word but to do what it says.

PRAYER:
Father God, I confess that I haven't always been obedient to your Word. I read it with great delight and expectation, but when it comes to the application of it, I fall far short. Please help me first of all to understand what I read and then to apply it to my life. Amen.

60. Faith That Works

In today's devotional, I continue to reflect on James' practical, down-to-earth approach to our faith in Jesus Christ.

In his epistle, James is writing to a group of people who did religion based on a works system. They believed that if they did some great works, it would be counted as righteousness, and they would achieve salvation from God. The independent nature of the human spirit struggles to admit that we can't make it into God's kingdom solely through our own efforts. So when God offers us the free gift of salvation through faith in Jesus Christ, our human nature says, "There must be a catch!" As humans, we love to boast that it was our efforts and good deeds that brought salvation to us. But as the prophet Isaiah observes, *"All of us have become like one who is unclean, and all our righteous acts are like filthy rags; we all shrivel up like a leaf, and like the wind our sins sweep us away"* (Isaiah 64:6).

We needed someone to stand in our place, and that's where the sacrifice of Jesus Christ on the cross comes in. By the grace of God, through faith in Jesus Christ, we were all given the free gift of salvation.

How do you usually respond when someone gives you a free gift, just out of the blue? We often struggle with receiving a free gift. Someone gives you a gift: What is the first thing that comes to mind? *I wonder why they gave it to me? What's in in for them? What strings are attached?* Right away, we start thinking of some ways to pay them back! "Let me take you out for coffee or dinner." We always feel that we need to do something to earn it!

That was the way many people in James' day felt—and may I say, even today. God has given us the free gift of salvation, but we feel we need to do other works to merit God's grace and complete the transaction. That way, we can boast about our own righteousness. But as we learn from scripture: *"For it is by grace you have been saved, through faith—and this is not from yourselves, it is the gift of God—not by works, so that no one can boast"* (Ephesians 2:8-9).

On the other side of the coin, there were those who were giving lip service only to their faith and not exhibiting any virtues or deeds that demonstrated a transformation in their lives. James starts off by asking this rhetorical question (one which the questioner doesn't expect a direct answer): *"What good is it, my brothers and sisters, if someone claims to have faith but has no deeds? Can such faith save them?"* (James 2:14). His audience would have either shrugged, because the answer was obvious, or they would have said certainly not!

James isn't saying that our works make us righteous before God but that real saving faith is demonstrated by good deeds. Faith in Christ always results in good works: *"Suppose a brother or a sister is without clothes and daily food. If one of you says to them, 'Go in peace; keep warm and well fed,' but does nothing about their physical needs, what good is it?"* (James 2:15-16). James says that kind of faith is useless faith and not saving faith.

We might conclude from James' epistle that neither the exhibition of works without faith or the profession of faith without any accompanying deeds amounts to anything. We need to exhibit a faith that works. When we do, our faith will bring pleasure to our Father in heaven, who delights in authentic faith. As Jesus said, *"Let you light so shine before others, so that they may see your good deeds* (works) *and glorify your father in heaven"* (Matthew 5:16).

Take a good look around you. Do you see some needs that could benefit from a deed of kindness? Put your faith into action. It will bring comfort and joy to someone and glorify your Father in heaven.

May the Lord bless you and help you to exhibit true faith by the loving deeds you demonstrate to others. Amen.

61. Sticks and Stones

Have you ever heard the saying, "Sticks and stones may break my bones but words could never hurt me"? The apostle James disagrees. Our words can totally wreck the life of someone else. In our culture today, and particularly in our schools, we hear of bullies who by their very words have brought death to someone else. Yes, words can kill.

Unfortunately, this kind of reckless use of our words isn't limited to our schools. Even in our day-to-day interactions with people, we may use words that destroy.

James calls the tongue a restless evil, full of deadly poison: *"All kinds of animals, birds, reptiles and sea creatures are being tamed and have been tamed by mankind, but no human being can tame the tongue. It is a restless evil, full of deadly poison"* (James 3:7–8). Since no human being can tame the tongue, what hope is there for us? James says it can be as venomous as a deadly snake.

In this devotional, I'm continuing to reflect on some of the practical illustrations from the book of James. Today, we consider "Taming the Tongue."

In this passage of scripture, James uses the "man on the moon" argument to get his point across. Have you heard this saying: How come they can put a man on the moon but they can't (you fill in the rest)? They can't make a good cup of coffee, or they can never get the trains to run on time. James says, "All kinds of animals, birds, reptiles and sea creatures are being tamed, but how come no one can tame the tongue?"

Not only can the tongue gossip and spread deadly rumours and damaging lies, but it can also put out enough deadly poison that can kill. You might be thinking that the tongue is only a tiny piece of flesh in the body that doesn't work independently of the rest. You are so right! So what is the problem? Where does this evil impulse come from?

The prophet Jeremiah says it so well! It comes from the *heart* of a person. When we read the word "heart" in the Bible, it's not referring to that muscle between the lungs that circulates blood throughout the body. The most common use of the word in scripture is to describe humanity's inclinations and personal will. It's what we use in making decisions. The human heart is the *rational will* coupled with *emotional desire*. It's the centre of who we are. Jeremiah says, *"The heart is deceitful above all things and beyond cure. Who can understand it?"* (Jeremiah 17:9).

James uses the examples of the bridle controlling the horse, and the rudder controlling a ship, to show how something so small can have such a large effect. In a similar way, the tongue can cause a lot of emotional and spiritual damage. We sometimes try to take back words spoken in anger. But words, like an arrow after it's been shot from the bow, can't be taken back. The damage and the injuries such cruel words inflict can last a lifetime.

So how do we make sure our words are kept in check in the first place? James says, *"My dear brothers and sisters, take note of this: Everyone should be quick to listen, slow to speak and slow to become angry, because human anger does not produce the righteousness that God desires"* (James 1:19–20).

People use will-power or some form of physical or psychological exercise to cure certain addictive behaviours. But James says that this kind of remedy or training doesn't work on the tongue. When it comes to the tongue, we see an overflow of what's in the heart. Jesus says, *"For out of the overflow of the heart the mouth speaks"* (Matthew 12:34).

The solution for taming of the tongue has to come from outside of ourselves. In order to tame our tongues, we require the Creator to give us a new heart and renew a right spirit within us. The psalmist prays in Psalm 141:3, "*Set a guard over my mouth, O Lord; keep watch over the door of my lips.*"

May that be your prayer as well today! The person who allows the Lord to supervise his/her heart, instead of speaking words that kill, will speak words of life, words of comfort, and words of peace and love.

So cling to the Lord and yield in obedience to Him. He will purify your heart and help you to watch your mouth.

62. Wisdom from Above

Where do you go to seek for wisdom when faced with a troubling problem that requires a wise decision? Do you go to a friend who you know will tell you just what you want to hear? Or do you seek out one who will instruct you wisely, even if it's not the answer you're hoping to hear? Have you ever thought about what makes a person wise?

Often we have strange ideas about what makes someone wise. Perhaps it's someone who wears glasses. Or someone with gray hairs. Maybe someone with a lot of degrees on his or her wall. Or someone who likes to read a lot of books. In this devotional, I reflect on the apostle James' description of wisdom and where it may be found: "*Who is wise and understanding among you? Let them show it by their good life, by deeds done in the humility that comes from wisdom*" (James 3:13).

In this passage, James focuses on wisdom, but not just any kind of wisdom. He focuses on wisdom from above. James has just been writing at length about how we use our words, and the destruction that can come from them when we don't keep a tight rein on our tongues. He now turns his attention to the deeper issue of wisdom. In this passage, James starts off with a provocative question: "*Who is wise and understanding among you?*"

How each of us answers this question will depend on whether our focus is limited to this life only or if it includes eternity. This is a test question that immediately challenges our personal pride, as we might be tempted to answer with "I am!"

But James answers his own question this way: "*Let them show it by their good deeds done in humility.*" In other words, "If you're wise, don't just say it. Do wise deeds." A truly wise person will demonstrate their wisdom with humility and by their good deeds. He compares the two basic sources of wisdom—wisdom from God and wisdom from the world around us.

In 1 Corinthians 3:19, the apostle Paul writes, "*For the wisdom of this world is foolishness in God's sight.*" James says:

> For where you have envy and selfish ambition, there you find disorder and every evil practice. But the wisdom that comes from heaven is first of all pure; then peace-loving, considerate, submissive, full of mercy and good fruit, impartial and sincere. (James 3:16–17)

Earthly wisdom is selfish and full of worldly ambition. But the characteristics of heavenly wisdom are given by God for the asking: "*If any of you lacks wisdom, you should ask God, who gives generously to all without finding fault, and it will be given to you*" (James 1:5).

How does Jesus describe a wise person?

> Therefore everyone who hears these words of mine and puts them into practice is like a wise man who built his house on the rock. The rain came down, the streams rose, and the winds blew and beat against that house; yet it did not fall, because it had its foundation on the rock. (Matthew 7:24–25)

Perhaps you've been seeking for wisdom but from all the wrong places, and you've discovered that such wisdom is the wisdom of this world, which is foolishness in God's sight. Seek the Lord and the wisdom that comes from above and you will discover that God gives it liberally to those who ask. May the Lord's blessings be yours today.

63. Sacred Submission

When you hear the word "submission," what do you think about? Do you think of a wrestler whose opponent has clearly defeated him, in which case he has no choice but to submit? Perhaps such an image keeps you from totally submitting yourself to the Lord. Submitting to the Lord is quite different. Today's devotional is about sacred submission.

In his epistle, James contrasts the gracious wisdom of God with the foolish "wisdom" of the world. Sometimes the foolish wisdom of this world presents a barrier to understanding the call of God on our lives. God invites us to come and have a more intimate relationship with Him, the gracious God of wisdom and love. But in order to do so, we need to submit our will to His. This kind of intimacy calls for submission, the kind of submission James talks about as a voluntary submission—a sacred submission: "*Submit yourselves, then, to God. Resist the devil, and he will flee from you. Draw near to God and he will draw near to you. Wash your hands, you sinners, and purify your hearts, you double-minded*" (James 4:7–8).

To submit oneself means to come into voluntary obedience to a person, to bend your will to theirs. In this case, to God. James tells us how to do it: "*Resist the devil, and he will flee from you*" (James 4:7b). The word "resist" means to set oneself against, to oppose, to withstand.

Our problem too often is that we're double-minded, James says. We cling to both our selfish desires *and* a desire to please God. But we must clearly take a stand against the things we know to be evil, and at the same time let go of those desires that give the devil power over us.

Resisting the devil means to stop flirting with his temptations, to say no to him and yes to God. "*He will flee from you*," James says, when you resist him.

As Martin Luther put it in his great hymn "A Mighty Fortress Is Our God," "*one little word can fell him.*" James says, "*Come near to God, and he will come near to you*" (4:8a).

What's the problem with double-mindedness? As long as we entertain thoughts of sin and serve them tea in the living rooms of our minds, we relegate God to the back porch. In order to resolve double-mindedness and submit ourselves to God, we need to resist the temptations of the devil, followed by drawing near to God.

You've probably learned from experience that this is easier said then done. In order to do so, we need to have our hearts and minds renewed.

> Therefore, I urge you, brothers and sisters, in view of God's mercy, to offer your bodies as a living sacrifice, holy and pleasing to God—this is your true and proper worship. Do not conform to the pattern of this world, but be transformed by the renewing of your mind. Then you will be able to test and approve what God's will is— his good, pleasing and perfect will. (Romans 12:1–2)

James commands us, on God's behalf to wash our hands. What does this mean? In the days of COVID-19, the command to wash your hands was everywhere. But James is talking about more than just a physical washing of the hands. The psalmist asks in Psalm 24:3–4: *"Who may ascend the mountain of the LORD? Who may stand in his holy place? The one who has clean hands and a pure heart."*

Sacred submission to God requires an ongoing humility in contrast to a life lived in rebellion against God. As you submit to Him today, you will find that it's much easier to let go of those things that have become a distraction to holding on to Him.

May the Lord bless you with a great sense of His presence as you submit your will to His. Amen

64. Beware of Boasting

How are you at making plans? Have you ever called something a "sure thing" because the outcome seemed so obvious? But then you soon discover that it was really a house of cards, as everything came crashing to the ground. The apostle James warns us about the folly of boasting about tomorrow.

> Now listen, you who say, "Today or tomorrow we will go to this or that city, spend a year there, carry on business and make money." Why, you do not even know what will happen tomorrow. What is your life? You are a mist that appears for a little while and then vanishes. (James 4:13–14)

There's a certain arrogance in boasting about tomorrow. When we do, we imagine that we have total control over the events of our own lives.

Do you remember at the start of year 2020, what great promises were made about the kind of year it was going to be? It was going to be a year of economic boom, a year of vision, and a year of prosperity. Needless to say, no one could have predicted the devastation COVID-19 would bring. Perhaps you'd made some sure-fire plans of your own that just couldn't fail. But they did! How do you recover from such a sense of failure and loss and regain your confidence in the need to plan for the future?

These businessmen in James' scenario were arrogantly assuming that they would wake up tomorrow, safely get to the city, and that their business ventures would be successful within a year. They were presuming all of these things about an unknown future, over which they had no control and no guarantees!

We must come to grips with the idea that we really don't know everything about the future. You might say, "I'm never going to plan again! I'm just going to let things take their own course." That wouldn't be the best approach. You see, if we fail to plan, we plan to fail.

It's not that we shouldn't plan for tomorrow; we should make our plans, but not to the exclusion of God's sovereignty. Because even with our best planning, everything is still subject to His will. Proverbs 16:9 says, *"In their hearts, humans plan their course, but the LORD establishes their steps."*

James asks, *"What is your life?" You are a mist* (a vapour) *that appears for a little while and then vanishes"* (James 4:14).

A vapour is short-lived. You see the steam coming out of your coffee cup, and in just a second it disappears into the air. James says life is like that. How does this knowledge prepare you for tomorrow? Not just the day after today, but for eternity? We must live each day as if it were our last.

James 4:15–16 goes on to say, "*Instead, you ought to say, 'If it is the Lord's will, we will live and do this or that.' As it is, you boast in your arrogant schemes. All such boasting is evil.*"

Not only does boasting leave the boaster with egg on the face, but we're told that all such boasting is evil. You may think that it's only those bad deeds we do to others that are considered evil or sinful. But James describes for us what makes something sinful or evil: "*If anyone, then, knows the good they ought to do and doesn't do it, it is sin for them*" (James 4:17). First and foremost, we must reorder our priorities by first seeking God and then get connected to Him—the giver of life, the One who holds the future.

Sometimes you hear the phrase, "this is a sure thing." It just can't fail. But I contend that there isn't any sure thing in this earthly life that you can count on. Jesus said:

> Do not lay up for yourselves treasures on earth, where moth and rust destroy, and where thieves break in and steal. But lay up for yourselves treasures in heaven, where neither moth nor rust destroys, and where thieves do not break in or steal. (Matthew 6:19–20).

Let's acknowledge God in everything we do, and plan with the understanding that at anytime God may overrule our plans. As His children, He cares deeply about the welfare of our lives and has our best interests at heart. May the Lord bless you. Amen.

Chapter 12:
Recalculating

> If we claim to be without sin, we deceive ourselves and the truth is not in us. If we confess our sins, he is faithful and just and will forgive us our sins and purify us from all unrighteousness.
>
> 1 John 1:8–9

65. Navigating the Unknown

Do you own a navigation device for your vehicle? Do you trust it? Sometimes it can be influenced by atmospheric conditions and give you erroneous directions. However, they can be quite reliable.

After you determine your destination and the route to get there, if conditions change, your device will try to get you back on a safe course. It will simply say, "Recalculating!" Then it will choose the next best route for you to follow.

Sometimes we try to override the instructions because we think we know a better route, only to find ourselves stuck on the wrong path. However, the navigating device is very patient. It doesn't call you some unflattering names. It just says, "Recalculating," and tries to get you back on course. It reminds me of the way God our Father deals with us, only His directions are sure.

September is usually the start of a new school year or fiscal year for many businesses. It's always a time to set objectives as to what you want to accomplish, and laying out a plan to achieve those goals. But very early into the journey, you may discover that those objectives are unrealistic and your goals unattainable.

If the last two or three years have taught us anything, it's that conditions along the journey can change quite rapidly. So is there a navigator that we can take on board that won't just recalibrate our settings but also provide wise counsel along the way?

Proverbs 3:5–6 say to us: "*Trust in the* L*ord* *with all your heart and lean not on your own understanding; in all your ways submit to Him, and He will make your paths straight.*" In today's devotional, my focus is on "Navigating the Unknown."

When Joshua was heading out to lead the children of Israel across the Jordan to possess the Promised Land, he was quite fearful, because there had been many missteps along the way. So he encouraged the people this way:

> When you see the ark of the covenant of the L*ord* your God, and the Levitical priests carrying it, you are to move out from your positions and follow it. Then you will know which way to go, since you have never been this way before. (Joshua 3:3–4)

The Ark of the Covenant of the Lord signified the presence of the Lord among the people. Following the ark was a guarantee that they would reach their destination. To say "We have never been this way before" would be a gross understatement. Each new year brings new discoveries and new challenges. But with God as our navigator, we will make it through.

Isaiah 30:21 reads: "*Whether you turn to the right or to the left, your ears will hear a voice behind you, saying, 'This is the way; walk in it.'*" So heed the voice of the Lord and follow His directions. He will lead you safely to your destination.

Perhaps you set a course in your life to rely on God more than you have been; you were going to read His Word more, pray more, and seek His direction for your life. But somewhere along the journey you discovered that you've fallen far short. It's never too late to make amends. God is the God of the second chance and more, meaning He will forgive your mistakes and shortcomings and re-order your life when you acknowledge that you have taken a wrong turn. Like your onboard navigator, He'll set a new course for you and direct your path on the journey. May the Lord bless you.

66. Unexpected Turns

On November 2, 2021, my friend Ron, a member of my discipleship group, landed in Hong Kong. His plans were to stay there for the holidays. He had planned to follow our group online and return to Toronto after the Christmas Holidays.

However, as he landed in Hong Kong, he received a text from his son-in-law that his daughter had suffered a brain aneurysm and had to be rushed to the hospital in serious condition. As any father would do, Ron took the next available flight back to Toronto to be with his family.

As human beings, we will never stop making plans, but a lesson for all of us is that we have to hold our plans loosely. On the journey of life, there are many perils and pitfalls, unexpected turns along the way that will throw us for a loop.

In this series of devotionals, I am endeavoring to show God as the one who helps us re-order our lives and gets us back on a safe and secure path. Today's devotional, "Unexpected Turns," focuses on letting go of our own plans and allowing God to navigate our lives, recognizing that He knows what's best for us and has ultimate control.

When asked about their predictions for 2023, people's number one answer was "change." The years 2020 to 2022 taught us that the only thing we can be certain of is change. If you have a smart navigation device on board your vehicle, and you trust it, it can get you through some unexpected turns. With all the distractions and confusions that we face daily, it's easy to lose our way or take a wrong turn somewhere along the journey.

When the children of Israel were on their way to the Promised Land, they wandered in the wilderness for a long time. Moses describes how God reoriented them: *"And the Lord spoke to me, saying, 'You have circled this mountain long enough. Now turn to the north'"* (Deuteronomy 2:2–3).

During those times on the journey when we can do no more than spin our wheels, God steps in and provides clear directions. Whether it's wrong decisions with career choices, relationships with friends and family, or even in our relationship with God, we may lose our way at times. But the wonder of God's grace is that He will guide us back to the right path. He does this through the Holy Spirit, who redirects our feet. He gives us knowledge and wisdom to discern the right path to follow. What great comfort to all of us that God has ultimate control!

We often come up against unexpected turns along the way that make us adjust our route or our plans. As this proverb puts it, *"The heart of man plans his way, but the Lord establishes his steps"* (Proverbs 16:9). Perhaps some of your plans had to be adjusted because of an unexpected event or situation that has caused you grief and heartache. You were sure you were on the right path, and everything seemed great for a while. But out of the blue, without any warning, conditions changed. Take heart and be of good courage, because the Lord knows what you're going through, and He promises to be with you.

Ron, in his unexpected situation, seemed to have taken everything in stride and has attributed his calmness to his belief that the Lord has the ultimate control. And thanks to the Lord and the medical professionals, his daughter is on the road to recovery.

As you seek to reorient your life, be sure to invite the Lord to be your navigator for the journey. He will lead, direct, and comfort you along the way.

67. Unrealistic Expectations

At the start of any new venture or adventure, we usually have high hopes and sometimes may set our goals further than our grasp. Whether it's the start of a new year or the end of the summer and you're making plans for September, make sure your goals and resolutions are within your grasp.

How many of you would admit to making New Year's resolutions? How many of them have actually come through? If the statistics are correct, by the end of January, many resolutions have already been broken. Today, I'm looking at the topic "Unrealistic Expectations."

According to Franklin Covey, it's much easier to keep just one resolution rather than several. One of the most common reasons we break our New Year's resolutions is that we get a little overzealous when we make them and we over-commit. As a result, 40 per cent of us blame our busy schedules for our lack of follow-through.

January 19 has been dubbed "Quitters Day," the day most people are likely to give up their New Year's resolutions. The key to successful goal-setting is not to be too hasty when you do it. Make resolutions and decisions you've thought through and are willing to dedicate your time and energy to accomplish.

In Luke 14:28, Jesus says *"Suppose one of you wants to build a tower. Won't you first sit down and estimate the cost to see if you have enough money to complete it?"* This same principle should apply when we make resolutions or set our goals. They should be realistic and achievable. Failure to achieve our goals can result in shame and discouragement. But failure is not a sign that we should give up.

Like the GPS that says "Recalculating" when you miss that turn, you must do a reassessment of your goals to see if they're in line with what God wants for you. Then ask Him to re-direct you and walk with you.

In John 15:5–6, Jesus gives us a sure-fire way to achieve our goals and be fruitful:

> I am the vine; you are the branches. If you remain in me and I in you, you will bear much fruit; apart from me you can do nothing. If you do not remain in me, you are like a branch that is thrown away and withers; such branches are picked up, thrown into the fire and burned. (John 15:5–6)

If we make our plans and set our goals in the absence of God's guidance, we will discover that, like the branch that's not connected to the vine, we will soon wither and our plans will die.

"*Plans fail for lack of good counsel, but with many advisers they succeed*" (Proverbs 15:22). Having our plans fail is disheartening enough, but when we fail personally, that can be quite devastating. But failing in an area of our life isn't the end of the world. Failure can only have mastery over your life if you give in and give up.

The God we serve isn't just the God of the second chance. He infinitely forgives and constantly invites us back into relationship with Himself. He says in Jeremiah 29:11, "*For I know the plans I have for you ... plans to prosper you and not to harm you, plans to give you hope and a future.*" God made this promise to His children as they we being taken away into exile. They had disobeyed His commands and had to suffer the consequences, but that wasn't going to be the end for them. He had already looked ahead on the journey and determined when their course would be readjusted.

He promised to hear their prayer and re-direct their path:

> "Then you will call on me and come and pray to me, and I will listen to you. You will seek me and find me when you seek me with all your heart. I will be found by you," declares the LORD, "and will bring you back from captivity." (Jeremiah 29:12–13)

It's never too late to seek the face of the Lord. He will forgive and abundantly pardon when you seek Him with all you heart.

May the Lord be with you and guide your steps along the journey.

68. Missing the Markers

Whenever I'm on a journey, especially travelling in unfamiliar territory, I always keep a close watch on the signs and markers along the way, because missing a sign could determine whether you arrive at your destination or not. In this devotional series, I focus on how to get back on track after we take a wrong turn, miss our goals, or move away from God's desire for our lives. We will discover that it's not the end of the world if we do, because we serve a God of the second chance and beyond.

I have titled this devotional, "Missing the Markers." It's about how our navigator—our loving God—makes corrections to our course along the way when we invite Him on the journey. On the journey of life, we usually start off well, but missing a sign or two along the way can lead to trouble. This is true for both our spiritual as well as our physical journey.

A few years ago, my daughter and I, after seeing a play in Stratford, Ontario for her birthday, decided that we would travel to London for the evening. But somewhere along the way, I missed the interchange that would take us to our destination. Since I didn't have a GPS, we ended up travelling around in circles for about an hour. It's no fun travelling along an unfamiliar highway, with streets with strange sounding names, when you really don't know where you are and if you're ever going to get back on track.

Eventually, my daughter, who is very wise. said, "I think we're lost. Why don't we stop at the next service station and ask for directions?" What she didn't realize was that men don't admit to being lost or stop and ask for directions. So after driving around for some time, I eventually stopped and went into a service station. But instead of asking for directions, I bought a map.

Now, a map is not a GPS, but it's a great navigational device. It shows you where you are, where you want to go, and the route to get there. It's kind of like the Bible. The Psalmist says in Psalm 119:105, *"Your Word is a Lamp onto my feet and a Light unto my path,"* and in Psalm 32:8, *"I will instruct you and teach you in the way you should go; I will counsel you with my loving eye on you."*

On the journey of life, we need to ask God for direction and guidance. But we also need to follow those directions. When we ignore them, we usually end up going around in circles. At other times, without intent, we may get side-tracked along the way and totally miss the sign.

Most of the time though, it seems like when we outright ignore God's directions, we find ourselves in the wilderness, as the children of Israel did on their way to the Promised Land. What was meant to be a five-week trek from Egypt to the Land of Canaan turned out to be a forty-year journey.

They eventually got to their destination when Moses' successor, Joshua, instructed the Israelites on how they were to move out:

> When you see the Ark of the Covenant of the LORD your God, and the Levitical priests carrying it, you are to move out from your positions and follow it. Then you will know which way to go, since you have never been this way before. (Joshua 3:2–4)

The Ark of the Covenant of the Lord signified the presence of the Lord among His people. When the presence of the Lord is with us, it is infinitely better than any GPS, because He is the unique and eternal One. He is the Ancient of Days who has been where we have never been, so He not only knows the way but is the WAY.

If you're like me, you might have taken a few wrong turns on your journey—not just to a designated city on this earth, but also on your spiritual journey to that Eternal City. Don't give up! Stop and ask the Lord for direction and invite Him on the journey. Like the GPS, He's very patient. He doesn't shame you for taking the wrong turn. Instead, He's in the business of re-calculating to get you to your desired destination. May your journey be filled with peace and joy.

69. Trusting the Navigator

How are you at trusting God? How are you at trusting when you're in the midst of a storm. Are you able to be at peace, knowing that you've invited the navigator on board? In this devotional series, I focus on those times when we get caught up in a storm. I call it "Trusting the Navigator."

It's easy to trust your on-board GPS on a clear day when the weather is fine! But are you able to trust it in a storm? What if all of a sudden a storm picks up that is beyond your ability to go through?

Psalm 107 gives us an account of merchants—experienced seamen—on the high seas who encountered a ferocious storm that threatened to overwhelmed their ship: "*They mounted up to the heavens and went down to the depths; in their peril their courage melted away. They reeled and staggered like drunkards; they were at their wits' end*" (Psalm 107:26–27).

Perhaps you've had a similar experience with storms in the recent past. Maybe it wasn't on the high seas, but a storm nevertheless. Perhaps it threw you for a loop, but God was with you and His faithfulness brought you through, so you can tell your story. Corrie Ten Boom said, "*When you are on a train and it goes through a tunnel and it gets dark, you don't throw away the ticket and jump off. You sit still and trust the engineer.*" [15]

What does the Bible say about trusting God? "*So do not fear, for I am with you; do not be dismayed, for I am your God. I will strengthen you and help you; I will uphold you with My righteous right hand*" (Isaiah 41:10). One of the most prominent themes throughout the scriptures is "trusting God," especially in times when it's difficult to do so. While we'll experience unexpected hardships in our lives, it's crucial for our spiritual health that we continue trusting God, as the Bible encourages.

During the past year, you might have experienced hardships that weren't your fault. As surely as spring follows winter, storms will come into our lives in the form of a calamity or hardship. You were just going about your business, when out of the blue a "storm" picked up. Sometimes they come in the form of an illness, a broken relationship, the loss of employment, or even the death of a loved one. The list goes on and on, none of which is attributable to something you've done. The merchants on the high seas in Psalm 107 weren't responsible for the onset of the storm. They just got caught up in it.

> Then they cried out to the LORD in their trouble, and he brought them out of their distress. He stilled the storm to a whisper; the waves of the sea were hushed. They were glad when it grew calm, and he guided them to their desired haven. (Psalm 107:28–30)

Yes, when we cry out to the Lord in our trouble, He hears and answers us. But even when the answer seems to be long in coming and the intensity of the storm remains unabated, we can trust the navigator on board.

In my more youthful days, I led the Christian Service Brigade boys group at our church. One time we went for a weekend camping trip at Terra Cotta Conservation Area. Weather wise it was a horrible weekend—pounding rain, lightening, thunder. Our tents soaked through, and we weren't able to do any of our campfire activities or play outdoor sports.

But spiritually we had a great time, as we were able to use one of the pavilions in the park for our spiritual activities. At around 1:00 PM on Sunday, we packed up and headed out. I drove three of the boys to the church so they could meet up with their parents.

On our way, driving through those huge hills and valleys and the winding road from Terra Cotta, the storm started again. It was the kind of rain in which wise people would pull off the road. There was a deafening silence in the back seat, and I could imagine how fearful the boys must be.

In order to break the tension, I said, "Some weekend, eh?" There was no answer. As I quickly glanced behind me, I saw, to my great surprise, that the three boys were all fast asleep. They were totally oblivious to the terrible summer storm that was raging. That Sunday afternoon, God drove home to me a wonderful lesson—the real meaning of trusting the navigator, even in the midst of a storm. May the Lord be with you on your journey. Amen.

15. Corie Ten Boom, *Favorite Quotes from Corie ten Boom*. (https://www.liveatthewell.org/quotes-from-corrie-ten-boom.html)

70. Seasons of Restraints

In Ecclesiastes 3:6–7, we read, "*There is a time to search and a time to give up, A time to keep and a time to throw away, A time to tear down and a time to mend.*" Even in searching, we have to exercise restraints. We have to know when to keep going and when to leave it all in God's hands. Sometimes we search for a reason or look for an explanation, or for the cause of something deep in our life. We may search for an explanation as to why a certain prayer remains unanswered. But as the Word says, there is a time to let go.

We've all had seasons of some deep soul searching, but sometimes God asks us to be content with where we are and the answers we don't yet have. We have to learn to recognize God's voice in all of these seasons of life.

We've all just emerged from a season in which we were asked to refrain from embracing, due to the pandemic. For many, this was a difficult thing to do. We asked when it would be a time to embrace again.

In Ecclesiastes 3:5, Solomon says, *"There is: a time to scatter stones and a time to gather them, a time to embrace and a time to refrain from embracing."* In these verses, Solomon is establishing a principle not just about the physical act of embracing, but also about how we are to exercise restraints in certain areas and activities of our lives. For example, in relationships, we need to know when it's time to end a friendship and when it's time to mend it. There comes a time in our lives when we should curtail certain friendships and make new ones.

All of this is God's wonderful plan for your life. The problem, of course, is that it's not always *our* plan or desire. If we were given the right to plan our lives, we would plan for no unpleasantness at all. But that would ruin us. You see, we gain strength as we emerge victorious from life's struggles.

In lifestyles and habits, there comes a time when we have to choose which ones to keep embracing and which ones to give up. You see, it's a principle that goes well beyond the physical and to the emotional and spiritual.

The apostle John, writing to the new followers of Jesus, wrote, *"Do not love the world or the things in the world. If anyone loves the world, the love of the Father is not in him"* (1 John 2:15–16). John goes on to describe what he means by the world: *"For all that is in the world—the lust of the flesh, the lust of the eyes, and the pride of life—is not of the Father but is of the world"* (1 John 2:15–16). These are some of the things that we need to refrain from embracing if we're to embrace the love and grace of God.

In Ecclesiastes 3, Solomon uses the practical aspects of life along with the spiritual to frame our understanding. He talks about gardens and buildings, birth and death, sadness and joy, mourning and dancing, holding on and letting go. These antitheses show us that God is in control of the various seasons of our lives. He wants us to understand that behind it all, there is purpose and order. In seasons of restraints, we're encouraged to see life God's way—not looking through rose-colored glasses, but understanding God's purpose. And so with sober reflection, we must proceed to make amends in those areas and activities in our lives that need to be changed.

Q. Is there something that you're embracing that you need to let go of? You're only able to embrace what God has for you after you release that which is already in your hands. May the Lord help you to embrace His way.

71. Let Justice Prevail

Just as we're not surprised when the seasons change each year, we shouldn't be surprised when seasons change in our lives as well. When we know we're entering the winter, we put away the things of summer and fall and grab our sweaters and heavy coats. Knowing the season we're currently in, or going into, helps us to prepare physically as well as emotionally. Sometimes the season we're in isn't one of the four calendar seasons. For example, we've been through a pandemic season. But as you know, all seasons come to an end, so hold on.

If ever there was a season to see justice done, it's today. We are living in a time when people are being ostracized and marginalized simply because of poverty, ethnicity, the colour of their skin, or cultural heritage. But the writer of the book of Ecclesiastes reminds us that *"There is nothing new under the sun"* (1:9). He says that this kind of systemic injustice has been going on for a long time. In Ecclesiastes 5:8, he writes: *"If you see oppression of the poor and perversion of justice and righteousness in the province, don't be astonished at the situation, because one official protects another official, and a higher official protect them."*

"*There is: a time to be silent and a time to speak, a time to love and a time to hate, a time for war and a time for peace*" (Ecclesiastes 1:7-8). In our society today, we see everywhere that it's not a time to be silent but a time to speak. In these contrasting seasons, one must be as Jesus said in Matthew 10:16: *"Look, I'm sending you out like sheep among wolves. Therefore, be as shrewd as serpents and as innocent as doves."*

There is a time to be silent and a time to speak. The tongue has the power of life and death, as the apostle James tells us. Fear of reprisal and personal recrimination may at times cause us to keep silent when we need to boldly speak truth in love. But as followers of Jesus, we must see justice given to the weak, the fatherless, the oppressed, and the marginalized. When we take a cowardly, silent back seat to injustice, we do more harm than good in. In Proverbs 31:8-9, we're told how we should go about making our voices heard: "*Speak up for those who cannot speak for themselves, for the rights of all who are destitute. Speak up and judge fairly; defend the rights of the poor and needy.*"

In Ecclesiastes 3:8, Solomon says: "*There is a time to love and a time to hate, a time for war and a time for peace.*" You might be thinking, *A time to hate? Aren't we to love everyone as we love ourselves?* Yes, but God also commands us to hate what is evil and to love what is good. But this kind of biblical hate is not what causes wars. Wars are caused by greed and man's inhumanity to man. But in the end, we see the Prince of Peace coming and restoring peace and justice.

We must not forget that God is the same in every season: "*He is the same yesterday, today, and forever*" (Hebrews 13:8). This means He is the same in your times of greatest triumph as well as in your time of greatest tragedy. His love, presence, and character are not seasonal—they are forever. And like the air we breathe, He is everywhere you go.

> He will judge between the nations and will settle disputes for many peoples. They will beat their swords into

plowshares and their spears into pruning hooks. Nation will not take up sword against nation, nor will they train for war anymore. (Isaiah 2:4)

There will be a season for peace! Hate and injustices will be over. Ask the Lord how you may fit into His plans to bring justice and peace to a troubled world.

PRAYER:
Father, as I take a look around me and at the world at large, I see so much hate, discrimination, and injustice that cry out for attention. I'm sorry for those times when I turned a blind eye or kept silent when I should have spoken up for those who couldn't speak for themselves. Please help me to speak up and judge fairly, and so defend the rights of the poor and needy. In Jesus' name. Amen.

Chapter 13:
New Beginnings

*Do not conform to the pattern of this world,
but be transformed by the renewing of your mind.
Then you will be able to test and approve what God's will is—
his good, pleasing and perfect will.*

Romans 12:2

72. Obedience

Have you ever had a longing? I mean a longing for something that could be a game changer in your life! What if after you have received it, you were asked by God to give it up, to submit it to Him, with no questions asked?

In this devotional today, I focus on Abraham and Isaac, the promised son. God made a promise to Abraham and Sarah that He would give them a son. Humanly speaking, this seemed impossible, since Sarah was barren and past her child-bearing years. It took twenty-five years for the promise to be fulfilled by God, so suffice it to say, Isaac was cherished and dearly loved by Abraham. But there came a time when God required both of them to submit in obedience to Him. For Abraham, it was to make the ultimate sacrifice, and for Isaac, it was submitting himself as the offering.

It's one thing to obey when the command is logical. It's another thing when something doesn't make sense. What might God be up to? Why would He make this seemingly unreasonable demand for obedience? Embracing a new beginning always requires obedience and submission—submission of self, submission of the will, and submission of plans to God.

In Proverbs 3:5-6, we read: *"Trust in the LORD with all your heart and lean not on your own understanding; in all your ways, submit to Him, and he will make your paths straight."* "Submit" is a military word that means to come under authority. Biblically, it means to arrange oneself under the command of God's sovereignty rather than live according to one's old way of life, based on human wisdom. It's a process in which we surrender in worship our own will to that of our Father, receiving in return that which we would never be able to achieve leaning on our own understanding. Obedience is the highest form of worship and the greatest evidence of love for God.

Abraham and Isaac, in submitting to God, received more than they could have imagined. Abraham not only received his son, as if back from the dead, but he also received the promise that on that mountain of sacrifice, God would provide the Lamb of God, the Saviour of the world. Isaac received new life, as one back from the dead, as we see in the book of Hebrews:

> Even though God had said to Abraham, "It is through Isaac that your offspring will be reckoned." Abraham reasoned that God could even raise the dead, and so in a manner of speaking he did receive Isaac back from death. (Hebrews 11:18-19)

New beginnings usually require us to unfold our arms or open our hands so that the things we're holding on to desperately can fall away, making room for what God is bringing into our lives. What would have happened had Abraham held jealousy to his son instead of letting go? Things would have been much different for all of us today. But he willingly submitted in obedience to God, believing that God who has promised is faithful.

"By faith Abraham, when God tested him, offered Isaac as a sacrifice. He who had embraced the promises was about to sacrifice his one

and only son" (Hebrews 11:17). The "attempted" sacrifice of Isaac on Mount Moriah that day was a fore-shadowing of the Lamb of God, who two thousand years later would climb the hill of Calvary with a rugged cross on His shoulders to offer His life as a sacrifice for your sins and mine.

God doesn't require us to obey and submit because He's a tyrant but because He's a loving Father who knows what's best for us. The blessings and peace we gain from humbly submitting ourselves to Him daily are a gift of grace to which nothing in this world can compare.

What might you be holding on to that's robbing you of the opportunity to receive something of greater worth from God? Let's be real—obedience and submission to a command that seems unreasonable can be hard. And honestly, it can be quite challenging to do this willingly. So how do we do that?

It means submitting our *heart, soul,* and *mind.* These are the human capacities with which we are to love the Lord. In submitting these, we submit our sinful tendencies, our selfish motives, our ungodly desires, and our anxieties about tomorrow. May the Lord bless you as you endeavour to live in obedience to Him.

73. Change of Identity

What's in a name? "That which we call a rose, by any other name, would smell just as sweet," says William Shakespeare. But that might not be true. You see, social scientists believe that names produce an effect that influences personality as well as how we're perceived. So if you hate the name given to you at birth, or later attributed to you, God has a new name for you. In today's devotional, I'm talking about "A Change of Identity."

When twin sons were born to Isaac and Rebecca, they named the first one Esau and the second Jacob (Genesis 25). The name Jacob means a scoundrel or a schemer, one who circumvents the established protocols in order to gain the upper hand. Jacob entered the world grabbing on to the heel of his twin brother, so he was named Jacob, or "Heel-grabber" (Gen. 25:26).

He lived a life of scheming, acquiring his brother's birthright through deception, which resulted in him travelling thousands of miles to get away from Esau, who wanted to kill him. His scheming continued when he used trickery to acquired the greater part of his uncle's livestock. So he set out for home, pursued by his uncle. On the way back home, he received news that his brother was on the way with four hundred men to confront him.

Not a pretty picture. You could say he was between a rock and a hard place. For the first time, Jacob sought the Lord in prayer: *"Jacob prayed to the* LORD, *humbly acknowledging his unworthiness, and for the Lord to Save him, from the hand of his brother Esau, who was on the way to kill him"* (Genesis 32:9–11).

Later that night, the Angel of the Lord wrestled with him until daybreak. Jacob was desperate and wouldn't let go unless he received a blessing from the Lord. Have you ever felt that kind of desperation, holding on to God in prayer until you got an answer?

"*The angel of the Lord asked him, 'What is your name?'*" (Genesis 32:27). Surely God knew his name. But I believe that God wanted to hear it from Jacob himself, as a kind of confession of the person he was—a schemer. So he answered and told God that his name was Jacob. "*Then God said, 'Your name will no longer be Jacob, but Israel—no longer a scoundrel, but a Prince. Because you have struggled with God and with humans and have overcome*'" (Genesis 32:28).

As you look back at your life and look toward a new beginning, perhaps you're looking for a change of identity as well. Perhaps who you are has become undesirable to you and those who know you! Perhaps you've left a trail of brokenness in your path, and life has become unbearable. Well, God wants to give you a new name—a change of identity—one that will transform your whole life.

In 2 Corinthians 5:17, Paul says, "*This means that anyone who belongs to Christ has become a new person. The old life is gone; a new life has begun!*" (2 Corinthians 5:17). I trust this has been the case for you! If not, will you ask the Lord to do a transforming work in your you—not just a name change, but a change of heart?

PRAYER:
Father God, I must confess that my life is not all that it might have been. I am ashamed of the way I've acted in my relationships with others. My quest to satisfy this worldly desire has left me desperate and broken. Please help me to turn around and find a new identity in you. In Jesus' name. Amen.

74. Patient Endurance

Are you a dreamer? No, I don't mean a daydreamer—one who has a series of pleasant thoughts that distract their attention from the present. I'm talking about stories that our minds create while we sleep, or which God creates in our minds. They can be vivid and seem perfectly rational, or they may be confusing.

In scripture, God uses dreams to predict the outcome of certain situations or events in people's lives. Such dreams were the kind that Joseph, the beloved son of Jacob, had as a youngster. These dreams predicted that Joseph would one day become a ruler, and that his entire family would pay homage to him.

But on the way to becoming a ruler, the path took him through hatred from his envious brothers, to a pit in the ground, to being sold as a slave and ending up in Egypt. In Egypt, he resisted temptation but was later put in prison before his dreams were fulfilled.

In today's devotional, I'm looking at the topic, "Patient Endurance." We can all benefit from one thing that Joseph learned: it's not always wise to share your dreams with others too soon. By sharing his dreams with his envious brothers, Joseph was seen as a boastful and prideful person who had to be silenced:

> When Joseph told his father as well as his brothers about his dreams, his father rebuked him and said, "What is this dream you had? Will your mother and I and your brothers actually come and bow down to the ground before you?" (Genesis 37:10)

Within a very short time, Joseph plummeted from being a favoured son to being a slave in Egypt. What a descent! How does one recover from such a precipitous place to move on to what God has in store for them? Psalm 40 describes the posture we need to take:

> I waited patiently for the LORD; he turned to me and heard my cry. He lifted me out of the slimy pit, out of the mud and mire; he set my feet on a rock and gave me a firm place to stand. He put a new song in my mouth, a hymn of praise to our God. Many will see and fear the LORD and put their trust in him. (Psalm 40:1–3)

It's not always easy to wait patiently. As impatient humans who would like to have things done yesterday and our prayers answered immediately, the words "patient endurance" aren't usually in our vocabulary. But the psalmist encourages us to wait patiently and keep trusting that God will hear our faintest cry and come to our rescue in due time.

When there's a God-ordained purpose in your life, try as hard as they may, no one will be able to hold back the hand of the Lord: "*There is no wisdom, no insight, no plan that can succeed against the* LORD" (Proverbs 21:30). Joseph's brothers had plotted to murder him, but his life was spared when some traders came by and his brothers decided to get rid of him instead by selling him off as a slave.

Perhaps God has birthed a dream in your heart but you're encountering obstacle after obstacle in your path to realizing your dream. Take heart! Endure patiently what you're going through, because God will one day bring it to pass.

Joseph didn't give up. He kept his dreams in front of his face, being confident of this: that God was going to bring to pass that which He'd promised. After years of imprisonment, God gave him a new beginning! What an amazing day that must have been for Joseph! Within hours, he was transfigured from living in a dungeon, forgotten, and seemingly without a future, to becoming a ruler in Egypt, second only to the king.

This picture points us again to Christ, who after suffering the depths of shame on a cross for our sake, died and was buried, and then was resurrected to life and ascended to the heights of heaven, making possible, our access to the Father. In similar fashion, we are to patiently endure until we receive that which God has promised.

God might have birthed a dream in your heart but you're still waiting to see its fulfilment. Don't give up! God is at work, perhaps in the background, but in His sovereign power He is orchestrating the process to bring it to pass in due time.

75. Change of Habit

What does your past whisper to you? Does it whisper guilt, shame, regret, condemnation, or even disqualification? Maybe these whispers haunt you from choices you made years ago. Or maybe those choices were yesterday.

In today's devotional, I'm looking at a character from the scriptures named Rahab. She was a *lady of the evening* running a house of ill-repute behind the walls of Jericho. But God found her there and changed her from *Madam to Matriarch*.

After wandering in the wilderness for forty years, Moses is now dead, and Joshua is charged with the responsibility of leading the children of Israel into the Promised Land. Jericho was the first city they faced. In Joshua 2, Joshua secretly sends out two spies to look over the city. So they went and entered the house of Rahab. It was a popular place, so they must have thought no one would have suspected that they were spies.

The King of Jericho, however, heard the news and sent a message to Rahab, *"To bring out the men who entered her house, because they had come to spy out the whole land."* But Rahab hid the spies and told the messenger that they had left and she didn't know which way they went. That night, as the two spies were safely hidden on her roof, Rahab made a bold claim and request. She said to the men: *"I know that the LORD has given you this land and that a great fear of you has fallen on us, so that all who live in this country are melting in fear because of you"* (Joshua 2:9).

The great exploits of the Hebrew people crossing over to Jericho had preceded the spies, and everyone was fearful of them. So Rahab made this bold statement of confession to the spies: *"When we heard of it, our hearts melted in fear and everyone's courage failed because of you, for the* LORD *your God is God in heaven above and on the earth below"* (Joshua 2:11).

Rahab had one hope, and she had pinned it on the One who is our only hope—God Himself. She confessed and surrendered herself to God's mercy. She asked for and received the word of the spies that they would save her when the city is destroyed. They gave her a sure sign that they'd be spared when the city falls. She was to tie a scarlet cord in one of her windows and bring her entire family into her house, otherwise they would perish.

The house of ill-repute would now become a house of refuge. Rahab made her decision, taking a bold step of faith. The scarlet cord dangling from her window as the walls of the city were being demolished by God was a sign that she was cutting with the past and moving on with the people of God.

It was also an emblem of the Passover, when God spared those who were under the blood covering their doorposts. The colour scarlet, which historically symbolizes sin and salvation, served as the sign that her entire home was to be saved.

In Acts 16:31, we read, *"They replied, 'Believe in the Lord Jesus, and you will be saved—you and your household.'"* Someone has said that there's a scarlet cord running all the way from cover to cover through the Bible, from the shedding of the blood of animals whose skins were used to cover the nakedness of Adam and Eve, to the blood shed on the cross by Jesus to cover us with His robe of righteousness.

Yes, through the grace and mercy of God, this woman who was a prostitute and an outsider served as a witness to truth and a role model of faith. God used her story to remind Israel that they were not chosen because they were a great and mighty nation; they were chosen to be God's people so that they could display God's compassion and mercy to the world.

In similar fashion, God chose Rahab, as well as us, to be His children.

As the city fell, the young spies went in and brought Rahab and her entire family out. They gave them a place outside the camp of

Israel. But God didn't leave Rahab outside the camp. He brought her to the centre of Jesus' family tree, as we see in Jesus' genealogy (Matthew 1:1-17). Salmon was the father of Boaz, whose mother was Rahab. In Hebrews 11, we also see a long list of people called heroes of Faith. We find Rahab among them: *"By faith the prostitute Rahab, because she welcomed the spies, was not killed with those who were disobedient"* (Hebrews 11:31).

Rahab's story is a picture of God's grace extended to sinful humans. He saves her, like he saves us—sinners considered, unclean. So regardless of who you are today, or what you've done, no one is outside the gracious arms of Jesus when they acknowledge Him as Lord of their life.

76. Shepherd Boy to King

Have you ever been surprised by grace, having something of great worth conferred upon you, who is so totally undeserving? Today I'm looking at David, the "Shepherd Boy to King." God took David from looking after his father Jesse's sheep and gave him a new beginning as King of Israel.

One day God instructed the prophet Samuel to go to Jesse's house and anoint one of his sons to become the next King of Israel. When Samuel arrived at Jesse's house and saw Jesse's eldest son, Eliab—tall and handsome, head and shoulders above his brothers—he thought, *Surely this is the one.*

> But the LORD said to Samuel, "Do not consider his appearance or his height, for I have rejected him. The LORD does not look at the things people look at. People look at the outward appearance, but the LORD looks at the heart." (1 Samuel 16:7)

David at the time was so insignificant in the eyes of his own family that he wasn't even invited to the party. He was out tending the sheep. Jesse passed six more of his sons before Samuel for his approval, but God rejected them all. "*So Samuel asked Jesse, 'Are these all the sons you have?' 'There is still the youngest,' Jesse answered. 'He is tending the sheep.' Samuel said, 'Send for him; we will not sit down until he arrives'"* (1 Samuel 16:11).

Do you feel insignificant today? Do you feel like you're unqualified, or that your past has disqualified you for the task God is calling you to do? I want you to know that God has great plans for your life. So avail yourself of what you believe God is calling you to become.

In Ephesians 10:2 Paul writes, "*For we are God's handiwork, created in Christ Jesus to do good works, which God prepared in advance for us to do.*"

Even though David was anointed to be king, it took him many years of struggle as God worked in his life to prepare him for what was ahead. Through the great trials and hardships, God made him into someone who was ready and prepared to rule over Israel.

When we experience those trials and testing in our own lives, we can be assured that our faith is being strengthened as God prepares us for what's ahead. As we see David rise, fall, and rise again, we learn from this shepherd/warrior-king, that there is no sin that can't be forgiven. Even when he had a great fall and his sin was pointed out to him, he was quick to repent and found forgiveness from a loving and compassionate God. Through the battles in David's life, we also learn that our God is a God of victory.

David's story reminds us that we can't afford to tolerate a Goliath in our own lives. If we do, he'll take over our territory, move into our camp, and steal our joy and rob us of our peace. We must deal with the Goliaths in our lives in whatever form they may take—sin, addiction, doubt, fear, or discouragement. David's praise to the Lord is written in words no modern poet could ever duplicate. He teaches us through the psalms that our hearts were made for the worship of God.

David on his throne foreshadowed Jesus Christ, as Jesus was born into the line of David, and promises that one day He will reign from the throne of David over not just Israel, but all the earth. When we reflect on David, we learn a lot about our God: He can take the most insignificant vessel and use it to bring honour and glory to His name.

Please remember the words of Ephesians 2:10: *"For we are God's handiwork, created in Christ Jesus to do good works, which God prepared in advance for us to do."*

May the Lord bless you and use you for His glory.

77. Change of Heart

What's your story? After meeting someone for the first time, the conversation inevitably turns to the question: So what's your story?

Everyone has a story, and there are few things more powerful and disarming than a story, particularly the story of how Jesus can change someone's heart.

Today I'm looking at the topic "A Change of Heart." Every follower of Jesus Christ has a story to tell that speaks of a changed heart, brought about by receiving the grace of God through the death of Jesus on the cross. Because regardless of what you've done, no one is beyond hope. That's the good news of the message of the gospel.

No sin in your past can trump the grace of God. If you have trouble believing that, think of Saul, that very zealous and brash Pharisee in the book of Acts. He persecuted the followers of Jesus, breathing out murderous threats and imprisoning them. Everything he thought, said, and did was dominated by his desire to destroy the church. Then the Lord met him and saved him on one of his murderous journeys on the Damascus Road. He gave him a new heart. And in the process, God made him a new creation. That's what makes grace so amazing!

The promise of a new heart was given by God way back in the Old Testament:

> I will give you a new heart and put a new spirit in you; I will remove from you your heart of stone and give you a heart of flesh. And I will put my Spirit in you and move you to follow my decrees and be careful to keep my laws. (Ezekiel 36:26–27)

That's what the Lord has done for all those who acknowledge their sins and fall on His mercy and grace.

As the freshly minted apostle Paul tells his story, he could have focussed on his devout religious upbringing, his impeccable knowledge of the law, or his great theological prowess. But instead he summarized his story this way:

> Indeed, I count everything as loss because of the surpassing worth of knowing Christ Jesus my Lord. For his sake I have suffered the loss of all things and count them as rubbish, in order that I may gain Christ and be found in him, not having a righteousness of my own that comes from the law, but that which comes through faith in Christ. (Philippians 3:8–9)

Paul, formerly Saul, a murderer of Christians, morphed into a preacher of the gospel. That's what happens when God takes out a heart of stone and gives a person a new heart. Even though your past may be soiled, anyone can find a new beginning with God. It's never too late for a new start in the direction that leads to abundant life in Jesus.

When Saul knelt before the King of Kings and the Lord of Lords on that Damascus Road that day, he finally faced the reality of his sin. Deep within his heart, Christ transformed his life and made him into a new creation. God's grace that made such a new beginning possible.

So don't get stuck where you are! Don't waste your time focusing on what you used to be or what might have been. Remember, the hope we have in Christ means there's a brighter tomorrow ahead. Sin has been forgiven, guilt and shame have been cancelled out, and we are no longer chained to a deep, dark pit of the past.

Grace will give you wings to soar above and beyond the darkness of the past. Yes, that's what so amazing about God's grace.

If you have experienced this grace, you will acknowledge that it's something that you didn't work for or deserve. That's what grace is: God's riches at Christ's expense. May He continue to bless you today!

OCTOBER – DECEMBER

Chapter 14:
Beauty from Ashes

> To appoint unto them that mourn in Zion,
> to give unto them beauty for ashes,
> the oil of joy for mourning, the garment of praise
> for the spirit of heaviness; that they might be called
> trees of righteousness, the planting of the LORD,
> that he might be glorified.
>
> Isaiah 61:3, KJV

78. Only Ashes

Have you ever asked the question "WHY?" It's the first question we ask when tragedy strikes, and it's the one that lingers the longest. Why, Lord? Why me? In Ecclesiastes 3:4, Solomon says that there is a time to weep and a time to laugh, a time to mourn and a time to dance. As you ask why, are you able to leave the outcome to God, trusting that in everything, He works for the good of those who love Him?

I trust that as you read and meditate on this series of devotionals, you'll discover something about yourself. But more importantly, that you will discover something about God. I trust you will discover that there is nothing beyond His ability to repair, nor is He ever unaware of our plight. Instead, He is constantly working on your behalf to bring beauty from ashes.

This story from the book of Ruth is told from the perspective of Naomi, the matriarch of the family. It begins with such great hope for a better tomorrow, but then tragedy strikes the whole family.

> In the days when the judges ruled, there was a famine in the land. So, a man from Bethlehem in Judah, named Elimelek, together with his wife Naomi, and their two sons, Mahlon and Kilion, went to live for a while in the country of Moab. They were Ephrathites from Bethlehem. And they went to Moab and lived there. (Ruth 1:1–2)

They did something that any of us would do. During hard times, it's natural to seek out a better future somewhere else. Unfortunately, sometimes all that glitters isn't gold but tears of sadness and regrets.

> Now Elimelek, Naomi's husband, died, and she was left with her two sons. They married Moabite women, one named Orpah and the other Ruth. After they had lived there about ten years, both her sons also died, and she was *left widowed* and *childless*. (Ruth 1:3–5, emphasis added)

Perhaps you identify with this story in some way because it mirrors some of the hardships and disappointments you've been through. You might have left your native land and travelled to another country, hoping for a better life, where things went well for a while. Then something like the global pandemic strikes, and now you've lost your job. Or perhaps even worse, the stress and mental anguish of trying to cope with life have resulted in some tragic consequences.

Naomi believed this was the direct hand of God's judgement against them. It's sometimes difficult to discern why tragic things happen the way they do. What is certain is that the change of scenery did not make things better for them.

To be a childless widow, especially in a foreign land, was to be among the lowest, most disadvantaged classes in the ancient world. There was no one to support you, and you had to live on the generosity of strangers. But as the book of Ruth unfolds, you'll discover that God is in the business of bringing beauty from ashes.

Naomi had no family in Moab, and no one else to help her. It was a desperate situation, so she decided to return home. In her grief, she cried out to God, blaming Him for making her life bitter instead of better, while all along neglecting to see the gift that God had placed in her path—Ruth, one of her daughters-in-law.

Have you been there? Have you ever been blinded by your grief and loss? As the story unfolds, you'll rejoice to know that we belong to a loving, faithful, and powerful God who has never failed to care and provide for His children.

In Isaiah 61:3, God promises to give you *beauty for ashes,* the oil of joy for mourning, and the garment of praise instead of the spirit of heaviness. Yes, regardless of your circumstances, be assured of this: God is still writing your story, and the end will be much more glorious than the beginning.

If you're anything like me, you can laugh and cry on the same day. That's the beauty of our Father God! He's in the business of reversals, of taking that which seems hopeless and turning it around. In the end, His children are blessed, and He receives the glory.

In every tear we shed, and each jolt of laughter we exude, God is right there with us in the good times and the bad. So whatever you may be facing today, don't give up! Keep trusting God, because there are better days ahead. May His blessings be yours today. Amen.

79. Against All Odds

Jesus was walking along the dusty roads of Galilee one day when someone shouted, *"Jesus, I'll follow you anywhere you go."* Jesus replied, *"Foxes have dens and birds have nests, but the Son of Man has no place to lay his head"* (Luke 9:57-58).

This was enough to dissuade even the most ambitious. It was the kind of question to be pondered, and it was the type of decision that two recently widowed young women had to make. They were Ruth and Orpah, Moabite women whose husbands, Mahlon and Kilion, had recently died. Naomi, the mother-in-law, whose husband had also died, came to the conclusion that the best thing for her to do would be to return home to Bethlehem, after she had heard that the famine was over: *"Then Naomi heard in Moab that the Lord had blessed his people in Judah by giving them good crops again"* (Ruth 1:6).

Naomi and her daughters-in-law got ready to leave Moab to return to her homeland, and they took the road that would lead them back to Judah.

But it's as if Naomi suddenly realized the futility of trying to take two foreigners back to Bethlehem with her. She must have thought, *What am I doing? I have nothing to offer these women* (Ruth 1:8). So, on the way, Naomi said to her two daughters-in-law, "Go back to your mothers' homes. And may the Lord reward you for your kindness to your husbands and to me. Then she kissed them good-bye, and they all broke down and wept. "No," they said. "We want to go with you to your people" (Ruth 1:8–10, paraphrased).

But like Jesus, Naomi laid out the reality for them: I have nothing back there! I have no house to lay my head, and I have no husband to give me more sons for you to marry. It was a hopeless situation for the women! At this point, Orpah, did the math—*Nothing plus nothing adds up to nothing*. She realized that following Naomi back to Bethlehem would be futile.

There are times when you may be called upon to take not a blind leap but a step of faith in the right direction. Have you ever been challenged to do that? Perhaps circumstances have sucked all your dreams away and left you hopeless. God wants to bring new hope to you, and move you in a new direction.

"And again the women wept together, and Orpah kissed her mother-in-law good-bye. 'Look,' Naomi said to Ruth, 'your sister-in-law has gone back to her people. You should do the same.' But Ruth clung tightly to her" (Ruth 1:13–15). Ruth also did the math, but she came up with a different answer than Orpah: For her, nothing plus the God of whom Naomi constantly talked added up to everything.

There must have been something about Naomi that made a lasting impression on Ruth. On the surface, Naomi appeared to be confused about what God was doing. And for sure, she wasn't brimming with hopefulness. Sometimes we think that as Christians, we have to be at our squeaky best to have a positive impact on others. But it's usually when we're going through some hardships in life, without any superficiality or pretence about our spirituality, that we have the greatest impact on those who are looking to us. Ruth's decision not to give up on Naomi reflected God's lovingkindness.

So against all odds, Ruth chose to follow Naomi back to Bethlehem. Not surprisingly, the name Ruth means "friend." But she wasn't just any friend. Proverbs 18:24 says that there are "friends" who destroy each other, but a real friend sticks closer than a brother or sister.

I don't know what you might be facing today. Perhaps your present circumstances have hindered you from taking that step of faith that would lead you to discover the person God wants you to be. Let me encourage you to go for it! There are blessings ahead. Amen.

80. Love beyond Measure

In the 1970 movie *Love Story*, Jenny Cavalleri, who had fallen in love with Oliver Barrett, said to him, "Love means never having to say you're sorry" after Oliver apologized to her for his anger.

In the Western world, love is based primarily on emotional feelings. It can be easily given and easily taken away. It's interesting to note that Orpah and Ruth had the same feelings toward their mother-in-law, Naomi. They both broke down and wept at the thought of leaving this seemingly destitute widow to go on alone to Bethlehem. They both had feelings of empathy for what she had gone through and what she was about to do. But only Ruth went beyond feelings.

For Ruth, love was not a feeling. It was a choice. And even though Naomi tried one last time to persuade Ruth to go back with her sister-in-law to her own people, Ruth was determined.

"Look," said Naomi, "your sister-in-law is going back to her people and her gods. Go back with her."

But Ruth replied with some of the most beautiful and gracious words one human being has ever spoken to another: *"Don't urge me to leave you or to turn back from following you. Where you go, I will go, and where you stay, I will stay. Your people will be my people and your God my God"* (Ruth 1:16).

Her moving vow of loyalty is often included in modern wedding ceremonies to communicate depth of devotion. But in the wedding ceremony, the vow usually ends with, "Until death do us part." Ruth's vow ends with the words: *"Where you die, I will die, and there I will be buried. May the LORD deal with me, be it ever so severely, if even death separates you and me"* (Ruth 1:17).

Faced with a difficult choice, Ruth gathered up all the information at hand and displayed it skilfully before her own heart. She was expressing love beyond all measure. Not even the perils of the journey, or the uncertainty of the destination, could have prevented Ruth from pledging her love so tenderly to Naomi.

In making such a vow, Ruth defied all conventions and took an enormous risk. She risked the ridicule and rejection from her adopted people, who hated all Moabites. They had been enemies for centuries. But she put her future squarely in the hands of the God of Israel.

Regardless of how bleak or perilous your situation may appear at the moment, you can face your future with certainty, because you know the God that Naomi knew and the one in whom Ruth came to place her trust. You too can remain devoted to Him, even in difficult times.

"So the two women went on, until they came to Bethlehem. When they arrived, the whole town was stirred because of them, and the women exclaimed, 'Can this be Naomi?'" (Ruth 1:19). The years had not been too kind to her. *"Don't call me Naomi,"* [a name which means pleasant] *she told them. "Call me Mara,* [which means bitter] *because the Almighty has made my life very bitter"* (Rugh 1:20).

She may have wanted to change her name, but <u>in the eyes of the Father, she was still the pleasant, beautiful one. And that's how the Father sees you today, regardless of how you may see yourself. You are who He says you are!</u>

Naomi said, *"I went away full, but the Lord has brought me back empty"* (Ruth 1:21a). But as you know, she was mistaken. She wasn't coming back empty at all. Whenever you feel that way, take another look. We have one who is called to walk with us. He is called the Paraclete—the Comforter. Naomi said this while unaware that the young Moabite woman who was walking alongside her that day was going to change the course of human history (stay tuned).

The story of Ruth and Naomi shows us what true love and loyalty are really like. Just as Ruth chose loyalty to Naomi and Naomi's God, we too should choose loyalty to God over any enticements this world has to offer. As Jesus said, *"Seek first his kingdom of God and His righteousness, and all these things* [your daily necessity] *will be given to you as well* (Matthew 6:33).

May the Lord help you to choose wisely and to love beyond measure. Amen.

81. God's Kindness

Have you ever been absolutely blown away by the extraordinary kindness of someone who provided for you just what was needed? As I continue to reflect on the book of Ruth, we see Naomi and Ruth arriving in Bethlehem at the beginning of the barley harvest.

The famine was over, and they had arrived just in time to share in the blessings God had provided. Then Ruth said to Naomi, *"Let me go to the fields and pick up the leftover grain behind anyone in whose eyes I find favor"* (Ruth 2:2). Ruth was asking permission to perform the ancient practice of gleaning. Gleaning was embedded in the laws of Israel as a means of providing social assistance to the poor and the needy. The needy person would follow behind the harvesters and collect grains left behind.

Naomi told her to go ahead, so she went out, entered a field, and began to glean behind the harvesters. As it turned out, she was gleaning in a field belonging to Boaz, who was from the clan of Elimelek, Naomi's deceased husband. This didn't happen by chance. You can probably attest to this in your own life, that the Lord arranges certain circumstances in order to accomplish His will. Where God is concerned, there are no coincidences! As the old adage goes, "A coincidence is a miracle in which God prefers to remain anonymous." The Lord led Ruth to the field belonging to Boaz. Boaz was a man of high standing, a pillar in the community.

As you've probably discovered on your journey, God doesn't always speak from a burning bush, or divide the Red Sea you come up against. Instead, He acts through circumstances and through the faithfulness of ordinary human beings like you and me to show His greatness and kindness. God's *kindness* is embodied in human action.

As Ruth was labouring in the fields, Boaz, the rich owner of the field, arrived. Being a foreigner, Ruth was immediately recognized by Boaz, who showed her great kindness. He provided her with food, drink, and protection. And he treated her in a very dignify way. Ruth was overwhelmed by the kindness of Boaz and wondered why this stranger would be so kind to her. She had been through a lot of hardships and excruciating loss. But even a blind person recognizes when the atmosphere is changing from darkness to light.

The tide was turning. Hope was being born: "*At this, Ruth bowed down with her face to the ground. She asked Boaz, 'Why have I found such favor in your eyes that you notice me—a foreigner?'*" (Ruth 2:10). You've probably asked questions like this when you've experienced the gracious kindness of someone. In this picture, I see Boaz as the Father God figure who, when we least expect it and totally undeserving of it, showers us with kindness—love with no strings attached.

There is only one answer to Ruth's question—it's God's mercy and grace, His unmerited favour. Why did God take notice of you and me? We were all strangers and foreigners to the commonwealth of God's kingdom when He noticed us: "*He saved us because of his mercy, and not because of any good things we have done*" (Titus 3:5). When we had no hope, when we were wandering in the barren land of guilt and shame, God noticed us and came to our rescue. And showed Himself to be the bread of life.

> Therefore I tell you, do not worry about your life, what you will eat or drink; or about your body, what you will wear. Is not life more than food, and the body more than

clothes? Look at the birds of the air; they do not sow or reap or store away in barns, and yet your heavenly Father feeds them. Are you not much more valuable than they? (Matthew 6:25–26)

Boaz pronounced this blessing on Ruth: "*May the LORD, under whose wings you have come to take refuge, bless you*" (Ruth 2:12).

Whatever you may be experiencing today that seems beyond your control, take heart, because your loving Father has it under His control. Weeping may last through the night, but rejoicing comes in the morning.

May the Lord bless you this day and fill you with hope. Amen.

82. God of the Harvest

Fall is usually a season of Thanksgiving, whether you reside in Canada or in the United States of America. It's a season when the seeds that were planted in the spring and summer have grown and produced their crops.

During this season, as we continue to reflect on Naomi and Ruth's journey to wholeness and redemption, we see Ruth being invited to a table of blessing to share a meal.

I don't know what your Thanksgiving Day was like if you've already celebrated it, or what it will be like when you do, but for many, Thanksgiving is a time of food, fellowship, and fun. Whether your dinner was a sumptuous one with all the trimmings, or just a simple meal, I trust that in your heart there was much for which to give God thanks.

These are strange times and difficult days, not unlike those Naomi and Ruth experienced. After they had returned to Bethlehem at the beginning of the barley harvest, Ruth soon discovered that God had gone ahead of her and directed her to the field belonging to Boaz to glean for food. During her hard toil in the field, Boaz, a kinsman of Naomi's deceased husband, extended an invitation for Ruth to join him at his table: "*At mealtime Boaz said to her, 'Come over here. Have some bread and dip it in the wine vinegar'*" (Ruth 2:14). When she sat down with the harvesters, he offered her some roasted grain. She ate all she wanted and had some left over.

To Ruth, this was an extraordinary gesture of kindness! Whether in ancient times or today, the invitation to share a meal is one of the greatest gestures of friendship and family one could receive. In that society where there was obvious discrimination against foreigners, Boaz invited Ruth to join him at his table. He extended grace to Ruth. God's grace had provided her with a people to whom she could belong. Boaz spoke dignity over Ruth. He wanted her to know that she wasn't going to be defined any longer by her past or her present circumstances. She was welcome among his people.

In the Song of Songs, Solomon delights in God's grace shown to him when he says, *"He has brought me to his banqueting house, and his banner over me is love"* (Song of Songs 2:4 KJV). Boaz, the master of the field, served the servant. This is a picture of compassion and love. This is a picture of restored dignity.

You are not defined by some arbitrary measures or by your past. You are defined by what the Redeemer says about you. You are family. You are a child of God! In Boaz, I see a picture of Jesus humbling himself to serve all of us, who are so undeserving of His grace: *"As she got up to glean, Boaz gave orders to his men, 'Let her gather among the sheaves and don't reprimand her'"* (Ruth 2:15).

She would now be gleaning from the bundles of grain the harvesters had gathered. This was beyond what she could have ever imagined. Boaz said, *"Even pull out some stalks for her from the bundles and leave them for her to pick up, and don't rebuke her"* (Ruth 2:16). Not only was God pulling out all the stops to bless Ruth, but Boaz was doing the same. The blessing was now progressing in its abundance. She was drawing from God's bountiful supply. After all, He is "God of the Harvest."

Ruth had enough left over to share with her mother-in-law. How do you usually respond to God's overwhelming show of kindness? Do you thanklessly lavish it all on yourself? Or do you share His blessings with others? When God blesses you with abundance, it's totally ungrateful to act in a selfish manner and hoard that blessing to yourself. Ruth blessed Naomi with what God had provided. And so should we.

Ruth discovered that the God of Naomi is a "way maker," as the song says. He is a miracle worker, a promise keeper, a light in the darkness. And even when we can't see it, He is working to bless His children.

I trust that you have found Him to be the same as you respond to His invitation to come and partake of the bread of life. After you have eaten it, you will never be hungry or thirsty again. May the Lord bless you during this season and make you a blessing. Amen.

83. God Covered Us

Have you ever been amazed at God's providence, the way He orchestrates certain events in order to accomplish His purposes? As we continue to reflect on Ruth's journey, we're captivated by a wonderful love story.

"*One day Ruth's mother-in-law Naomi said to her, 'My daughter, I must find a home for you, where you will be well provided for'*" (Ruth 3:1). I can imagine that every time Naomi looked at Ruth and remembered her sacrifice in leaving her people behind to follow her back to Bethlehem that she was overcome with love and gratitude and wanted only the best for her.

As the story unfolds, Ruth has found favour in the eyes of Boaz, who as a near relative of her deceased husband, and according to Jewish law and tradition, *could* become Ruth's husband. As a near kinsman, he was considered one of her Guardian Redeemers, and therefore the responsibility could fall on him to redeem Elimelek's property and continue his name.

Naomi then became a matchmaker: "*Naomi said to her, Now Boaz, with whose women you have worked, is a relative of ours. Tonight, he will be winnowing barley on the threshing floor*" (Ruth 3:2). After the day's harvest, to separate the grains from the chaffs, farmers usually made a pile with the grains and slept close to it to guard against robbers during the night. Naomi encouraged Ruth to make herself nice, go down to Boaz's threshing floor, and lie down at his feet after he went to sleep.

> Wash, put on perfume, and get dressed in your best clothes. Then go down to the threshing floor, but don't let him know you are there until he has finished eating and drinking. When he lies down, note the place where he is lying. Then go and uncover his feet and lie down. He will tell you what to do. (Ruth 3:3–4).

At midnight as Boaz turned in his sleep, you can imagine his amazement when he discovered someone lying there: *"'Who are you?' he asked. 'I am your servant Ruth,' she said. 'Spread the corner of your garment over me, since you are a guardian-redeemer of our family'"* (Ruth 2:9).

Ruth identified herself and made quite a bold request—*"Spread the corner of your garment over me."* This was a culturally relevant way to say, "I am a widow; take me as your wife, since you're one of our Kinsmen Redeemers."

Here she boldly asked Boaz to take her in marriage, to figuratively take her under his wings.

"The wings" used here is a metaphor for protection and belonging, as an eagle would cover the young eaglet under its wings. Boaz had blessed Ruth earlier by saying: *"May you be richly rewarded by the LORD, the God of Israel, under whose wings you have come to take refuge"* (Ruth 2:12). At the time, Boaz was saying, "God has provided a place of safety and rest for you." Ruth was now asking Boaz to do the same for her.

Now it's Boaz's turn to be flattered that Ruth, a younger woman, would notice him, an older gentleman: "The Lord bless you, my daughter," he replied. "This kindness is greater than that which you showed earlier: You have not run after the younger men, whether rich or poor. ¹¹ And now, my daughter, don't be afraid. I will do for you all you ask. All the people of my town know that you are a woman of noble character (Ruth 3:10–11). <u>What Ruth asked Boaz to do for her is what God had done for Israel long before.</u>

In Ezekiel 16:8, God reminds His people what He did for them. Describing how He betrothed Israel, God says:

> Later I passed by, and when I looked at you and saw that you were old enough for love, I spread the corner of my garment over you and covered your naked body. I gave you my solemn oath and entered into a covenant with you, declares the Sovereign LORD, and you became mine.

God uses the same image to describe us—His church, the bride of Christ, His betrothed. Christ is our Kinsman Redeemer. He has provided a covering for us. When God looked at you and me in our sinful state, He extended a covering over us. He took us under His wings and extended the corner of His garment over us. Like Ruth, He saw us as aliens, poor, destitute, and naked, and He covered us with His robe of righteousness and called us his own.

He did this when He sent His Son, Jesus Christ, to redeem us at a great price. He gave us His solemn oath and entered into a love covenant with us. It is the greatest love story ever told. He brought beauty from ashes and gave us a garment of praise. May we all recognize today that we are no longer aliens, outcasts, and strangers but His Bride—the Church. Amen.

84. Redemption

Have you ever given much thought to the word "redemption"? To redeem means to *buy back* or to *buy out*. As we continue to reflect on the book of Ruth, we come to a very important concept: the concept of redemption.

In Ruth 3, Ruth makes a passionate request of Boaz, *"Extend the corner of your garment over me, since you are a kinsman redeemer of our family"* (v. 9). This young Moabite widow was asking Boaz to take her in marriage. Boaz agreed, but there was a potential problem. You see, there was a nearer kinsman, who according to the law would have the first right either to refuse or to redeem Naomi's property and to marry Ruth.

In Ruth 3:12–13, Boaz responds to Ruth:

> Although it is true that I am a guardian-redeemer of our family, there is another who is more closely related than I. Stay here for the night, and in the morning if he wants to do his duty as your guardian-redeemer, good; let him redeem you. But if he is not willing, as surely as the Lord lives, I will do it. Lie here until morning.

Boaz was a man of integrity and selflessness. True to form, he wasn't willing to cut corners. He would do God's will, God's way. How about you? Do you sometimes seize the day to accomplish your own agenda? Boaz knew that if it was really of the Lord, then it would be done orderly and properly. Boaz believed that if this was God's doing, then God would work out the details.

He spoke honourably of Ruth as a virtuous woman and made her a solemn promise. So Boaz went up to the town gate, where legal transactions took place, just as the nearer Kinsman Redeemer came along.

Boaz related the story of Naomi and Ruth to him and suggested that he should step forward, being the nearer kinsman. Boaz said to him, *"If you will redeem* [the land], *do so. But if you will not, tell me, so I will know. For no one has the right to do it except you, and I am next in line"* (Ruth 4:4).

The kinsman agreed to redeem it, and then Boaz said, *"'On the day you buy the land from Naomi, you also acquire Ruth the Moabite, the deceased man's widow, in order to maintain his name with his property.' At this, the guardian-redeemer said, 'Then I cannot redeem it because I might endanger my own estate. You redeem it yourself. I cannot do it'"* (vv. 5–6).

These must have been glorious words in the ears of Boaz, who loved Ruth dearly. A moment earlier, all seemed lost when the nearer kinsman had agreed to redeem the land. But now Boaz could joyfully fulfill his desire to marry Ruth.

Sadly, the decision of this nameless nearer kinsman to reject the offer of redemption kept him from experiencing the joy of becoming one of God's heroes in the Bible. He will forever remain *nameless* and be remembered only as the one who was given a great opportunity but rejected it, because he didn't want to endanger his estate.

In Philippians 2, on the other hand, we see Jesus our Redeemer, who did not cling jealously to His position but humbled himself by becoming a servant, redeeming us through His obedience and death—even death on a cross! But God exalted him to the highest place and gave him the name that is above every name.

What is even sadder is that every day people are invited by God to go beyond their comfort zones and embrace something of far greater worth. But quite often, the cost is too great. This nearer kinsman, when he heard the conditions of the transaction, refused it. In the same way, many are reluctant to receive the great redemption offered by God. They may think the cost is too high and reject it for fear that it will endanger their own worldly pursuits. That's why Jesus said, "What would it profit a person if they were to gain the whole world and lose their own soul?" (Mark 8:36, paraphrased).

The application of the term "redemption" to Christ's death on the cross is quite telling. Since Christ "redeemed us," we have been bought back. This must mean that God was our prior owner. You see, we were made in His image, but we chose another master.

The prophet Isaiah says, "*We all like sheep have gone astray, we have turned each one to his own way. But the Lord laid on Jesus all of our sins*" (Isaiah 53:6). God has purchased our freedom. And thanks be to Him, we do not have to live as slaves to sin any longer. He redeemed us, not with corruptible things such as silver or gold, but with the precious blood of Jesus Christ.

May the Lord bless you today as you reflect on the cost of your redemption. Amen.

85. Something Beautiful

Have you ever heard the saying, "If only I knew then what I know now, life would have been so much more pleasant"? Hindsight is always 20/20, as the saying goes.

This might have been Naomi's reflection as she held her newborn grandson—Ruth's baby—in her arms. As we come to our final reflection on the book of Ruth, Boaz has married Ruth: "*So Boaz took Ruth and she became his wife. When he made love to her, the LORD enabled her to conceive, and she gave birth to a son. The LORD enabled her to conceive*" (Ruth 4:13)

The gift of children was never taken for granted in Israel. It was very precious. The fact that Boaz and Ruth were able to raise up a son to the deceased Mahlon was evidence of God's blessing: "*The women said to Naomi: 'Praise be to the LORD, who this day has not left you without a guardian-redeemer. May he become famous throughout Israel!*'" (v. 14).

It's fitting that at the end of Ruth, attention should return to Naomi to admire her radical reversal of fortune: "*Then Naomi took the child in her arms and cared for him. The women living there said, 'Naomi has a son!' And they named him Obed. He was the father of Jesse, the father of David*" (Ruth 4:16–17).

It was through the ancestry of David that Jesus came to earth. In this grandson, Naomi's hopes were renewed—hopes she had lost when her husband and two sons died in Moab. Dreams she never dreamed when her loving daughter-in-law refused to let her go to Bethlehem alone.

I want you to picture her now, filled with joy! She's probably sitting on a rocking chair on the porch, holding baby Obed in her arms and reflecting on her recent past. Pain can make people either bitter or better. She once was bitter, but now she is better. Perhaps as she held little Obed in her arms, her thoughts went back to Moab—how she was then, and where she is now. How she felt about God then, and how she feels about Him now. It might have been a moment of praise but also one of confession to God.

Along with the lullaby she might be singing to little Obed, she might have been asking God to pardon her disbelief and lack of trust in His ability to provide for His children. She might have been reflecting on her confusion about God's wrath toward her, realizing now that God not only understood but, in due time, made something beautiful of her life. God had restored her name back to Naomi! She was once again someone pleasant, someone beautiful. From the ashes of her life, God brought beauty.

The imagery of Jesus can be seen throughout the pages of this scripture passage. In the person of Boaz, He is pictured as the Kinsman Redeemer, who had to be a family member. And so we see Jesus coming to earth, adding humanity to His eternal deity. In order for Him to be our kinsman and to redeem us, He had to become one of us:

> Therefore, it was necessary for him to be made in every respect like us, his brothers and sisters, so that he could be our merciful and faithful High Priest before God. Then he could offer a sacrifice that would take away the sins of the people. (Hebrews 2:17, NLT)

God might have sent an angel to redeem us, but the angel wouldn't have been our *kinsman*. A great prophet or priest would be our *kinsman*, but his own sin would have disqualified him as our *redeemer*. Only Jesus, the eternal God who added humanity to His eternal deity, could be both *the kinsman* and *the redeemer* for all humanity!

Spiritually, we all have to come to Bethlehem, *the House of Bread*, where we will discover that Jesus is "The bread of life." In John 6:35, Jesus declares, "*I am the bread of life. Whoever comes to me will never go hungry, and whoever believes in me will never be thirsty.*"

What can we learn about ourselves and God from these few devotional thoughts? How do we trust Him, even when the outcome seems quite despairing? We learn that we can't trust our feelings, as they can be deceptive. We learn that if we have the determination to go on, we will find the courage and strength in God. And we learn that God's plan is perfect and filled with love, that He is never against us but always for us. We learn that He never stops working on our behalf, even when we can't feel it or see it.

Regardless of what you may be facing today, please know that you belong to a loving, faithful, and powerful God who never fails to care and provide for His children, in the good times and the bad. May the Lord bless and give you hope during this season

PRAYER:
Father God, like Naomi, I have experienced circumstances from which I thought there could be no redemption. I've felt the sting of loss and grief in my life and began to doubt your goodness and your promises to be my provider in every situation. But now I can see how your goodness has followed me. Please restore my faith and hope and give me the strength to patiently endure, knowing that in due time, you will bring from the ashes of my life, beauty. Amen.

Chapter 15:
A Time for Waiting

> But they that wait upon the Lord
> shall renew their strength;
> they shall mount up with wings as eagles;
> they shall run, and not be weary;
> and they shall walk, and not faint.
>
> Isaiah 40:31

86. Waiting on the Lord

Waiting is one of the hardest things to do! Whether you're waiting on your spouse, a friend, or waiting on a call from your doctor, it's an exhausting exercise. And if you're waiting on God for the answer to a particular problem, the wait becomes even more unbearable.

As humans we want quick answers, quick solutions. We may even try to help God out by running ahead of Him to accomplish our plans. But when we do, not only do we miss out on what God has in store for us, but we usually make a mess of the situation and complicate our lives even further.

Today's devotional is about "Waiting on the Lord." Let's see what the prophet Isaiah has to say about waiting.

> Have you not known? Have you not heard? The LORD is the everlasting God, the Creator of the ends of the earth. He does not faint or grow weary; His understanding

is unsearchable. He gives power to the faint, and
to him who has no might He increases strength.
(Isaiah 40:28–29)

Although these words were addressed to Israel during their time of distress and their call on God for deliverance, they have significant application in the lives of *all* God's children everywhere and at all times. These words are a call to all of us to turn from our own self-reliance and anxiety and rely on God's strength.

The Lord is always faithful to His promise and has never gone back on His word. God's greatness is not just that He is strong, but that He is strong for us.

> Even youths shall faint and be weary, and young men shall fall, exhausted; But they that wait upon the LORD shall renew their strength; they shall mount up with wings as eagles; they shall run, and not be weary; and they shall walk, and not faint. (Isaiah 40:30–31)

This promise of hope was given when the Israelites were worn out from their hardship and were beginning to lose their faith and trust in God. They had lived in exile in Babylon for several decades, and their perspective was darkened by their own despairing thoughts about God: "*Our way is hidden from the Lord, and our right is disregarded by our God*" (Isaiah 40:27).

They thought God either couldn't help or didn't care. Have you ever felt that way? Isaiah uses a pair of words—*faint* and *weary*—several times in this passage, indicating Israel's state of being. They were exhausted and burdened from the circumstances of life.

They weren't just weak in body; they were weak in spirit. How could they endure the hard circumstances of life any longer? I wonder if you've ever felt that faint and weary waiting for the Lord? Isaiah 40 contains great promises of strength for the weary: "*Even youths shall faint and be weary; and young men shall fall exhausted.*" In other words, even those in their prime, with perfect health, have limits. We need a stronger strength to match our weakness and, at times, deep discouragements.

So how do we get it? There is only one answer, and here we come to the great promise of this text: *"They who wait for the Lord shall renew their strength."* These are words that we can rely on. It doesn't say those who *work* for the Lord, but those who *wait* for Him. This isn't about doing our part and asking God to do the rest. No! God's greatness isn't just that He is strong but that He is strong for us.

We have to acknowledge that we need the strength only God can give as we wait for Him, which is more than just passing time. This kind of waiting carries with it a sense of hopeful expectation. So in the midst of hardship, let us look to Him as the One who works all things together for our good.

As Christians, we look to Jesus, who extends this wonderful invitation to us:

> Come to me, all you who are weary and burdened, and I will give you rest. Take my yoke upon you and learn from me, for I am gentle and humble in heart, and you will find rest for your souls. For my yoke is easy and my burden is light. (Matthew 11:28–30)

He carried the burden of our sin and judgement upon Himself on the cross. And He rose again and sent His Spirit to empower us and strengthen us in all our weakness. Therefore, we can rely on His great strength today.

87. Soar Like the Eagle

In today's devotional, I want to focus on soaring with wings as eagles. Isaiah says, *"They that wait upon the LORD shall mount up with wings as eagles"* (Isaiah 40:31). Waiting on the Lord enables us to soar to great heights. Not only does waiting enable us to mount up with wings as eagles, but it gives us a sense of joy and fulfillment when God's plan is accomplished.

Twenty-five years! That's how long Abraham waited between hearing God's promise and holding his son Isaac in his arms.

Abraham and Sarah lived it day by day, waiting, waking up more than nine thousand mornings with the promise still unfulfilled. Three times during those twenty-five years, God appeared to Abraham to reaffirm His word. Yet they waited in silence, with open hands and an empty womb. Abraham was a waiting man who trusted in God. As his seventy years advanced into the eighties and turned into the nineties, he waited. He waited as his body weakened and as his wife grew gray. He waited.

I suppose God could have brought Isaac sooner, or Abraham could have been given the promise later, closer to Isaac's birth. Instead, God sent Abraham into the "wilderness of waiting" for twenty-five years.

Have you been waiting on God to fulfill a promise? How is that going? Getting tired? Waiting was part of God's good plan for Abraham. And so it is for us. Our verse today tells us: *"But they that wait upon the* LORD *shall renew their strength; they shall mount up with wings as eagles."* This is one of God's great exhortation verses in the Bible. It promises strength to those who wait and trust in God. God knows that as humans, we're prone to take matters into our own hands, which often leads to failure or disappoint.

As we see in Abraham and Sarah's case, when they took matters into their own hands and went ahead of God's plan by producing a son, Ishmael, by Sarah's maidservant, that was not the "son of promise." But when the appointed time came, Abraham and Sarah were filled with joy and soared like the eagle with delight as they held their promised son, Isaac, in their arms:

> Now the LORD was gracious to Sarah as He had said, and the LORD did for Sarah what he had promised ... Sarah said, "God has brought me laughter, and everyone who hears about this will laugh with me."
> And she added, "Who would have said to Abraham that Sarah would nurse children? Yet I have borne him a son in his old age." (Genesis 21:1, 6–7)

Every obedient child of God will eventually be filled with joy and lifted and sustained by His Spirit, as an eagle is lifted by the wind. Why does Isaiah use the analogy of a soaring eagle to bolster the faith of the Israelites?

In order to understand God's comparison of our faith-walk to the flight of an eagle, let's take a brief look at the eagle's wings.

Eagles are born with large, heavy wings. It's part of the survival mechanism that helps them fly without expending a lot of energy flapping their wings. They learn very early that in order to soar without expending a lot of energy, they must wait for what are called wind thermals to come up on them. Does this remind you of the disciples waiting in the upper room?

Sometimes eagles will remain perched for days as they wait to catch a good, strong wind thermal. Then they can launch onto the strong wind to get them to where they want to go. That's why the Bible teaches that we as believers can possess the characteristics of an eagle. The eagle doesn't run from the storm! It actually uses the storm to lift itself higher. In the same way, when we're faced with trials or obstacles, we will rise above them as we wait on the Lord and allow our strength to be renewed by His Holy Spirit.

Perhaps like Abraham and Sarah, you've been waiting a very long time for the fulfilment of a promise. Not only has the waiting been long, but the journey has been a turbulent one. Take comfort from the eagle and allow the storm to not only make you stronger in the end but enable you to soar above it, through the power of the Holy Spirit.

88. Run and Not Be Weary

In the Movie *The Ten Commandments*, Pharaoh says to Moses, "Your Commander is a poor strategist; he has left you no way of escape." This is said in response to the predicament Moses and thousands of escaping Jews found themselves in.

After waiting on the Lord for over four hundred years for their deliverance from slavery in Egypt, the children of Israel were finally given their freedom. But when Pharaoh realized that his whole labour force was gone, he changed his mind and began to pursue them. Pharaoh and his army chased them to the edge of the Red Sea. Supposing that he had won because there was no way for Hebrew slaves to go, the Pharaoh made the condescending remark.

But Pharaoh was in for a rude awakening, not realizing he was up against the unstoppable God. He'd pursued them to the edge of the Red Sea, where humanly speaking they were facing an impossible situation. You could say they found themselves between a *rock and a hard place*, literally between the *devil and the deep blue sea*.

But nothing shall be impossible with the Lord. As Moses called upon the Lord and waited for their deliverance, God showed Pharaoh that He is the greatest strategist of all time. In Isaiah 40:31, the prophet says, *"But they that wait upon the LORD shall renew their strength; they shall mount up with wings as eagles; they shall run, and not be weary; and they shall walk, and not faint"*

In this devotional, I'm focusing on "They Shall Run and Not Be Weary."

Have you ever found yourself in a predicament where only the hand of God could deliver you? All of us at one point or another will face situations from which only God can deliver us.

> If the LORD had not been on our side when people attacked us, then they would have swallowed us alive when their anger exploded against us. Then the floodwaters would have swept us away. An overflowing stream would have washed us away. (Psalm 124:2–4)

The King of Egypt, like all those whose strength is in the number of their chariots or their own human resources, under-estimated the power of the Lord Almighty. When the Israelites looked up and saw that the Egyptians were coming after them, they were terrified, so they cried out to the Lord. They even wanted to turn back, saying, *"Didn't we tell you in Egypt, 'Leave us alone! Let us go on serving the Egyptians'? It would have been better for us to serve the Egyptians than to die in the desert!"* (Exodus 14:12). The trouble with being delivered from the tentacles of oppression is that we sometimes have short-term memory loss. You'll see that memory loss in abusive relationships, in addictive behaviours, and in being delivered from sinful habits. People will look back and think, *It really wasn't that bad.* There's always a tendency to revert to the old life, even though to do so could mean death in many of its facets. It was no different with the children of Israel. They had forgotten what it meant to be enslaved. Let us not forget what God has delivered us from!

It 's during those times when we feel the pressure of the journey and have the overwhelming desire to turn back that we should remember the words of the prophet Isaiah: "*They that wait upon the LORD shall renew their strength; they shall mount up with wings as eagles; they shall run, and not be weary; and they shall walk, and not faint*" (Isaiah 40:31).

Moses reminded the people to wait on God, or to stand still: "*Moses answered the people, Don't be afraid! Stand still, and see what the LORD will do to save you today. You will never see these Egyptians again. The LORD is fighting for you! So be still!*" (Exodus 14:13-14).

Moses reminded the people about the power of the Lord—the unstoppable God who had called him from the burning bush to go to Egypt to set His people free. He wasn't about to abandon Moses now: "*Then Moses stretched out his hand over the sea, and turned the sea into dry ground. The water divided, and the Israelites went through the middle of the sea on dry ground*" (Exodus 14:21–22). You are wrong, Pharaoh! Our God is a great strategist. He always provides a way of escape.

Does your situation look impossible? Wait on the Lord, because they that wait on the Lord shall run and not be weary.

89. Walk and Not Faint

After the children of Israel had wandered around the wilderness for forty years, it was time for them to advance and possess the land promised to their forefathers as an inheritance.

> After the death of the LORD's servant Moses, the LORD said to Moses' assistant Joshua, son of Nun, "My servant

> Moses is dead. Now you and all these people must cross the Jordan River into the land that I am going to give the people of Israel. I will give you every place on which you set foot, as I promised Moses. (Joshua 1:1–3)

Very soon afterwards they broke camp and crossed the Jordan, miraculously. As soon as the priests carrying the Ark of the Covenant came to the edge of the Jordan River and set foot in the water, the water stopped flowing from upstream. Again, as was the case with the Red Sea, they crossed over on dry ground.

Sometimes in life things seem to go so smoothly, there's no doubt that the Lord's hand is in the situation. But at times we come up against an immovable object. What do you do? According to the prophet Isaiah, we wait on the Lord. We wait on the Lord, remembering His faithfulness, and listen to hear His voice for the next steps.

Such was the case when the children of Israel reached the City of Jericho. This was a walled city that stood in the way of the Israelites advancing to their appointed destination.

Q. What lesson was God going to teach them?

In this devotional, I'm looking at "Walking without Fainting." Again, this was an impossible situation from which only the hand of God could bring deliverance.

> Now the gates of Jericho were securely barred because of the Israelites. No one went out and no one came in. Then the LORD said to Joshua, "See, I have delivered Jericho into your hands, along with its king and its fighting men. (Joshua 6:1–2)

Does it sound like God has a sense of humour?

The children of Israel saw the wall. But God saw rubble on the ground along with captives.

Q. What walls might you be facing today? Do they look impenetrable? What is God saying to you about your wall?

God said to Joshua, "*March around the city once with all the armed men. Do this for six days*" (Joshua 6:3). This required not just faith but strength. The prophet Isaiah says, "*They that wait on the Lord shall renew their strength ... they shall walk and not be weary*" (Isaiah 40:31c).

You see, it wasn't going to be through human ingenuity, or through a multitude of chariots, that the wall of Jericho was going to fall, but by the power of God. God said to Joshua:

> Have seven priests carry trumpets of rams' horns in front of the ark. On the seventh day, march around the city seven times, with the priests blowing the trumpets. When you hear them sound a long blast on the trumpets, have the whole army give a loud shout; then the wall of the city will collapse and the army will go up, everyone straight in. (Joshua 6:4–5)

God's ways are so much different than ours. His thoughts are so much higher. He acts in mysterious ways to perform His wonders. Our duty is to walk in obedience and observe the Lord as He brings to pass that which He has ordained. With God, one thing is sure: walls must come down.

When God brings down the walls we face, He does it quite differently than what the world does. He does it through the obedience, praise, and worship by His children. Do you face a wall? Wait on the Lord and walk in obedience, because obedience is the highest form of worship. So walk in obedience and keep praising the Lord as you go.

On the seventh day, the seventh time around, when the priests sounded the trumpet blast, and the army shouted. At the sound of the trumpet, when the men gave a loud shout, the wall of the city collapsed. The walls came crashing to the ground! Not with the blast of a cannon, not with bulldozers, and not with hammers, chisels, and other tools like those used to chip away at the Berlin Wall until it crumbled. No, it collapsed through the power of the Almighty God.

The outcomes may not be instant, but when we wait on the Lord, He renews our strength, enabling us to walk without fainting. So keep waiting on the Lord.

Today we were reminded of how crucial it is to wait on God and put our trust in Him, because that's when the impossible becomes possible. May the Lord bless you.

Chapter 16:
Lost and Found

> Bring the fattened calf and kill it.
> Let's have a feast and celebrate.
> For this son of mine was dead and is alive again;
> he was lost and is found.' So they began to celebrate
>
> Luke 15:23–24

90. The Lost Sheep

On August 5, 2010, thirty-three miners in northern Chile were considered lost after a copper and gold mine collapsed, trapping them half a mile underground. But the families and friends, who believed in God, never gave up hope that they would be found alive, even though the miners weren't able to communicate with emergency officials.

Engineering and mining experts from around the world worked tirelessly to free them with little success. On August 22, rescuers were able to drill a small hole from the surface down to the miners—2,300 feet underground. Not long after, the men sent up a note that read: "We are fine in the shelter, the thirty-three of us."

Apparently, after the collapse, the men, ranging in age from nineteen to sixty-three, moved to an underground emergency shelter area with a limited supply of food and water. While the miners were underground, Elizabeth Segovia, the wife of one of the trapped men, gave birth to a girl she named Esperanza, the Spanish word for "hope."

On October 13, after more than two months, the miners were lifted out safely, one by one, through a narrow escape tunnel in a rescue capsule painted blue, red, and white—the colours of the Chilean flag. It took just under twenty-three hours to lift all thirty-three men safely to the surface. They had been trapped for sixty-nine days. It's believed that more than one billion people around the world watched the rescue live on TV.

There was no TV two thousand years ago, but if there were, the population of the whole world would have watched as the greatest rescue ever to take place was put into action. When the righteous Son of God died on the cross that day, He rescued us from being trapped in sin's domain and spiritual darkness, bringing us out into the Kingdom of God. *Halleluiah*!

In this devotional series, I reflect on how God our Father found us and rescued us when we were lost and without hope. I have titled this devotional "The Lost Sheep."

In Luke 15, Jesus tells the parable of the lost sheep. This was in response to the Pharisees and the teachers of the law, who were accusing Him of welcoming sinners and eating with them. For whatever reason, tax collectors and those labeled sinners were all gathering around to hear Jesus.

> Then Jesus told them this parable: "Suppose one of you has a hundred sheep and loses one of them. Doesn't he leave the ninety-nine in the open country and go after the lost sheep until he finds it? And when he finds it, he joyfully puts it on his shoulders and goes home. Then he calls his friends and neighbors together and says, 'Rejoice with me; I have found my lost sheep.'"
> (Luke 15:3–6)

In this parable, Jesus is emphasizing that He didn't come for the ones who sit smugly in their self-righteous state but for "sinners"— those who acknowledge their own lostness and poverty of spirit.

Jesus says that when such people are found by God, there is rejoicing in heaven. Jesus is also focusing on the importance of the *one* who repents. You see, when Jesus died on the cross, He gave His life for the whole world. But the offer is for the whosoever—the one that believes.

Jesus concludes the parable by saying, *"I tell you that in the same way there will be more rejoicing in heaven over one sinner who repents than over ninety-nine righteous persons who do not need to repent"* (Luke 15:7).

Of all domesticated animals, sheep are the most helpless. They'll spend their entire day grazing, wandering from place to place, never looking up. As a result, they often become lost. Isaiah, explaining why Jesus had to come to earth and die on a cross, says, *"We all, like sheep, have gone astray, each of us has turned to our own way; and the LORD has laid on him the iniquity of us all"* (Isaiah 53:5).

Sheep follow the leader. If the leader walks off a cliff, the others will follow, resulting in their death. As humans, we were born with that same inherent tendency and have followed after the sin of Adam and Eve in the Garden of Eden. You could say that we have followed them off a cliff. But God so loved us that He sent His one and only Son to rescue us: *"He* (Jesus) *was crushed for our iniquities; the punishment that brought us peace was on him, and by his wounds we are healed"* (Isaiah 53:5).

The rescued miners from the collapsed Chilean mine shaft gave thanks to God for the incredible miracle they received from His hand. In the same way, those of us who were lost in sin and iniquity but have been rescued by Jesus give praise and thanks to God for the wonderful miracle of a transformed life.

I don't know what season you're in at the moment; perhaps you feel lost and would like Jesus to come and save you. He's as close as your very breath. So whisper this prayer to Him.

PRAYER:
Oh God, like that sheep that has wandered off and gotten lost, I feel the loneliness and burden of my sin weighing heavily on me. I now

believe that Jesus died on the cross to save me. I accept your gift of salvation. Please come into my heart by your Spirit and save me. Thank you, God. Amen.

91. The Lost Coin

His name was John Newton and he was nurtured by a Christian mother who taught him the Bible at an early age. But after she died, he was raised by his father, whose character was not conducive to raising a young boy. By age eleven, he was accompanying his father on sea voyages.

At age eighteen he was pressed into service with the Royal Navy, but after attempting to desert, he was relieved of his post and sent aboard a passing slave vessel. He became attracted to the transatlantic slave trade as "an easy and creditable way of life," and later served as a sailor aboard several ships involved in the slave trade.

Newton had largely abandoned the faith of his childhood, and in his own words, he was lost. But March 10, 1748, was a turning point for him. While steering his slave ship through a fierce thunderstorm, he didn't think he would survive. So he started praying to God for mercy. When he made it through the storm, he attributed his safety to the grace of God. It was this event that started his conversion and led to him eventually becoming a clergyman.

He wrote many hymns, including "Amazing Grace." In many ways, this hymn reflects on Newton's own conversion to following the Lord. In it, he expressed the truth of what had happened to him: "I once was lost, but now I'm found; was blind but now I see." [16]

In Luke 15, Jesus tells three parables about things that had been lost but were found again: the parables of the lost sheep, the lost coin, and the lost son. The Parable of the Lost Coin is about a coin, one in a collection of ten silver coins, that was lost somewhere in the house.

> Suppose a woman has ten silver coins and loses one. Doesn't she light a lamp, sweep the house and search carefully until she finds it? And when she finds it, she calls her friends and neighbors together and says,

> 'Rejoice with me; I have found my lost coin.' In the same way, I tell you, there is rejoicing in the presence of the angels of God over one sinner who repents. (Luke 15:8–10)

Jesus told this parable because the ultra-religious leaders, as well as the teachers of the law, complained about Jesus associating with people who were considered outcasts or of ill-repute and who often came to listen to Him. He even had meals with some of them.

This parable demonstrates the importance of the *one*—the lost *one*. Throughout Jesus' ministry, He demonstrated his love and care for the *one*, the least and the lost. Whether it was a rich young ruler; Zacchaeus, a notorious tax collector; or the blind beggar Bartimaeus, Jesus' desire was always to find and connect with that one lost soul.

In the case of Zacchaeus, Jesus said, "*Today salvation has come to this house, because this man, too, is a son of Abraham. For the Son of Man came to seek and to save the lost*" (Luke 19:9–10). The parable of the lost coin ends with Jesus saying, "*In the same way, there is joy in the presence of God's angels when even one sinner repents*" (Luke 15:11).

Like the people in Luke 15 who lost something and searched for it, Jesus came looking for you and me. But He didn't just look. No, He did more than that—He gave himself for the lost one, for us. Whether you identify with the lost sheep, the lost coin, the lost son, or the lost slave ship captain, please know this: Jesus loves you, cares for you, and will pursue you until you are found.

If you take one thing away from this devotional today, let it be this: Regardless of how far you've gone or to what depth you've sunk, Jesus is always there with open arms, waiting to welcome you home. He did it for John Newton in 1748, He did it for me in 1963, and He will do it for you today.

Won't you respond to Him today by taking hold of His extended hand. He has come to rescue you. He has come to set you free from whatever you may be facing—anxieties, fears, or a feeling of separation from God. Because He loves you.

May the Lord bless you this day as you receive His love and tender care.

16. John Newton, *Amazing Grace* (1772), Onley England.

92. The Lost Son

Jesus was intentional in everything He did. His chief concern was for lost people, so He went out of his way to find them and bring them back home. Whether it was the woman at the well (John 4), the woman caught in adultery (John 9), tax collectors, or prostitutes, He was always very caring and compassionate toward them.

When He was criticized for being found with them, His only answer was: "*It is not the healthy who need a doctor, but the sick. I have not come to call the righteous, but sinners*" (Mark 2:17). It was in one of these conversations with the Pharisees and teachers of the law that He told the parable of the lost son.

This parable is so multifaceted, but primarily it speaks to the love of Father God toward His children. Jesus pulls out all the stops in conveying to us what the love of the Father is like. He wants us to know that there is nothing we can do, nowhere we can go, no depth to which we can sink where the love of our heavenly Father can't reach us.

In speaking to the Pharisees and the teachers of the law one day, Jesus painted a picture for them regarding the reason why He was always so caring and compassionate to those considered "sinners." In this devotional I'm reflecting on "The Lost Son."

> Jesus continued: "There was a man who had two sons. The younger one said to his father, 'Father, give me my share of the estate.' So, he divided his property between them. "Not long after that, the younger son got together all he had, set off for a distant country and there squandered his wealth in wild living. After he had spent everything, there was a severe famine in that whole country, and he began to be in need. (Luke 15:11–14)

What this younger son did was reprehensible in Jewish culture. He really should have been cast out without a penny to his name. What the young son was saying amounted to, "Father, I wish you were dead already so I could have my inheritance. Give it to me now." But the father was full of grace and gave him the desire of his heart.

When you presume upon the grace of God, you'll discover that the thing you so long for usually turns to ashes in your hand, leaving you with emptiness and a deep void that nothing in this world could satisfy. Jesus continued:

> So he went and hired himself out to a citizen of that country, who sent him to his fields to feed pigs. He longed to fill his stomach with the pods that the pigs were eating, but no one gave him anything. (Luke 15:15–16)

When someone wanders away from the love and security of the Father's house to pursue, as the Bible refers to it, the *world*, the *flesh*, and the *devil*, not only do they discover that it's a futile pursuit, but they soon discover that they're at the end of their own human resources.

It's usually at the point where you have to look up to see the bottom that redemption starts to happen. Jesus said:

> When he came to his senses, he said, "How many of my father's hired servants have food to spare, and here I am starving to death! I will set out and go back to my father and say to him: Father, I have sinned against heaven and against you. I am no longer worthy to be called your son; make me like one of your hired servants." So he got up and went to his father. (Luke 15:17–20)

The son reasoned that the best place to be at a time like this was in his father's house. He took a bold step, not knowing the outcome. But he surmised that anywhere else, any kind of favourable reception, even that of being a hired hand, would be better than the hopeless place in which he found himself.

> So he got up and went to his father. But while he was still a long way off, his father saw him and was filled with compassion for him; he ran to his son, threw his arms around him and kissed him. (Luke 15:20)

When you take one step toward the Father, my friend, you will find His arms open wide. The father seeing him afar off means that he was in constant look-out for him, perhaps from the very day he left home. Not only did the father see him afar off, but he ran to him.

My friend, the Father is on the look-out for you, because His heart has been grieving ever since the day you wandered off and got lost. But He is ready at a moment's notice to run to you.

"*The son said to him, 'Father, I have sinned against heaven and against you. I am no longer worthy to be called your son'*" (Luke 15:21). But in such a joyous moment, those words would have served to remove the dagger that had pierced the father's heart when he believed that his son was lost.

> But the father said to his servants, "Quick! Bring the best robe and put it on him. Put a ring on his finger and sandals on his feet. Bring the fattened calf and kill it. Let's have a feast and celebrate. For this son of mine was dead and is alive again; he was lost and is found." So, they began to celebrate. (Luke 15:22–24)

My friend, as Jesus says: "*I tell you that in the same way there will be more rejoicing in heaven over one sinner who repents than over ninety-nine righteous persons who do not need to repent*" (Luke 15:7).

93. The Wanderer

As I was meditating on Psalm 107 recently, it struck me how we sometimes forget to give thanks for all the good things we've received from others. In those instances, it's sad that we forget to say thanks. But how much sadder it is when we forget to be thankful not just for the kindness shown to us by others, but for the blessings God bestows on us. We often take so many things for granted.

In Psalm 107, the author earnestly encourages the people to be thankful to God by repeating on four occasions the phrase: *"Let them give thanks to the Lord for his unfailing love and his wonderful deeds to mankind."* I can tell you the one thing that I am grateful for above any other is that Jesus found me and rescued me when I was a wanderer, lost and hopeless.

In this devotional, I'm focusing on our need to be grateful to God for rescuing us. Today we consider "The Wanderer."

Are you feeling lost and hopeless? The children of Israel were on their way to the Promised Land, but they got lost on the way, sidetracked by their disobedience and unbelief. This caused them to wander around for forty years: *Some wandered in desert wastelands, finding no way to a city where they could settle. They were hungry and thirsty, and their lives ebbed away"* (Psalm 107:4–5)

And as we follow them through their wilderness journey, we recall how God fed them with manna, the bread of life, from heaven. And after they had their fill of manna, we recall how God provided quail for them to eat, until they were satisfied. We also recall how God provided water from a rock after they'd been travelling for days without any water to drink and were at the point of death. But God found them and provided for them again: *"Then they cried out to the Lord in their trouble, and he delivered them from their distress. He led them by a straight way to a city where they could settle"* (Psalm 107:5–7).

Our human nature is so prone to forget. The children of Israel, once their needs were met, not only forgot the goodness of the Lord, but they carried on in their sinful ways. So the psalmist admonished them not to forget to give thanks for all that the Lord had done for them.

You might never have been through a desert experience, but perhaps it felt that way. Perhaps like the children of Israel, you felt like you were lost and wandering in a trackless wasteland, where the winds of time quickly covered over your footprints in the sand, causing you to think God had abandoned you. If you did cry out to God to come to your rescue, I'm sure He heard you and delivered you. He eventually led you by a straight way to your destination. The psalmist says you should exalt the Lord in the congregation of the people and praise Him in the assembly of the elders. The dominant theme in one of my favourite songs, "Amazing Grace," is *I once was lost but now I'm found.*

The psalmist says, "*Let them give thanks to the* LORD *for his unfailing love and his wonderful deeds for mankind, for he satisfies the thirsty and fills the hungry with good things* (Psalm 107:8–9). He satisfies the thirsty and fills the hungry with good things! Has that been your experience? You and I were not lost in a physical wilderness, but the consequences were the same. We were lost in a dominion of darkness, enslaved by our sin and guilt. But the Lord opened wide our prison door and set us free.

The apostle Paul, writing to the Colossians, said, "*For he has rescued us from the dominion of darkness and brought us into the kingdom of the Son he loves, in whom we have redemption, the forgiveness of sins*" (Colossians 1:13–14).

As you reflect on this Psalm, be reminded of how the Lord brought deliverance through your trials, healings for you and your loved ones, guidance in difficult situations, provision in unexpected ways, and protection from the pestilences around you. There is so much to be thankful for! The psalmist concludes by saying, "*Let the one who is wise heed these things and ponder the loving deeds of the* LORD" (Psalm 107:43). When we do this, the upright, seeing the goodness of the Lord, will rejoice. But all the wicked will shut their mouths.

Perhaps as you're meditating on this devotional, you recognize that you're not in a good place. Your foundation is slipping from under you. Reach out a hand to Jesus! He is reaching out to you! Invite Him to become your solid foundation!

PRAYER:
Jesus, I confess that I have wandered very far from you, and the consequences of my actions are driving me even farther away. Please reach out your hand and rescue me, for I am in need of your

protection and guidance. I now surrender my life to you and cast myself on your mercy and grace. Amen.

94. He Sets Prisoners Free

Psalm 107 speaks of God's deliverance of His people in so many ways. The concept of being "lost and found" is ever present in this psalm. In today's devotional, I'm sharing with you the thought that "God Sets Prisoners Free."

The Psalmist describes how God delivered His children from darkness and prison, and he admonishes us not to forget what He had done for us:

> Some sat in darkness, in utter darkness, prisoners suffering in iron chains, because they rebelled against God's commands and despised the plans of the Most High. So he subjected them to bitter labor; they stumbled, and there was no one to help. (Psalm 107:10–12)

We know from the history of the children of Israel that on several occasions, they were subjected to earthly taskmasters who abused them, holding them in both physical and spiritual bondage. They suffered because of their sin and rebellion against God. They sat in darkness in exile, subjected to the jeers and insults of their evil taskmasters, as a consequence of their rebellion against God's commands. At times there seemed to be no hope. But Psalm 107:13 says, *"Then they cried to the LORD in their trouble, and he saved them from their distress."*

We must ask ourselves how this relates to us today? Many people we know may be going through a very difficult situation. Many may be wandering aimlessly through life, restless, depressed, hostile, or even bitter. Maybe you even identify with some of this. There seems to be no way out. They are held prisoner by their attitude, outlook, or habit. Or perhaps they are sick, or emotionally unwell.

Some may be fearful, troubled by a crisis in which they find themselves, imprisoned by the consequences of their own actions. These are all things that God's children may be going through, so, if this is your situation today, stop and think about what has brought you to this juncture in your life and turn around. Know that God accepts you and that He loves you; ask Him to come and deliver you.

The psalmist says, "*Then they cried to the* LORD *in their trouble, and he saved them from their distress*" (Psalm 107:13). This is a reflection of the sinner's deliverance from an even worse confinement than the physical bars of a prison. Having struggled in vain for deliverance through our own efforts, we find that our only help is through the mercy and grace of God. When confession is made of our own sin, guilt, and shame, God extends His forgiveness and grace and delivers us from our prison cell. He forgives and sets us free by breaking the bars of our prison so that we can walk in freedom. The psalmist says, "*He brought them out of darkness, the utter darkness, and broke away their chains*" (Psalm 107:14).

God is deeply concerned about you and me. He'll meet us right where we are and take us just as we are. But He won't be satisfied to let us remain just as He found us. He will bring us out of darkness and break away our chains. But when He does, don't forget to give Him praise: "*Let them give thanks to the* LORD *for his unfailing love and his wonderful deeds to mankind, for he breaks down gates of bronze and cuts through bars of iron*" (Psalm 107:15–16).

The Message Translation puts it this way:

> Some of you were locked in a dark cell, cruelly confined behind bars; Punished for defying God's Word, for turning your backs on the High God's counsel—A hard sentence, and not a soul in sight to help. Then you called out to God in your desperate condition; He got you out in the nick of time. (Psalm 107:10–12, MSG)

Thank God for His marvelous love! You once were lost, but now you have been found. Your deeds had imprisoned you, but Jesus sets you free. The apostle Paul put it this way:

> Thanks be to God, who always leads us in triumphal procession in Christ and through us spreads

everywhere the fragrance of the knowledge of him.
For we are to God the aroma of Christ among those
who are being saved and those who are perishing. (2
Corinthians 2:14–16)

Let's not forget, or pass up the opportunity, to thank the Lord for what He has done for us, and to tell our redemption story of God's amazing grace. For the Lord is good, and His love and faithfulness endure forever.

95. Darkness to Light

As frail human beings, we are so much like our Jewish brothers and sisters of the past who received so much from the hand of the Lord but soon forgot His wonderful goodness. Psalm 107 is a psalm of thanksgiving, extolling God for delivering His people from a variety of troubles. He sought them, found them, and delivered them, breaking their yoke of bondage and setting them free.

In this devotional series, I'm reflecting on the way God brings out His people from "Darkness to Light." The author earnestly encourages the people to be thankful to God by repeating this phrase on four occasions: *"Let them give thanks to the* Lord *for his unfailing love and his wonderful deeds for mankind."*

The psalm begins with these three introductory verses:

> Give thanks to the Lord, for He is good; His love
> endures forever. Let the redeemed of the Lord tell their
> story, those he redeemed from the hand of the foe, those
> he gathered from the lands, from east and west, from
> north and south.

I think this admonition applies to all of us today. The psalmist also describes the many ways in which a loving God has been faithful to His children by reflecting on His *deliverance*, His *guidance*, His *provision*, *protection*, and many *blessings*.

Do you remember the day and time when God delivered you from darkness? For some it was a gradual deliverance, a gradual clearing of their spiritual site, until one day they discovered that the darkness was gone and they now could see. Regardless of how your transformation took place, whether it was instant or gradual, you must never forget to always give thanks.

A week ago I had surgery to remove a cataract from my right eye. Five years ago my optometrist advised me that cataracts were beginning to appear. Every year, he told me that I needed to have them removed. He informed me that the surgery wasn't a painful one, but when seeing becomes uncomfortable, I should have it done.

Psalm 107 tells the story of God's deliverance of His children from darkness to light, and they're admonished to never forget what the Lord had done for them: "*Some sat in darkness, in utter darkness, prisoners suffering in iron chains, because they rebelled against God's commands and despised the plans of the Most High*" (Psalm 107:10–11).

They had been suffering because of their sin and rebellion against God. They had been exiled on several occasions and felt the darkness that engulfed them. This was the consequence of their rebellion.

In my physical condition, I wasn't sitting in darkness, but my, my, how wonderful to be able to see things again so clearly—to be able to watch TV without my glasses on. Considering the painlessness of the surgery, I often wondered why I hadn't done it before.

The sad thing is, many people today are walking in spiritual darkness, even though God offers them deliverance from their darkness. But in rebellion, they carry on in their own way, groping in the dark to find a way out. The psalmist says, "*Some sat in darkness, in utter darkness, prisoners suffering in iron chains, because they rebelled against God's commands and despised the plans of the Most High*" (Psalm 107:10–11).

But God is patient with us—those who know Him and those who are far off. He is full of compassion toward us, not willing that any should perish but that all would come to a knowledge of Him and His great love. The psalmist describes what life was like for those whom God rescued, and perhaps those who are still feeling the effects of their rebellion and sin—the darkness of disobedience.

The psalmist says that some of you were sick because you'd lived a bad life and found yourself immersed in the darkness of this world. Your bodies felt the effects of your sin; you couldn't stand the sight of those things that you once craved earnestly. You were so miserable that you came to the conclusion life was no longer worth living. Then you called out to God in your desperate condition, and He got you out in the nick of time. He restored your sight and made you whole: "*He sent out his word and healed them; he rescued them from the grave*" (Psalm 107:20).

The psalmist says, "*Let the redeemed of the Lord tell their story—those he redeemed from the hand of the foe*" (Psalm 107:2). So thank God for His marvelous love, for His wonderful mercy and grace toward you, the child He loves. Offer thanksgiving and the sacrifice of praise to Him, and tell the world what He's done!

Perhaps you aren't quite there yet. You have seen flashes of light in the darkness, but you're covering your face because you can't bear to see what is being exposed by the light. Put your shields down! Allow the light of God's presence to transform you and bring you out of darkness into His marvelous light. Ask the Lord to deliver you as He has so many, and when He does, remember to give Him praise. For the Lord is good, and His mercy endures forever. May the Lord bless you this day. Amen.

96. The Lord Our Healer

Psalm 107 is a psalm of thanksgiving, extolling God for delivering His people from a variety of troubles. Not only does it recount all the wonderful things God has done for His children, but it also admonishes them not to forget to give Him thanks and praise.

In our reflection today, we're looking at how God sent his Word and healed them. It's a reminder to us today that the Lord is Our healer!

The psalmist says, "*Some became fools through their rebellious ways and suffered affliction because of their iniquities. They loathed all food and drew near the gates of death*" (Psalm 107:17–18).

During their sojourn through the wilderness, we see how their disobedience caused the children of Israel to suffer afflictions (Numbers 21:4–9). The people had become discouraged along the way and spoke harshly against both God and Moses. They questioned why God and His servant Moses had brought them out into such a desolate land, where they had neither food nor water. They felt lost and abandoned.

This lack of faith and show of disobedience displeased the Lord greatly. So as a consequence for their sin and evil words, the Lord God sent fiery serpents among the people to bite them, and many of the people died. But the people acknowledged their sin and asked Moses to pray to the Lord to remove the serpents from them. But God is always merciful. He listens to the faintest cry of His children when they acknowledge their sins. God commanded Moses to make a bronze serpent and lift it up on a pole so that anyone bitten by the serpents could look at the serpent and live rather than die: "*Then they cried to the* LORD *in their trouble, and he saved them from their distress. He sent out his word and healed them; He rescued them from the grave*" (Psalm 107:19–20, emphasis added).

But because they were so prone to forget the goodness of the Lord, they had to be reminded time and time again: "*Let them give thanks to the* LORD *for his unfailing love, and his wonderful deeds for mankind. Let them sacrifice thank offerings and tell of his works with songs of joy*" (Psalm 107:21–22).

We too are prone to forget what the Lord has done for us. We constantly need to be reminded to thank and praise the Lord. One thing we shouldn't forget to praise God for is this: "*Just as Moses lifted up the snake in the wilderness, so the Son of Man must be lifted up, that everyone who believes may have eternal life in him*" (John 3:14–15).

We must never forget that God sent His Word and healed us. The apostle John reminds us who is the Word—the Word that heals us. Moses lifting up the snake on a pole in the wilderness provided healing for those who'd been bitten by a snake. But it was also symbolic of Jesus, "the Word" being lifted up on a cross so that all of humanity, who had been bitten by the *snake* of sin, can look upon Him and be healed. He sent His Word and healed us.

The apostle John writes, "*In the beginning was the Word, and the Word was with God, and the Word was God*" (John 1:1). Jesus was this Word God sent to heal us when we were dead in our trespasses and sins. He saved us through His atoning work on the cross.

The prophet Isaiah, looking ahead to the cross many hundreds of years in the future, saw the Word becoming flesh and being wounded on a cross to heal us:

> Surely, he took up our pain and bore our suffering, yet we considered him punished by God, stricken by him, and afflicted. But he was pierced for our transgressions, he was crushed for our iniquities; the punishment that brought us peace was on him, and <u>by his wounds we are healed</u>. (Isaiah 53:4–5, emphasis added)

The apostle James reminds us, "*Every good gift and every perfect gift is from above, coming down from the Father of lights, with whom there is no variation or shadow due to change*" (James 1:17). <u>Without gratitude, we become arrogant and self-centred. Giving thanks reminds us of how much we do have, and what God has done for us.</u>

Let's remember the words of the Lord, spoken by His servant Moses as they journeyed along the way:

> <u>If you will diligently listen to the voice of the Lord your God, and do that which is right in his eyes, and give ear to his commandments and keep all his statutes, I will put none of the diseases on you that I put on the Egyptians, for I am the Lord, your healer</u> (Exodus 15:26, emphasis added)

Chapter 17:
The Season of Incarnate Love

*But when the set time had fully come,
God sent his Son, born of a woman,
born under the law, to redeem those under the law,
that we might receive adoption to sonship.*

Galatians 4:4–5

97. Bethlehem, House of Bread

Bethlehem is a small city in Judah. The name means "House of Bread." It was also called "the City of David." It's first mentioned in scripture as the place where Rachel died and was buried by the wayside, directly to the north of the city (Genesis 48:7). It was seemingly such an insignificant city that the prophetic announcement that the Messiah would be born there would have raised a few eyebrows.

You're going to hear the name Bethlehem time and time again during the Christmas season, but have you ever given any thought to the name? In this devotional series, I'm focusing on "Bethlehem House of Bread"—The Promise.

It's impossible for darkness to overcome light. If you were to enter the darkest room and turn on the smallest light, the light would dispel the darkness. Darkness and light cannot co-exist. In Matthew's Gospel, he interprets Isaiah 9:12 as the prophecy of Jesus, the light, coming into the darkness of the world: *"The people living in darkness have seen a great light; on those living in the land of the shadow of death a light has dawned"* (Matt. 4:16). But as we approach this particular season, there's another aspect I want us to think about.

Approximately seven hundred years before the birth of Jesus, the prophet Micah gave this extra-ordinary prophecy from God: *"But you, Bethlehem Ephrathah, though you are small among the clans of Judah, out of you will come for me one who will be ruler over Israel, whose origins are from of old, from ancient times"* (Micah 5:2).

The real Bethlehem wasn't quite what the picture books depict. For one thing, it was very little, hence the Christmas carol "O Little Town of Bethlehem." It was so insignificant, it wasn't even included in the lengthy list of the cities of Judah in Joshua.15. Yet the place Bethlehem appears about fifty times in the Bible.

Bethlehem was the place where the prophet Samuel anointed David as king. Bethlehem was central to King David's early activities, and it's home to Rachel's tomb, which draws many pilgrims yearly. But there are some other compelling accounts involving Bethlehem in the scriptures.

The story of Ruth the Moabitess, who married Boaz from the tribe of Judah and was introduced into the bloodline of Jesus the Messiah, took place there. Boaz was Ruth's Kinsman Redeemer, the only relative able and willing to redeem her. Taking Ruth as wife, Boaz redeemed the name, the land, and the legacy of his deceased relative—a picture of the promised Redeemer who would also come from Bethlehem years later to redeem His Bride.

It was Ruth's faith, devotion, and courage as a non-Hebrew woman, casting her lot in with the people of God, that earned her a place in Messiah's bloodline, and Bethlehem is where it all happened.

In the Hebrew language, the city's name means "House of Bread." And how can we miss the connection to Jesus' own declaration:

> I am the living bread which came down from heaven. If anyone eats of this bread, he will live forever; and the bread that I shall give is my flesh, which I shall give for the life of the world. *(John 6:51)*

Indeed, Jesus, who was born in the House of Bread, is the "Bread of Life." The apostle John sees Him as the living Bread, the manna that sustained the children of Israel during their wilderness journey to the Promised Land. And indeed, it was in Bethlehem that the Son of God was born, clothed in human flesh, preparing to offer Himself as the perfect sacrifice according to the will of His heavenly Father. Think of it, of all the places God could have chosen to bring forth the Saviour, Bethlehem was His choice.

The insignificant nature of His birthplace should have been a clue to the kind of person and ministry Jesus was destined to have. Born in a stable and in a manger instead of a palace, wrapped in swaddling clothes instead of royal robes. This was an indication of how His heart would be broken for sinners, the outcasts, the marginalized, the lost—those on the fringes of society.

As we saw later in His ministry, with love and compassion He endeavoured to bring everyone from the fringes into the centre of God's redeeming love. As we think about Bethlehem this Christmas season, let's not miss its significance to our salvation story.

Perhaps you're reading this during the Christmas season, or maybe it's just one of those busy seasons where you feel pressurized and anxious. Please don't miss the connection that Jesus is the Bread of Life, and that it is He alone who is able to satisfy your deepest hunger. May the Lord bless you during this season!

98. The Awakening

God's redemption story didn't just begin in Bethlehem where the Redeemer was born. It actually began way back in the Garden of Eden, when animals were killed to make coverings for Adam and Eve, whose sin had revealed their nakedness.

Throughout the Bible, God had been revealing bits and pieces of His redemption plan through the prophets. But only those with vision and ears to hear what the Spirit of God was saying recognized and looked forward to the fulfilment of His promise.

It had been four hundred years since the children of Israel, or anyone else, had heard from the Lord. The prophet Malachi had given his last prophecy, after which there was only silence. But all of a sudden, there was a voice.

In this devotional, I'm looking at the "Awakening." Have you ever received a promise from your boss or a friend, but the fulfilment was so long in coming that you got used to the status quo. You adjusted your mindset and your expectation and became accustomed to the way things were? You might even have lost hope. Such was the case with the children of Israel waiting for the fulfilment of God's promised Redeemer.

Malachi had proclaimed the Word of God that said, "*I will send my messenger, who will prepare the way before me. Then suddenly the Lord you are seeking will come to his temple; the messenger of the covenant, whom you desire, will come,*" says the Lord Almighty (Malachi 3:1). But since then, there had been silence for four hundred years.

But all of a sudden there was a Voice—there was an *Awakening*. God, who is faithful to His promise, had not forgotten His children, who were groping in the darkness. And just as surely, He hasn't forgotten you. John the Baptist, God's messenger, had arrived on the scene.

> In those days John the Baptist came, preaching in the wilderness of Judea and saying, "Repent, for the kingdom of heaven has come near." This is he who was spoken of through the prophet Isaiah: "A voice of one calling in the wilderness, 'Prepare the way for the LORD, make straight paths for him.'" (Matthew 3:1–3)

God had sent His messenger to turn the hearts of the people back to God. John came preaching a message of repentance and baptizing those who heard the message and were convicted of their sins. He had come to shake up the status quo.

John had a compelling message that was hard to ignore. The religious elite (Pharisees and Sadducees) who had been living lives of hypocrisy had been called out by John, so many of them went reluctantly, either to observe or to be baptized, seeking forgiveness from the Lord. But John had seen through their hypocrisy and had some very harsh words for them: "*But when he saw many of the Pharisees and Sadducees coming to where he was baptizing, he said to them: 'You brood of vipers! Who warned you to flee from the coming wrath? Produce fruit in keeping with repentance'*" (Matthew 3:7–8).

The name "brood of vipers" clearly connects these people to the deceiving serpent in the Garden of Eden. John asked them who had warned them to flee from God's impending wrath. His prophecy of the coming of the Kingdom of Heaven was good news for those who were seeking to lead holy lives, but terrible news for those who continued in sin.

A "voice in the wilderness" is an English idiom for someone who expresses an idea or opinion that's not popular or is unique to that person, usually suggesting that the opinion is ignored. But literally, John was crying out from the Judean wilderness.

John the Baptist's self-description as "the voice of one calling in the wilderness" was profoundly fitting. Not only did John minister in the wilderness of Judea, but God also chose him to introduce the nation of Israel to Jesus Christ and prepare the people's hearts to receive their Saviour and Redeemer.

John preached boldly, calling people to repent of their sins and turn to God, because the Kingdom of Heaven was near. After people confessed their sins, they demonstrated repentance by being baptized and then living transformed lives. John stood all alone against the status quo. He was a messenger with the good news that the Kingdom of Heaven was at hand.

Jesus would later arrive on the scene, as John had prophesized. God was faithful to His promise and had sent His Son to redeem the world. Like John, Jesus wants us to be different, to be able to stand up for the truth and not conform to the pattern of this world.

So today, let's join our voices with John's, proclaiming the message of Christ's salvation to a lost and dying world so that the glory of the Lord will be revealed, and all people will see it and turn to the Lord in repentance as we wait for the return of the Lord, our Saviour, from heaven.

99. The Fulfillment

During the days of John the Baptist, as he ministered to the people in the Judean wilderness, many were baptized as a form of repentance from their sin. John had convinced them that he was not the Christ, just the one preparing the way for Him.

This devotional is about "The Fulfilment" of God's promise of the Redeemer and how we shouldn't lose hope. Instead, with expectant hearts, we must wait for what the Lord has promised, because He is faithful. After John the Baptist had announced that the promised Redeemer would soon appear, people were waiting with expectant hearts for the coming of the Messiah. Those who were familiar with prophecies would have known about "The Promise," which was made by God and announced by the prophet Micah hundreds of years earlier: "But you, Bethlehem Ephrathah, though you are small among the clans of Judah, out of you will come for me one who will be ruler over Israel, whose origins are from of old, from ancient times" (Micah 5:2).

As the prophets had foretold, God sent the angel Gabriel to Nazareth, a town in Galilee, to a virgin named Mary. We read in Luke 1:26-27: "*In the sixth month of Elizabeth's pregnancy, God sent the angel Gabriel to Nazareth, a town in Galilee, to a virgin pledged to be married to a man named Joseph, a descendant of David. The virgin's name was Mary.*"

After Mary recovered from her fright and amazement, God informed her of His plans, and that she had been chosen as the one through whom this Messiah would be born. The angel Gabriel went on to say to Mary: "*He will be great and will be called the Son of the Most High. The Lord God will give him the throne of his father David, and he will reign over Jacob's descendants forever; his kingdom will never end*" (Luke 1:32-33). God, who always keeps His word, fulfilled His promise, and Jesus was born to Joseph and Mary in Bethlehem.

Although Bethlehem was considered insignificant, it was the place God chose as the birthplace for His Son. The choice of this place, and the nature of Jesus' birth, give us an understanding of the kind of life and ministry Jesus was to have. He was the king of the universe, but He didn't come wearing a crown of gold or dressed in purple robes. He was the King of Kings and Lord of Lords, but He wasn't born in a palace but in a smelly stable among the animals, dressed in strips of cloth and laid in a trough, in which the animals fed. He didn't come with edicts that compelled people to follow Him. Instead, with the soft and tender touch of a baby's hand, He gently knocks at our heart's door, inviting us to give him entrance.

It came to pass one day, as John the Baptist was baptizing people at Bethany on the other side of the Jordan, that he was asked many questions as to whether he was the Messiah or not. When he explained that he wasn't the Messiah, then asked why he was baptizing: "'I baptize with water,' John replied, 'but among you stands one you do not know. He is the one who comes after me, the straps of whose sandals I am not worthy to untie'" (John 1:26–27). But when God's time had come for the unveiling of the Messiah to the people, Jesus showed up for all to see:

> The next day John saw Jesus coming toward him and said, "Look, the Lamb of God, who takes away the sin of the world! This is the one I meant when I said, 'A man who comes after me has surpassed me because he was before me.'" (John 1:29–30)

He came as the Lamb of God who would take away the sin of the world. We all came into the world with the expectation of our parents that we would live. Jesus came into the world with the expectation that He was going to die. But His life wasn't taken from Him. He freely laid it down for you and me. And through His loving sacrifice on the cross, He has transformed the lives of many by extending His grace.

Ironically, it was the shepherds, one of the lowliest professions in Jesus' day, who were the first recipients of the good news that the Messiah was born. Then came the wisemen from the East—Gentile Magi who had seen His star and had followed it to Bethlehem. Right from the very beginning, the birth of Jesus in Bethlehem had worldwide implications. The news began locally but crossed national and international lines, going beyond ethnic boundaries and cultures. It speaks to the ever-widening scope and impact Jesus the Messiah would have on the entire world.

God's promise had been fulfilled, and people could now leave behind their heavy burden of sin, guilt, and shame by surrendering them at the foot of the cross, where sin's demands and penalty were paid. If you're reading this devotional in the season of Christmas, go one step farther and let it be the season of God's redemption story for you. Indeed, let Him be the reason for the season. Wise men and women still seek Him today.

100. Waiting for the Lord's Return

After His resurrection, Jesus spent many days with His disciples, instructing them about the hope they had in Him. Not surprising, they still didn't understand that He would be soon departing this world to be with the Father in heaven.

> "LORD, are you at this time going to restore the kingdom to Israel?" He said to them: "It is not for you to know the times or dates the Father has set by his own authority. But you will receive power when the Holy Spirit comes on you; and you will be my witnesses in Jerusalem, and in all Judea and Samaria, and to the ends of the earth." After He said this, He was taken up before their very eyes, and a cloud hid Him from their sight. They were looking intently up into the sky as He was going, when suddenly two men dressed in white stood beside them. "Men of Galilee," they said, "why do you stand here looking into the sky? This same Jesus, who has been taken from you into heaven, will come back in the same way you have seen him go into heaven." (Acts 1:6–8)

Since then, there has been an upward look by the children of God, waiting for the return of Jesus. It's been almost two thousand years, and Jesus' promise to return hasn't been fulfilled. Even in the days of the apostles, people were already getting anxious that the Lord hadn't returned as He'd promised. The apostle Peter had to remind them, and us, that God is faithful to His promise.

> Dear friends, this is now my second letter to you. I have written both of them as reminders to stimulate you to wholesome thinking. I want you to recall the words spoken in the past by the holy prophets and the command given by our Lord and Savior through your apostles. Above all, you must understand that in the last days scoffers will come, scoffing and following their own evil desires. They will say, "Where is this 'coming' He promised? Ever since our ancestors died, everything goes on as it has since the beginning of creation." 2 Peter 3:1–4

Waiting can be quite exhausting, but the prophet Isaiah reminds us that they that wait on the Lord shall walk and not faint. You see, our walk is a walk of faith, not one of sight only. This promise is a promise of God's supernatural strength for the journey: "*So, I say, walk by the Spirit, and you will not gratify the desires of the flesh*" (Galatians 5:16).

Many people missed the first coming of Jesus, even though it had been prophesied thousands of years before, so we must be careful and on guard as we wait to ensure that His coming doesn't surprise us as a thief in the night. As we wait for Him, we should wait not with passive resignation, feeling helpless about the situation in our world, or just by doing "busy work." We are to do what Jesus said we should do: "*And he called his ten servants, and delivered them ten pounds, and said unto them, Occupy till I come*" (Luke 19:13).

In similar fashion, as we wait for the return of Jesus, we are to be using the talents He has given us to enrich His kingdom, here on earth and in heaven. The apostle James reminds us what true and pure religion looks like: "*Religion that God our Father accepts as pure and faultless is this: to look after orphans and* widows *in their distress and to keep oneself from being polluted by the world*" (James. 1:27).

While you wait for the return of the Lord, let your light shine before others, doing those good deeds that bring glory to the Father in heaven. Jesus' first coming, though prophesized hundreds of years before, was met with disbelief and skepticism. So keep waiting and watching with joyful expectation.

He was to be called the *Desire of Nations*, but only a few desired Him when He came the first time—born in a stable, in the insignificant city of Bethlehem, grew up in Nazareth, of which the question was asked, "Can anything good come from there?"

He was hated by even his own brothers, and finally, He died on a cruel cross for the sins of the whole world. So, you see, we have to be careful that His second coming doesn't take us unawares: *"Be dressed, ready for service and keep your lamps burning, like servants waiting for their master to return from a wedding banquet, so that when He comes and knocks, they can immediately open the door for him"* (Luke 12:35–36).

Whatever you may be going through today, wait patiently for your deliverance from heaven. Because He who has promised is faithful.

101. Come, Lord Jesus

It's been almost two thousand years since Jesus was taken up to heaven in the sight of His disciples, and since then, there is a joyful expectation that the Lord will soon return. Hymn writers have written about it; we have sung about it, and we have even prayed about it, as indicated at the end of Revelation: *"He who testifies to these things says, 'Yes, I am coming soon.' Amen. Come, Lord Jesus"* (Revelation 22:20).

The Apostle John writes in Revelation 1:9–11:

> I John, your brother and companion in the suffering and kingdom and patient endurance that are ours in Jesus, was on the island of Patmos because of the word of God and the testimony of Jesus. On the Lord's Day I was in the Spirit, and I heard behind me a loud voice like a trumpet, which said: "Write on a scroll what you see

and send it to the seven churches: to Ephesus, Smyrna, Pergamum, Thyatira, Sardis, Philadelphia and Laodicea.

It was now approximately sixty years following the death, burial, resurrection, and ascension of Jesus Christ to the Father in heaven. His followers had gone through persecution and had been scattered across the Roman Empire, with churches in Asia Minor.

Some of these churches were doing well in certain areas, but others were starting to assimilate into the culture, bringing alongside the truth of God's Word some very dangerous heresies. So Jesus had a message for those churches that had begun to depart from the narrow way. He chose the apostle John as His messenger.

> I turned around to see the voice that was speaking to me. And when I turned, I saw seven golden lampstands, and among the lampstands was someone like a Son of man, dressed in a robe reaching down to his feet and with a golden sash around his chest. (Revelation 1:12–13)

The apostle John goes on to describe what he saw. It was an awesome and at the same time terrifying sight.

> When I saw him, I fell at his feet as though dead. Then he placed his right hand on me and said: "Do not be afraid. I am the First and the Last. I am the Living One; I was dead, and now look, I am alive for ever and ever! And I hold the keys of death and Hades." (Revelation 1:17–18)

This is the same John, the beloved apostle, who always sat close to Jesus. At the Last Supper, he was sitting right next to Jesus when Jesus made the shattering statement that one of the disciples would betray Him. Some of the others asked John to find out from Jesus who it was that was going to betray Him. You could say they were like "bosom buddies."

But that was then. Now Jesus is glorified, and He who was from the beginning, whom they had heard, whom they had seen with their eyes, whom they had looked upon and touched, now existed in unapproachable splendour. John said, *"When I saw him, I fell at his feet as though dead"* (Revelation 1:17).

Sometimes you hear people say, "I've gone through so much suffering in this life. I just can't wait until I see Jesus to aske Him what's up with that." But from John's reaction, I think such a question will be the last thing on your mind.

Throughout the scriptures, anytime someone encounters the living God, falling to the ground is their inevitable posture: Abraham when called by God, Moses at the burning bush, Joshua at the entrance to the City of Jericho, Ezekiel when he saw God on His throne chariot, Peter, James, and John at the Transfiguration, or John the Beloved here in Revelation. They all fell to the ground at the awesome sight, in worship to God.

Whenever we experience the risen Lord, as we do from time to time in some transcendent moments of praise and worship, our inevitable posture is to fall to the ground. So even though we may say with great gusto and sincerity, "Amen. Come, Lord Jesus," it will be quite amazing when we see Him. Because He alone is worthy of worship.

Jesus placed His right hand on John and said, *"Do not be afraid. I am the First and the Last. I am the Living One; I was dead, and now look, I am alive for ever and ever! And I hold the keys of death and Hades"* (Revelation 1:17a–18).

At this scene, we see both the imminence and the transcendence of God—transcendent because He dwells in unapproachable light, but imminent because He is the God at hand, the One who is able to empathise with what we're going through. One who feels our pain and weeps with us in our grief, or even when we're being persecuted.

Our world is at a crucial point in its history, but we remember the words of Jesus when He said, *"And when these things begin to come to pass, then look up, and lift up your heads; for your redemption draweth nigh"* (Luke 21:28, KJV).

So together with the hymn writers and the book of Revelation, we say, "*Amen. Come, Lord Jesus!*" But let us be dressed and ready for when He comes.

Doxology

To him who is able to keep you from stumbling and to present you before his glorious presence without fault and with great joy— to the only God our Savior be glory, majesty, power and authority, through Jesus Christ our Lord, before all ages, now and forevermore! Amen (Jude 1:24-25).

Printed in Canada